DEFINITIONS AND CONCEPTIONS OF GIFTEDNESS

Essential Readings in Gifted Education

Series Editor

Sally M. Reis

1 **Robert J. Sternberg**
Definitions and Conceptions of Giftedness

2 **Joseph S. Renzulli**
Identification of Students for Gifted and Talented Programs

3 **Linda E. Brody**
Grouping and Acceleration Practices in Gifted Education

4 **Joyce VanTassel-Baska**
Curriculum for Gifted and Talented Students

5 **Carol Ann Tomlinson**
Differentiation for Gifted and Talented Students

6 **Alexinia Y. Baldwin**
Culturally Diverse and Underserved Populations of Gifted Students

7 **Susan Baum**
Twice-Exceptional and Special Populations of Gifted Students

8 **Sidney M. Moon**
Social/Emotional Issues, Underachievement, and Counseling of Gifted and Talented Students

9 **Enid Zimmerman**
Artistically and Musically Talented Students

10 **Donald J. Treffinger**
Creativity and Giftedness

11 **Carolyn M. Callahan**
Program Evaluation in Gifted Education

12 **James J. Gallagher**
Public Policy in Gifted Education

Robert J. Sternberg
EDITOR

DEFINITIONS AND CONCEPTIONS OF GIFTEDNESS

A Joint Publication of Corwin Press and the National Association for Gifted Children

ESSENTIAL READINGS IN GIFTED EDUCATION
Sally M. Reis, SERIES EDITOR

For information:

Corwin Press
A Sage Publications Company
2455 Teller Road
Thousand Oaks, California 91320
www.corwinpress.com

Sage Publications Ltd
1 Oliver's Yard
55 City Road
London EC1Y 1SP
United Kingdom

Sage Publications India Pvt. Ltd.
B-42, Panchsheel Enclave
Post Box 4109
New Delhi 110 017 India

Printed in the United States of America

Library of Congress Cataloging-in-Publication Data

A catalog record for this book is available from the Library of Congress.

ISBN 1-4129-0427-7

This book is printed on acid-free paper.

04 05 06 07 08 10 9 8 7 6 5 4 3 2 1

Acquisitions Editor: Kylee Liegl
Editorial Assistant: Jaime Cuvier
Production Editor: Sanford Robinson
Typesetter: C&M Digitals (P) Ltd.
Cover Designer: Tracy E. Miller
Graphic Designer: Tracy E. Miller

NAGC Publications Coordinator: Jane Clarenbach

Contents

About the Editors

Sally M. Reis is a professor and the department head of the Educational Psychology Department at the University of Connecticut where she also serves as principal investigator of the National Research Center on the Gifted and Talented. She was a teacher for 15 years, 11 of which were spent working with gifted students on the elementary, junior high, and high school levels. She has authored more than 130 articles, 9 books, 40 book chapters, and numerous monographs and technical reports.

Her research interests are related to special populations of gifted and talented students, including: students with learning disabilities, gifted females, and diverse groups of talented students. She is also interested in extensions of the Schoolwide Enrichment Model for both gifted and talented students and as a way to expand offerings and provide general enrichment to identify talents and potentials in students who have not been previously identified as gifted.

She has traveled extensively conducting workshops and providing professional development for school districts on gifted education, enrichment programs, and talent development programs. She is co-author of *The Schoolwide Enrichment Model, The Secondary Triad Model, Dilemmas in Talent Development in the Middle Years*, and a book published in 1998 about women's talent development titled *Work Left Undone: Choices and Compromises of Talented Females*. Sally serves on several editorial boards, including the *Gifted Child Quarterly*, and is a past president of the National Association for Gifted Children.

Robert J. Sternberg is IBM Professor of Psychology and Education and Director of the Center for the Psychology of Abilities, Competencies, and Expertise at Yale. This Center is dedicated to the advancement of theory, research, practice, and policy advancing the notion of intelligence as developing expertise—as a construct that is modifiable and capable, to some extent, of development throughout the life span. The Center seeks to have an impact on science, on education, and on society. Sternberg is the 2003 President of the American Psychological Association.

Sternberg received his Ph.D. from Stanford University in 1975 and his B.A. summa cum laude, Phi Beta Kappa, from Yale University in 1972. He also holds honorary doctorates from the Complutense University of Madrid, Spain; the University of Leuven, Belgium; the University of Cyprus; and the University of Paris V, France.

Sternberg is the author of over 950 journal articles, book chapters, and books. The central focus of his research is on intelligence, creativity, and wisdom, and he also has studied love and close relationships as well as hate. This research has been conducted in five different continents.

Sternberg is also a Fellow of the American Academy of Arts and Sciences, the American Association for the Advancement of Science, the American Psychological Association (in 14 divisions), the American Psychological Society, the Connecticut Psychological Association, the Royal Norwegian Society of Sciences and Letters, the International Association for Empirical Aesthetics, and the Society of Experimental Psychologists. He has received the Arthur W. Staats Award from the American Psychological Foundation and the Society for General Psychology, the E. L. Thorndike Award for Career Achievement in Educational Psychology Award, the Distinguished Award for an Early Career Contribution to Psychology, and Boyd R. McCandless Award from APA; the Palmer O. Johnson, Research Review, Outstanding Book, and Sylvia Scribner Awards from AERA; the James McKeen Cattell Award from APS; the Distinguished Lifetime Contribution to Psychology Award from the Connecticut Psychological Association; the International Award of the Association of Portuguese Psychologists; the Cattell Award of the Society for Multivariate Experimental Psychology; the Award for Excellence of the Mensa Education and Research Foundation; the Distinction of Honor SEK, from the Institucion SEK (Madrid); the Sidney Siegel Memorial Award of Stanford University; and the Wohlenberg Prize of Yale University. He has held a Guggenheim Fellowship and Yale University Senior and Junior Faculty Fellowships as well as an NSF Graduate Fellowship. He also has held the Honored Visitor Fellowship of the Taiwan National Science Council and the Sir Edward Youde Memorial Visiting Professorship of the City University of Hong Kong. He has served as Editor of the *Psychological Bulletin* and is Editor of *Contemporary Psychology.* Sternberg is most well known for his theory of successful intelligence, investment theory of creativity (developed with Todd Lubart), theory of thinking styles as mental self-government, balance theory of wisdom, and for his triangular theory of love and his theory of love as a story.

Series Introduction

Sally M. Reis

The accomplishments of the last 50 years in the education of gifted students should not be underestimated: the field of education of the gifted and talented has emerged as strong and visible. In many states, a policy or position statement from the state board of education supports the education of the gifted and talented, and specific legislation generally recognizes the special needs of this group. Growth in our field has not been constant, however, and researchers and scholars have discussed the various high and low points of national interest and commitment to educating the gifted and talented (Gallagher, 1979; Renzulli, 1980; Tannenbaum, 1983). Gallagher described the struggle between support and apathy for special programs for gifted and talented students as having roots in historical tradition—the battle between an aristocratic elite and our concomitant belief in egalitarianism. Tannenbaum suggested the existence of two peak periods of interest in the gifted as the five years following *Sputnik* in 1957 and the last half of the decade of the 1970s, describing a valley of neglect between the peaks in which the public focused its attention on the disadvantaged and the handicapped. "The cyclical nature of interest in the gifted is probably unique in American education. No other special group of children has been alternately embraced and repelled with so much vigor by educators and laypersons alike" (Tannenbaum, 1983, p. 16). Many wonder if the cyclical nature to which Tannenbaum referred is not somewhat prophetic, as it appears that our field may be experiencing another downward spiral in interest as a result of current governmental initiatives and an increasing emphasis on testing and standardization of curriculum. Tannenbaum's description of a valley of neglect may describe current conditions. During the late 1980s, programming flourished during a peak of interest and a textbook on systems and models for gifted programs included 15 models for elementary and secondary programs (Renzulli, 1986). The Jacob Javits Gifted and Talented Students Education Act passed by Congress in 1988 resulted in the creation of the National Research Center on the Gifted and Talented, and dozens of model programs were added to the collective knowledge in the field in areas related to underrepresented populations and successful practices. In the 1990s, reduction or elimination of gifted programs occurred, as budget pressures exacerbated by the lingering recession in the late 1990s resulted in the reduction of services mandated by fewer than half of the states in our country.

Even during times in which more activity focused on the needs of gifted and talented students, concerns were still raised about the limited services provided to these students. In the second federal report on the status of education for our nation's most talented students entitled *National Excellence: A Case for Developing America's Talent* (Ross, 1993), "a quiet crisis" was described in the absence of attention paid to this population: "Despite sporadic attention over the years to the needs of bright students, most of them continue to spend time in school working well below their capabilities. The belief espoused in school reform that children from all economic and cultural backgrounds must reach their full potential has not been extended to America's most talented students. They are underchallenged and therefore underachieve" (p. 5). The report further indicates that our nation's gifted and talented students have a less rigorous curriculum, read fewer demanding books, and are less prepared for work or postsecondary education than the most talented students in many other industrialized countries. Talented children who come from economically disadvantaged homes or are members of minority groups are especially neglected, the report also indicates, and many of them will not realize their potential without some type of intervention.

In this anniversary series of volumes celebrating the evolution of our field, noted scholars introduce a collection of the most frequently cited articles from the premiere journal in our field, *Gifted Child Quarterly*. Each volume includes a collection of thoughtful, and in some cases, provocative articles that honor our past, acknowledge the challenges we face in the present, and provide hopeful guidance for the future as we seek the optimal educational experiences for all talented students. These influential articles, published after a rigorous peer review, were selected because they are frequently cited and considered seminal in our field. Considered in their entirety, the articles show that we have learned a great deal from the volume of work represented by this series. Our knowledge has expanded over several decades of work, and progress has been made toward reaching consensus about what is known. As several of the noted scholars who introduce separate areas explain in their introductions, this series helps us to understand that some questions have been answered, while others remain. While we still search for these answers, we are now better prepared to ask questions that continue and evolve. The seminal articles in this series help us to resolve some issues, while they highlight other questions that simply refuse to go away. Finally, the articles help us to identify new challenges that continue to emerge in our field. Carol Tomlinson suggests, for example, that the area of curriculum differentiation in the field of gifted education is, in her words, an issue born in the field of gifted education, and one that continues to experience rebirth.

Some of the earliest questions in our field have been answered and time has enabled those answers to be considered part of our common core of knowledge. For example, it is widely acknowledged that both school and home experiences can help to develop giftedness in persons with high potential and that a continuum of services in and out of school can provide the greatest likelihood that this development will occur. Debates over other "hot" issues such as grouping and acceleration that took place in the gifted education community 30 years ago are now largely unnecessary, as Linda Brody points out in her introduction to a series of articles in this area. General agreement seems to have been reached, for example, that grouping, enrichment and acceleration are all necessary to provide appropriate educational opportunities for gifted and talented learners. These healthy debates of the past helped to strengthen our field but visionary and reflective work remains to be done. In this series, section editors summarize what has been learned and raise provocative questions about the future. The questions alone are some of the most thoughtful in our field, providing enough research opportunities for scholars for the next decade. The brief introductions below provide some highlights about the series.

DEFINITIONS OF GIFTEDNESS (VOLUME 1)

In Volume 1, Robert Sternberg introduces us to seminal articles about definitions of giftedness and the types of talents and gifts exhibited by children and youth. The most widely used definitions of gifts and talents utilized by educators generally follow those proposed in federal reports. For example, the Marland Report (Marland, 1972) commissioned by the Congress included the first federal definition of giftedness, which was widely adopted or adapted by the states.

The selection of a definition of giftedness has been and continues to be the major policy decision made at state and local levels. It is interesting to note that policy decisions are often either unrelated or marginally related to actual procedures or to research findings about a definition of giftedness or identification of the gifted, a fact well documented by the many ineffective, incorrect, and downright ridiculous methods of identification used to find students who meet the criteria in the federal definition. This gap between policy and practice may be caused by many variables. Unfortunately, although the federal definition was written to be inclusive, it is, instead, rather vague, and problems caused by this definition have been recognized by experts in the field (Renzulli, 1978). In the most recent federal report on the status of gifted and talented programs entitled *National Excellence* (Ross, 1993), a newer federal definition is proposed based on new insights provided by neuroscience and cognitive psychology. Arguing that the term *gifted* connotes a mature power rather than a developing ability and, therefore, is antithetic to recent research findings about children, the new definition "reflects today's knowledge and thinking" (p. 26) by emphasizing talent development, stating that gifted and talented children are

> children and youth with outstanding talent performance or show the potential for performing at remarkably high levels of accomplishment when compared with others of their age, experience, or environment. These children and youth exhibit high performance capability in intellectual, creative, and/or artistic areas, possess an unusual leadership capacity, or excel in specific academic fields. They require services or activities not ordinarily provided by the schools. Outstanding talents are present in children and youth from all cultural groups, across all economic strata, and in all areas of human endeavor. (p. 26)

Fair identification systems use a variety of multiple assessment measures that respect diversity, accommodate students who develop at different rates, and identify potential as well as demonstrated talent. In the introduction to the volume, Sternberg admits, that just as people have bad habits, so do academic fields, explaining, "a bad habit of much of the gifted field is to do research on giftedness, or worse, identify children as gifted or not gifted, without having a clear conception of what it means to be gifted." Sternberg summarizes major themes from the seminal articles about definitions by asking key questions about the nature of giftedness and talent, the ways in which we should study giftedness, whether we should expand conventional notions of giftedness, and if so, how that can be accomplished; whether differences exist between giftedness and talent; the validity of available assessments; and perhaps most importantly, how do we and can we develop giftedness and talent. Sternberg succinctly summarizes points of broad agreement from the many scholars who have contributed to this section, concluding that giftedness involves more than just high IQ, that it has noncognitive and cognitive components, that the environment is crucial in terms of whether potentials for gifted performance will be realized, and that giftedness is not a single thing. He further cautions that the ways we conceptualize giftedness greatly influences who will have opportunities to develop their gifts and reminds readers of our responsibilities as educators. He also asks one of the most critical questions in our field: whether gifted and talented individuals will use their knowledge to benefit or harm our world.

IDENTIFICATION OF HIGH-ABILITY STUDENTS (VOLUME 2)

In Volume 2, Joseph Renzulli introduces what is perhaps the most critical question still facing practitioners and researchers in our field, that is how, when, and why should we identify gifted and talented students. Renzulli believes that conceptions of giftedness exist along a continuum ranging from a very conservative or restricted view of giftedness to a more flexible or multidimensional approach. What many seem not to understand is that the first step in identification should always be to ask: identification for what? For what type of program or experience is the youngster being identified? If, for example, an arts program is being developed for talented artists, the resulting identification system must be structured to identify youngsters with either demonstrated or potential talent in art.

Renzulli's introductory chapter summarizes seminal articles about identification, and summarizes emerging consensus. For example, most suggest, that while intelligence tests and other cognitive ability tests provide one very important form of information about one dimension of a young person's potential, mainly in the areas of verbal and analytic skills, they do not tell us all that we need to know about who should be identified. These authors do not argue that cognitive ability tests should be dropped from the identification process. Rather, most believe that (a) other indicators of potential should be used for identification, (b) these indicators should be given equal consideration when it comes to making final decisions about which students will be candidates for special services, and (c) in the final analysis, it is the thoughtful judgment of knowledgeable professionals rather than instruments and cutoff scores that should guide selection decisions.

Another issue addressed by the authors of the seminal articles about identification is what has been referred to as the distinction between (a) convergent and divergent thinking (Guilford, 1967; Torrance, 1984), (b) entrenchment and non-entrenchment (Sternberg, 1982), and (c) schoolhouse giftedness versus creative/productive giftedness (Renzulli, 1982; Renzulli & Delcourt, 1986). It is easier to identify schoolhouse giftedness than it is to identify students with the potential for creative productive giftedness. Renzulli believes that progress has been made in the identification of gifted students, especially during the past quarter century, and that new approaches address the equity issue, policies, and practices that respect new theories about human potential and conceptions of giftedness. He also believes, however, that continuous commitment to research-based identification practices is still needed, for "it is important to keep in mind that some of the characteristics that have led to the recognition of history's most gifted contributors are not always as measurable as others. We need to continue our search for those elusive things that are left over after everything explainable has been explained, to realize that giftedness is culturally and contextually imbedded in all human activity, and most of all, to value the value of even those things that we cannot yet explain."

ACCELERATION AND GROUPING, CURRICULUM, AND CURRICULUM DIFFERENTIATION (VOLUMES 3, 4, 5)

Three volumes in this series address curricular and grouping issues in gifted programs, and it is in this area, perhaps, that some of the most promising practices have been implemented for gifted and talented students. Grouping and curriculum interact with each other, as various forms of grouping patterns have enabled students to work on advanced curricular opportunities with other talented students. And, as is commonly known now about instructional and ability grouping, it is not the way students are grouped that matters most, but rather, it is what happens within the groups that makes the most difference.

In too many school settings, little differentiation of curriculum and instruction for gifted students is provided during the school day, and minimal opportunities are offered. Occasionally, after-school enrichment programs or Saturday programs offered by museums, science centers, or local universities take the place of comprehensive school programs, and too many academically talented students attend school in classrooms across the country in which they are bored, unmotivated, and unchallenged. Acceleration, once a frequently used educational practice in our country, is often dismissed by teachers and administrators as an inappropriate practice for a variety of reasons, including scheduling problems, concerns about the social effects of grade skipping, and others. Various forms of acceleration, including enabling precocious students to enter kindergarten or first grade early, grade skipping, and early entrance to college are not commonly used by most school districts.

Unfortunately, major alternative grouping strategies involve the reorganization of school structures, and these have been too slow in coming, perhaps due to the difficulty of making major educational changes, because of scheduling, finances, and other issues that have caused schools to substantially delay major change patterns. Because of this delay, gifted students too often fail to receive classroom instruction based on their unique needs that place them far ahead of their chronological peers in basic skills and verbal abilities and enable them to learn much more rapidly and tackle much more complex materials than their peers. Our most able students need appropriately paced, rich and challenging instruction, and curriculum that varies significantly from what is being taught in regular classrooms across America. Too often, academically talented students are "left behind" in school.

Linda Brody introduces the question of how to group students optimally for instructional purposes and pays particular concern to the degree to which the typical age-in-grade instructional program can meet the needs of gifted students — those students with advanced cognitive abilities and achievement that may already have mastered the curriculum designed for their age peers. The articles about grouping emphasize the importance of responding to the learning needs of individual students with curricular flexibility, the need for educators to be flexible when assigning students to instructional groups, and the need to modify those groups when necessary. Brody's introduction points out that the debate about grouping gifted and talented learners together was one area that brought the field together, as every researcher in the field supports some type of grouping option, and few would disagree with the need to use grouping and accelerated learning as tools that allow us to differentiate content for students with different learning needs. When utilized as a way to offer a more advanced educational program to students with advanced cognitive abilities and achievement levels, these practices can help achieve the goal of an appropriate education for all students.

Joyce VanTassel-Baska introduces the seminal articles in curriculum, by explaining that they represent several big ideas that emphasize the values and relevant factors of a curriculum for the gifted, the technology of curriculum development, aspects of differentiation of a curriculum for the gifted within core subject areas and without, and the research-based efficacy of such curriculum and related instructional pedagogy in use. She also reminds readers of Harry Passow's concerns about curriculum balance, suggesting that an imbalance exists, as little evidence suggests that the affective development of gifted students is occurring through special curricula for the gifted. Moreover, interdisciplinary efforts at curriculum frequently exclude the arts and foreign language. Only through acknowledging and applying curriculum balance in these areas are we likely to be producing the type of humane individual Passow envisioned. To achieve balance, VanTassel-Baska recommends a full set of curriculum options across domains, as well as the need to nurture the social-emotional needs of diverse gifted and talented learners.

Carol Tomlinson introduces the critical area of differentiation in the field of gifted education that has only emerged in the last 13 years. She believes the diverse nature of the articles and their relatively recent publication suggests that this area is indeed, in her words, "an issue born in the field of gifted education, and one that continues to experience rebirth." She suggests that one helpful way of thinking about the articles in this volume is that their approach varies, as some approach the topic of differentiation of curriculum with a greater emphasis on the distinctive mission of gifted education. Others look at differentiation with a greater emphasis on the goals, issues, and missions shared between general education and gifted education. Drawing from an analogy with anthropology, Tomlinson suggests that "splitters" in that field focus on differences among cultures while "lumpers" have a greater interest in what cultures share in common. Splitters ask the question of what happens for high-ability students in mixed-ability settings, while lumpers question what common issues and solutions exist for multiple populations in mixed-ability settings.

Tomlinson suggests that the most compelling feature of the collection of articles in this section—and certainly its key unifying feature—is the linkage between the two areas of educational practice in attempting to address an issue likely to be seminal to the success of both over the coming quarter century and beyond, and this collection may serve as a catalyst for next steps in those directions for the field of gifted education as it continues collaboration with general education and other educational specialties while simultaneously addressing those missions uniquely its own.

UNDERREPRESENTED AND TWICE-EXCEPTIONAL POPULATIONS AND SOCIAL AND EMOTIONAL ISSUES (VOLUMES 6, 7, 8)

The majority of young people participating in gifted and talented programs across the country continue to represent the majority culture in our society. Few doubts exist regarding the reasons that economically disadvantaged, twice-exceptional, and culturally diverse students are underrepresented in gifted programs. One reason may be the ineffective and inappropriate identification and selection procedures used for the identification of these young people that limits referrals and nominations and eventual placement. Research summarized in this series indicates that groups that have been traditionally underrepresented in gifted programs could be better served if some of the following elements are considered: new constructs of giftedness, attention to cultural and contextual variability, the use of more varied and authentic assessments, performance-based identification, and identification opportunities through rich and varied learning opportunities.

Alexinia Baldwin discusses the lower participation of culturally diverse and underserved populations in programs for the gifted as a major concern that has forged dialogues and discussion in *Gifted Child Quarterly* over the past five decades. She classifies these concerns in three major themes: *identification/selection, programming,* and *staff assignment and development.* Calling the first theme **Identification/Selection**, she indicates that it has always been the Achilles' heel of educators' efforts to ensure that giftedness can be expressed in many ways through broad identification techniques. Citing favorable early work by Renzulli and Hartman (1971) and Baldwin (1977) that expanded options for identification, Baldwin cautions that much remains to be done. The second theme, **Programming**, recognizes the abilities of students who are culturally diverse but often forces them to exist in programs designed "for one size fits all." Her third theme relates to **Staffing and Research,** as she voices concerns about the diversity of teachers in these programs as well as the attitudes or mindsets of researchers who develop theories and conduct the research that addresses these concerns.

Susan Baum traces the historical roots of gifted and talented individuals with special needs, summarizing Terman's early work that suggested the gifted were healthier, more popular, and better adjusted than their less able peers. More importantly, gifted individuals were regarded as those who could perform at high levels in all areas with little or no support. Baum suggests that acceptance of these stereotypical characteristics diminished the possibility that there could be special populations of gifted students with special needs. Baum believes that the seminal articles in this collection address one or more of the critical issues that face gifted students at risk and suggest strategies for overcoming the barriers that prevent them from realizing their promise. The articles focus on three populations of students: twice-exceptional students—gifted students who are at risk for poor development due to difficulties in learning and attention;

gifted students who face gender issues that inhibit their ability to achieve or develop socially and emotionally, and students who are economically disadvantaged and at risk for dropping out of school. Baum summarizes research indicating that each of these groups of youngsters is affected by one or more barriers to development, and the most poignant of these barriers are identification strategies, lack of awareness of consequences of co-morbidity, deficit thinking in program design, and lack of appropriate social and emotional support. She ends her introduction with a series of thoughtful questions focusing on future directions in this critical area.

Sidney Moon introduces the seminal articles on the social and emotional development of and counseling for gifted children by acknowledging the contributions of the National Association for Gifted Children's task forces that have examined social/emotional issues. The first task force, formed in 2000 and called the Social and Emotional Issues Task Force, completed its work in 2002 by publishing an edited book, *The Social and Emotional Development of Gifted Children: What Do We Know?* This volume provides an extensive review of the literature on the social and emotional development of gifted children (Neihart, Reis, Robinson, & Moon, 2002). Moon believes that the seminal studies in the area of the social and emotional development and counseling illustrate both the strengths and the weaknesses of the current literature on social and emotional issues in the field of gifted education. These articles bring increased attention to the affective needs of special populations of gifted students, such as underachievers, who are at risk for failure to achieve their potential, but also point to the need for more empirical studies on "what works" with these students, both in terms of preventative strategies and more intensive interventions. She acknowledges that although good counseling models have been developed, they need to be rigorously evaluated to determine their effectiveness under disparate conditions, and calls for additional research on the affective and counseling interventions with specific subtypes of gifted students such as Asian Americans, African Americans, and twice-exceptional students. Moon also strongly encourages researchers in the field of gifted education to collaborate with researchers from affective fields such as personal and social psychology, counseling psychology, family therapy, and psychiatry to learn to intervene most effectively with gifted individuals with problems and to learn better how to help all gifted persons achieve optimal social, emotional, and personal development.

ARTISTICALLY AND CREATIVELY TALENTED STUDENTS (VOLUMES 9, 10)

Enid Zimmerman introduces the volume on talent development in the visual and performing arts with a summary of articles about students who are talented in music, dance, visual arts, and spatial, kinesthetic, and expressive areas. Major themes that appear in the articles include perceptions by parents, students, and teachers that often focus on concerns related to nature versus nurture in arts talent development; research about the crystallizing experiences of artistically talented students; collaboration between school and community members about identification of talented art students from diverse backgrounds; and leadership issues related to empowering teachers of talented arts students. They all are concerned to some extent with teacher, parent, and student views about educating artistically talented students. Included also are discussions about identification of talented students from urban, suburban, and rural environments. Zimmerman believes that in this particular area, a critical need exists for research about the impact of educational opportunities, educational settings, and the role of art teachers on the development of artistically talented students. The impact of the standards and testing movement and its relationship to the education of talented students in the visual and performing arts is an area greatly in need of investigation. Research also is needed about students' backgrounds, personalities, gender orientations, skill development, and cognitive and affective abilities as well as cross-cultural contexts and the impact of global and popular culture on the education of artistically talented students. The compelling case study with which she introduces this volume sets the stage for the need for this research.

Donald Treffinger introduces reflections on articles about creativity by discussing the following five core themes that express the collective efforts of researchers to grasp common conceptual and theoretical challenges associated with creativity. The themes include **Definitions** (how we define giftedness, talent, or creativity), **Characteristics** (the indicators of giftedness and creativity in people), **Justification** (Why is creativity important in education?), **Assessment** of creativity, and the ways we **Nurture** creativity. Treffinger also discusses the expansion of knowledge, the changes that have occurred, the search for answers, and the questions that still remain. In the early years of interest of creativity research, Treffinger believed that considerable discussion existed about whether it was possible to foster creativity through training or instruction. He reports that over the last 50 years, educators have learned that deliberate efforts to nurture creativity are possible (e.g., Torrance, 1987), and further extends this line of inquiry by asking the key question, "What works best, for whom, and under what conditions?" Treffinger summarizes the challenges faced by educators who try to nurture the development of creativity through effective teaching and to ask which experiences will have the greatest impact, as these will help to determine our ongoing lines of research, development, and training initiatives.

EVALUATION AND PUBLIC POLICY (VOLUMES 11, 12)

Carolyn Callahan introduces the seminal articles on evaluation and suggests that this important component neglected by experts in the field of gifted education for at least the last three decades can be a plea for important work by both evaluators and practitioners. She divides the seminal literature on evaluation, and in particular the literature on the evaluation of gifted programs into four categories, those which (a) provide theory and/or practical guidelines, (b) describe or report on specific program evaluations, (c) provide stimuli for the discussion of issues surrounding the evaluation process, and (d) suggest new research on the evaluation process. Callahan concludes with a challenge indicating work to be done and the opportunity for experts to make valuable contributions to increased effectiveness and efficiency of programs for the gifted.

James Gallagher provides a call-to-arms in the seminal articles he introduces on public policy by raising some of the most challenging questions in the field. Gallagher suggests that as a field, we need to come to some consensus about stronger interventions and consider how we react to accusations of elitism. He believes that our field could be doing a great deal more with additional targeted resources supporting the general education teacher and the development of specialists in gifted education, and summarizes that our failure to fight in the public arena for scarce resources may raise again the question posed two decades ago by Renzulli (1980), looking toward 1990: "Will the gifted child movement be alive and well in 2010?"

CONCLUSION

What can we learn from an examination of our field and the seminal articles that have emerged over the last few decades? First, we must **respect the past** by acknowledging the times in which articles were written and the shoulders of those persons upon whom we stand as we continue to create and develop our field. An old proverb tells us that when we drink from the well, we must remember to acknowledge those who dug the well, and in our field the early articles represent the seeds that grew our field. Next, we must **celebrate the present** and the exciting work and new directions in our field and the knowledge that is now accepted as a common core. Last, we must **embrace the future** by understanding that there is no finished product when it comes to research on gifted and talented children and how we are best able to meet their unique needs. Opportunities abound in the work reported in this series, but many questions remain. A few things seem clear. Action in the future should be based on both qualitative and quantitative research as well as longitudinal studies, and what we have completed only scratches the surface regarding the many variables and issues that still need to be explored. Research is needed that suggests positive changes that will lead to more inclusive programs that recognize the talents and gifts of diverse students in our country. When this occurs, future teachers and researchers in gifted education will find answers that can be embraced by educators, communities, and families, and the needs of all talented and gifted students will be more effectively met in their classrooms by teachers who have been trained to develop their students' gifts and talents.

We also need to consider carefully how we work with the field of education in general. As technology emerges and improves, new opportunities will become available to us. Soon, all students should be able to have their curricular needs preassessed before they begin any new curriculum unit. Soon, the issue of keeping students on grade-level material when they are many grades ahead should disappear as technology enables us to pinpoint students' strengths. Will chronological grades be eliminated? The choices we have when technology enables us to learn better what students already know presents exciting scenarios for the future, and it is imperative that we advocate carefully for multiple opportunities for these students, based on their strengths and interests, as well as a challenging core curriculum. Parents, educators, and professionals who care about these special populations need to become politically active to draw attention to the unique needs of these students, and researchers need to conduct the experimental studies that can prove the efficacy of providing talent development options as well as opportunities for healthy social and emotional growth.

For any field to continue to be vibrant and to grow, new voices must be heard, and new players sought. A great opportunity is available in our field; for as we continue to advocate for gifted and talented students, we can also play important roles in the changing educational reform movement. We can continue to work to achieve more challenging opportunities for all students while we fight to maintain gifted, talented, and enrichment programs. We can continue our advocacy for differentiation through acceleration, individual curriculum opportunities, and a continuum of advanced curriculum and personal support opportunities. The questions answered and those raised in this volume of seminal articles can help us to move forward as a field. We hope those who read the series will join us in this exciting journey.

REFERENCES

Baldwin, A.Y. (1977). Tests do underpredict: A case study. *Phi Delta Kappan, 58,* 620-621.

Gallagher, J. J. (1979). Issues in education for the gifted. In A. H. Passow (Ed.), *The gifted and the talented: Their education and development* (pp. 28-44). Chicago: University of Chicago Press.

Guilford, J. E. (1967). *The nature of human intelligence.* New York: McGraw-Hill.

Marland, S. P., Jr. (1972). *Education of the gifted and talented: Vol. 1. Report to the Congress of the United States by the U.S. Commissioner of Education.* Washington, DC: U.S. Government Printing Office.

Neihart, M., Reis, S., Robinson, N., & Moon, S. M. (Eds.). (2002). *The social and emotional development of gifted children: What do we know?* Waco, TX: Prufrock.

Renzulli, J. S. (1978). What makes giftedness? Reexamining a definition. *Phi Delta Kappan, 60*(5), 180-184.

Renzulli, J. S. (1980). Will the gifted child movement be alive and well in 1990? *Gifted Child Quarterly, 24*(1), 3-9. **[See Vol. 12.]**

Renzulli, J. (1982). Dear Mr. and Mrs. Copernicus: We regret to inform you . . . *Gifted Child Quarterly, 26*(1), 11-14. **[See Vol. 2.]**

Renzulli, J. S. (Ed.). (1986). *Systems and models for developing programs for the gifted and talented.* Mansfield Center, CT: Creative Learning Press.

Renzulli, J. S., & Delcourt, M. A. B. (1986). The legacy and logic of research on the identification of gifted persons. *Gifted Child Quarterly, 30*(1), 20-23. **[See Vol. 2.]**

Renzulli J., & Hartman, R. (1971). Scale for rating behavioral characteristics of superior students. *Exceptional Children, 38,* 243-248.

Ross, P. (1993). *National excellence: A case for developing America's talent.* Washington, DC: U.S. Department of Education, Government Printing Office.

Sternberg, R. J. (1982). Nonentrenchment in the assessment of intellectual giftedness. *Gifted Child Quarterly, 26*(2), 63-67. **[See Vol. 2.]**

Tannenbaum, A. J. (1983). *Gifted children: Psychological and educational perspectives.* New York: Macmillan.

Torrance, E. P. (1984). The role of creativity in identification of the gifted and talented. *Gifted Child Quarterly, 28*(4), 153-156. **[See Vols. 2 and 10.]**

Torrance, E. P. (1987). Recent trends in teaching children and adults to think creatively. In S. G. Isaksen (Ed.), *Frontiers of creativity research: Beyond the basics* (pp. 204-215). Buffalo, NY: Bearly Limited.

Introduction to Definitions and Conceptions of Giftedness

Robert J. Sternberg

Yale University

Just as people have bad habits, so can academic fields have bad habits. A bad habit of much of the gifted field is to do research on giftedness, or worse, identify children as gifted or not gifted, without having a clear conception of what it means to be gifted. We can thereby end up with a label—"giftedness"—that has no clear content. The seminal articles from *Gifted Child Quarterly* in this volume address this issue of what giftedness is. They thereby inform our efforts to do research on giftedness and to identify children as gifted.

What are some of the major issues raised in these articles, and what are examples of some ideas proposed to address each of these issues?

- What is the nature of giftedness and talent?
  - One can learn more about the nature of giftedness through viewing responses to enrichment activities than through conventional tests (Passow, 1981).
  - Giftedness involves excellence, rarity, productivity, demonstrability, and value attached to the skills/products of the individual (Sternberg & Zhang, 1995).
- How should we study giftedness?
  - We need more to use the techniques of mainstream psychological research to study giftedness (Jackson, 1993).

- Should we expand conventional notions of giftedness, and if so, how should we do so?
  - Metacognition is crucial to giftedness (Shore & Dover, 1987).
  - Creativity is an important facet of giftedness (Runco, 1993).
  - Wisdom is an important kind of giftedness (Sternberg, 2000).
- How, if at all, are giftedness and talent different?
  - Giftedness refers to domains of human abilities, talents, to domains of human accomplishments (Gagné, 1985).
- Are there different profiles of giftedness and talent, and if so, what are they?
  - Six profiles of giftedness and talent are successful, challenging, underground, dropouts, double-labeled, and autonomous (Betts & Neihart, 1988).
  - Different kinds of gifted individuals (e.g., statesmen versus religious leaders) develop through different profiles of strengths and weaknesses (Walberg, Tsai, Weinstein, Gabriel, Rasher, Rosecrans, Rovai, Ide, Trujillo, & Vukosavich, 1981).
- How do giftedness and talent develop?
  - They develop in part through certain kinds of overexcitabilities, namely, psychomotor, sensual, intellectual, imaginational, and emotional (Piechowski & Colangelo, 1984).
  - Prodigies develop in a way that is different from that of most gifted individuals in part as a function of opportunities made available to them in their environments (Feldman, 1993).
  - Giftedness can be understood in part in terms of the interaction of the organism and the environment, which produces diverse developmental outcomes (Horowitz, 1987).
- How valid are available assessments of giftedness and talent?
  - Measures of multiple intelligences appear, in general, to be reliable but not particularly valid (Plucker, Callahan, & Tomchin, 1996).

It would, of course, be delightful if a consensus could be found on all or even many of these issues, but consensus is hard to find. Nevertheless, there appear to be at least several points of broad agreement.

- Giftedness involves more than just high IQ.
- Giftedness has noncognitive (e.g., motivationally driven) components as well as cognitive ones.
- Environment is crucial in terms of whether potentials for gifted performance will be realized.

- Giftedness is not a single thing: There are multiple forms Hence, one-size-fits-all assessments or programs are lik narrow.
- Measures for identifying or evaluating gifted individuals nee posed to operationalize theories, and then they need to be uated rather than merely being assumed to be valid.

Thus, progress has been made in the definition and conceptualization of giftedness, and series such as this, that this progress will continue into the future. Research that is summarized in these seminal articles raise important points for both researchers and teachers to consider and broadened definitions and conceptions of giftedness will result in more enlightened choices about the decisions we make about who is able to participate in the programs we develop.

I end on a cautionary note. The way we conceptualize giftedness greatly influences who will have greater and lesser opportunities to contribute to future society. People who are identified as gifted are given opportunities to succeed that people who are not so identified are not given. Thus, it is important to consider not only the skills individuals have, but also how they will use them. Will, for example, abilities, in Gagné's sense of the term, be transformed into talents that are useful to society? Will individuals who are intellectually able make creative contributions, or will they merely replicate what is already known, however well they may replicate it? Will able individuals use their knowledge wisely, or for destructive ends? In a world beset by conflict and turmoil, perhaps these are the most important questions we presently need to address.

REFERENCES

Betts, G. T., & Neihart, M. (1988). Profiles of the gifted and talented. *Gifted Child Quarterly, 32*(2), 248-253. **[See Vol. 1, p. 97]**

Feldman, D. H. (1993). Child prodigies: A distinctive form of giftedness. *Gifted Child Quarterly, 37*(4), 188-193. **[See Vol. 1, p. 133]**

Gagné, F. (1985). Giftedness and talent: Reexamining a reexamination of the definitions. *Gifted Child Quarterly, 29*(3), 103-112. **[See Vol. 1, p. 79]**

Horowitz, F. D. (1987). A developmental view of giftedness. *Gifted Child Quarterly, 31*(4), 165-168. **[See Vol. 1, p. 145]**

Jackson, N. E. (1993). Moving into the mainstream? Reflections on the study of giftedness. *Gifted Child Quarterly, 37*(1), 46-50. **[See Vol. 1, p. 29]**

Passow, A. H. (1981). The nature of giftedness and talent. *Gifted Child Quarterly, 25*(1), 5-10. **[See Vol. 1, p. 1]**

Piechowski, M. M., & Colangelo, N. (1984). Developmental potential of the gifted. *Gifted Child Quarterly, 28*(2), 80-88. **[See Vol. 1, p. 117]**

Plucker, J., Callahan, C. M., & Tomchin, E. M. (1996). Wherefore art thou, multiple intelligences? Alternative assessments for identifying talent in ethnically diverse and low income students. *Gifted Child Quarterly, 40*(2), 81-92 . **[See Vol. 1, p. 155]**

Runco, M. A. (1993). Divergent thinking, creativity, and giftedness. *Gifted Child Quarterly, 37*(1), 16-22. **[See Vol. 1, p. 47]**

Shore, B. M. & Dover, A. C. (1987). Metacognition, intelligence and giftedness. *Gifted Child Quarterly, 31*(1), 37-39. **[See Vol. 1, p. 39]**

Sternberg, R. J. (2000). Wisdom as a form of giftedness. *Gifted Child Quarterly, 44*(4), 252-260. **[See Vol. 1, p. 63]**

Sternberg, R. J., & Zang, L. (1995). What do we mean by giftedness? A pentagonal implicit theory. *Gifted Child Quarterly, 39*(2), 88-94. **[See Vol. 1, p. 13]**

Walberg, H. J., Tsai, S., Weinstein, T., Gabriel, C. L., Rasher, S. P., Rosecrans, T., Rovai, E., Ide, J., Trujillo, M., & Vukosavich, P. (1981). Childhood traits and environmental conditions of highly eminent adults. *Gifted Child Quarterly, 25*(3), 103-107. **[See Vol. 1, p. 107]**

1

The Nature of Giftedness and Talent

A. Harry Passow

Any discussion of the nature of giftedness and talent will depend on how one defines those terms. Who is gifted? Who is talented? How are giftedness and talent manifested?

Perhaps the widest used definition these days—"used" in the sense that a good deal of the literature alludes to it and a great many school systems assert that it is the definition which guides their planning—is the so-called U.S. Office of Education definition. This definition suggested by an advisory panel to the then-Commissioner of Education, Sidney Marland, Jr., and presented in the Marland Report is as follows:

> Gifted and talented children are those identified by professionally qualified persons who, by virtue of outstanding abilities, are capable of high performance. These are children who require differentiated educational programs and/or services beyond those normally provided by the regular school program in order to realize their contribution to self and society. (p. IX)

Editor's Note: From Passow, A.H. (1981). The nature of giftedness and talent. *Gifted Child Quarterly, 25*(1), 5–10.

Children capable of high performance include those with demonstrated achievement and/or potential ability in any of the following areas, singly or in combination:

1. general intellectual ability;
2. specific academic aptitude;
3. creative or productive thinking;
4. leadership ability;
5. visual and performing arts;
6. psychomotor ability.

It should be noted that "psychomotor ability" was deleted from the areas suggested by the Marland Report by PL 95–561, leaving only five areas in the OE definition.

For the most part, the OE definition has been accepted quite uncritically and, as Renzulli (1978) has pointed out, "has served the very useful purpose of calling attention to a wider variety of abilities that should be included in a definition of giftedness. . . ." However, he adds, "at the same time it has presented some major problems" (p. 181).

From 1868 on, when William T. Harris instituted flexible promotion as a way of providing for abler pupils in the St. Louis schools, various school systems instituted programs to meet the needs of the "pupils of more than average capability," "brilliant children," "pupils of supernormal mentality," "gifted" and a variety of other terms—all of which referred to individuals with high intelligence quotients and/or high scholastic attainments. "Rapid advancement classes" were started in New York City in 1900. These were classes for exceptionally bright children. By 1915, what eventually became known as the "SP" classes were designed to hasten the progress of bright children by enabling them to complete seventh, eighth, and ninth grades in two years (Henry, 1920, p. 31).

The reviews of programs and provisions (or gifted in the early years which appeared in the National Society for the Study of Education, 19th and 23rd yearbooks (Henry, 1920 & Whipple, 1924), clearly indicate that it was the highly intelligent and high academic achiever who were considered gifted, and it was the traits and characteristics of such individuals which determined the nature of giftedness. It was Guy M. Whipple who was credited with having established the "term 'gifted' as the standard designation of children of supernormal ability," having used it in Monroe's *Cyclopedia of Education* (Henry, 1920, p. 9).

Although there was a good deal of activity and some research prior to the start of Terman's so-called *Genetic Studies of Genius* in 1922—the bibliography in the 19th NSSE Yearbook contains 163 items and the 23rd NSSE Yearbook includes an annotated bibliography of 453 items—represented the first large-scale longitudinal study of the nature of the gifted. The Stanford Study "was designed to discover what physical, mental, and personality traits are characteristic of gifted children as a class, and what sort of adult the typical gifted child becomes" (Terman & Oden, 1951, p. 21). Increasing the knowledge about the origin and the physical and mental traits of gifted children was not viewed by Terman as an end unto itself. Rather, as he pointed out, in the first report:

> When the sources of our intellectual talent have been determined, it is conceivable that means may be found which would increase the supply. When the physical, mental, and character traits of gifted children are better understood it will be possible to set about their education with better hope of success. . . . In the gifted child, nature has moved far back the usual limits of educability, but the realms thus thrown open to the educator are still *terra incognita.* It is time to move forward, explore, and consolidate. (Terman, 1925 & 1926, pp. 16–17)

Terman's search for subjects was aimed at locating "subjects with a degree of brightness that would rate them well within the top one percent of the school population" (Terman, 1925 & 1926, p. 19). A 140 IQ on the Stanford-Binet test and, for high school subjects, a 135 IQ on the Terman Group Intelligence Test was, as Terman pointed out, the arbitrary standard set for inclusion in the study.

The initial Terman study and the subsequent follow-up studies (which still continue although Terman died in 1956) have lent support to the hypothesis that early promise of intellectually gifted students in the elementary school is likely to culminate in relative outstanding achievement during adulthood. Among the many findings was the fact that, contrary to popular belief, mentally gifted youngsters were far superior to their less highly endowed age peers in general health and physique, mental health and adjustment, adult intelligence, occupational status and earned income, publications and patents, and even "contentment."

One of Terman's co-workers, Catherine Cox (1926), took a reverse path by studying biographical and historical records of some 301 eminent persons in order to estimate their IQ's as accurately as possible. Two IQ estimates were made—one, an average rating on records of development to age 17 (AI), and the other an average for the development from age 17 to 26 (AII). The range of the estimated IQ's was from 100 to 190. Thirteen cases were rated between 100–110 while another 30 cases were estimated to be between 110–120. After various corrections were made, Cox concluded that *"the true IQ's of the subjects of this study average above 160. It further indicates that many of the true IQ' s are above 180, while but few of them are below 140"* (p. 85). [Italics in original.]

Cox (1926) drew three major conclusions from her study. She observed that, in general, those youths who achieve eminence in later life:

1. Have above-average heredity and superior advantages in their early environment.

2. Display childhood behaviors which indicate an unusually high IQ.

3. *"Are characterized not only by high intellectual traits, but also by persistence of motive and effort, confidence in their abilities, and great strength of force of character"* (p. 218). [Italics in original.]

Increasingly, superior intelligence, defined in various ways such as a percentage of the population (e.g., highest 1 or 2 percent in general intelligence) or a particular cut-off score on a test of intelligence (e.g., 125 IQ or 135 IQ) was considered as gifted and programs and provisions were made in schools for nurturing the intellectually superior child. Lists of the mental, emotional, social, and physical characteristics of children who scored high on individual or group tests of intelligence and/or high scholastic achievers have been prepared by a number of writers (see, for example, Durr, 1964, pp. 33–51; Clark, 1979, pp. 20–34; and Tuttle & Becker, 1980, pp. 11–38).

Leta S. Hollingworth was actively involved with studying the nature and needs of the gifted in New York City at the same time that Terman was conducting his longitudinal studies in California. Hollingworth defined gifted children as those "who are in the top 1 percent of the juvenile population in *general intelligence*" which, in her view, was the "power to achieve literacy and to deal with its abstract knowledge and symbols" (Pritchard, 1951, p. 49). Nevertheless, in 1931 she wrote:

> By a gifted child, we mean one who is far more educable than the generality of children are. This greater educability may lie along the lines of one of the arts, as in music or drawing; it may lie in the sphere of mechanical aptitude; or it may consist in surpassing power to achieve literacy and abstract intelligence. It is the business of education to consider all forms of giftedness in pupils in reference *to how unusual individuals may be trained for their own welfare and that of society at large.* (Pritchard, 1951, p. 49; italics added)

As early as the 1940's, writers were pointing to the limitations of intelligence tests in defining and identifying the gifted. Witty, for instance, wrote:

> If by gifted we mean those youngsters who give promise of creativity of a high order, it is doubtful if the typical intelligence test is suitable for use in identifying them. For creativity points to originality, and originality implies successful management, control, and organization of new materials or experiences. Intelligence tests contain over-learned materials. . . . The content of the intelligence is patently lacking in situations which disclose originality or creativity. (Pritchard, 1951, p. 81)

Writing in the American Association for Gifted Children's 1951 publication, Lally and LaBrant pointed out that since schools had been traditionally concerned with academic subjects, "the search for gifted children has usually discovered the brilliant student in such areas" and that identification procedures tended to parallel the school emphasis—excluding those students talented in the arts (Lally & LaBrant, 1951, p. 243). They noted that far less was known about special gifts than about the mentally gifted:

> How far talents are related; to what degree general high quality behavior may be channeled early in life; to what degree certain children are especially acute in various sensory perceptions of sound, space, or color, we are not able to state definitely. Nor do we know too much about the effects of various stimuli provided during the earliest years. (p. 244)

Since the AAGC publication, definitions of gifted and talented have become more inclusive or, as Renzulli puts it, "more liberal" (Renzulli, 1978). Passow et al. (1955) defined talent as the capacity for superior achievement in any socially valuable area of human endeavor, but limiting the areas to "such academic fields as languages, social sciences, natural sciences, and mathematics; such art fields as music, graphic and plastic arts, performing arts and mechanic arts; and the field of human relations" (p. 6).

The Ford Foundation–sponsored program for the gifted in the Portland (Oregon) Public School (1959) took the position "that a definition of giftedness limited to academic aptitude was much too narrow and that there was a variety of socially useful abilities which should be identified and developed (p. 13). Portland's definition of giftedness "included approximately the upper ten percent of the most intellectually talented pupils and also the same proportion of the most talented in each of seven special aptitudes . . . art, music, creative writing, creative dramatics, creative dance, mechanical talent, and social leadership" (p. 13). Portland was one of the few school systems which defined giftedness broadly and attempted to identify and nurture a broad array of gifts and talents.

For the 1957 yearbook of the National Society for the Study of Education, Witty (1958) "recommended that the definition of giftedness be expanded and that we consider any child gifted whose performance, in a potentially valuable line of human activity, is consistently remarkable" (p. 62). Witty's definition advocated a broad conception of the nature of giftedness. Phrases such as "potentially valuable line of human activity" and "consistently remarkable" raised a good many problems in terms of specificity and meaning.

Getzels and Jackson's (1958) studies of highly creative and highly intelligent youth led them to speculate that if a precedent be set by "allowing an exception to the practice of labelling only high IQ as 'gifted,' the possibility of expanding the concept to include other potentially productive groups become a genuine challenge to both educators and research workers" (p. 277).

The work of such researchers as Torrance, Taylor, Barron, and others helped revise perceptions of the nature of giftedness and to include creativity—variously defined—as either a component of giftedness and talent or as a kind of giftedness and talent to be identified and nurtured. Creativity research has focused on at least seven areas, according to Taylor (1975): "(1) the creative personality; (2) creative problem formulation; (3) the creative process; (4) creative products; (5) creative climates; (6) creativity and mental health; and (7) creativity and intelligence" (p. 12).

Creativity—defined in a number of ways—has been viewed as a necessary ingredient of intellectual giftedness and as a kind of giftedness. Gallagher and Weiss (1979) have pointed out:

> There have been numerous attempts to sort out the special characteristics of the creative child—that child who possesses superior ability to generate, visualize, dramatize, or illustrate a new idea, concept, or product. While there is a close relationship between high mental ability and creativity, it has become clear that there are particular intellectual skills and personality traits that predispose certain children and adults to creative activity. (pp. 6–7)

Researchers during the past two decades have come to the conclusion that creativity can be nurtured. Parnes (1962) for example, asserts that: "the evidence of the current research does point to a definite contradiction of the age-old notion that creativity cannot be developed." I. Taylor (1975), for instance, initiated a creative development program which focuses on: "(1) transposing one's ideas into the environment; (2) formulating basic or generic problems; (3) transforming ideas through reversals and analogies; (4) generating outcomes with creative characteristics; and (5) facilitating these processes through exposure to direct sensory stimulation" (p. 26).

Calvin Taylor asserts that research indicates "that we have talents of many different types, not just 'general intelligence.'" Taylor has proposed a Multiple Talent Teaching Approach—the talents identified include academic, creative, planning, communicating, forecasting, and decision making. Taylor asserts that the Multiple Talent Totum Pole Approach helps move us "toward the goal of developing fully functioning, effectively talented people. It enriches and enlivens the students and their teachers and administrators, and thereby humanizes the entire educational process" (Taylor & Ellison, 1975, 213).

Some researchers have focused on gifted performance of adults rather than on the potential for outstanding achievement by students. The Goertzels, (Goertzels & Goertzel, 1962; Goertzel, et al., 1978) for instances, have conducted two studies of some seven hundred "eminent personalities," individuals who have achieved success in various areas—sciences, business, literature and drama, etc. The Goertzels have studied the family background which eminent personalities were formed; the personal lives of the eminent individuals, particularly as adults; and the work which brought them the fame which represents their impact on society. The Goertzels (1978) have built composite portraits of the eminent or the gifted and talented which provide some insights into the nature of gifted. Some of the observations that they make include the following:

> The eminent man or woman is likely to be the firstborn or only child in a middle-class family where the father is a businessman or professional man and the mother is a housewife. In these families there are rows of books on shelves, and parental expectations are high for all children. . . .
>
> Children who become eminent love learning but dislike school and school teachers who try to confine them to a curriculum not designed for individual needs. They respond well to being tutored or to being left alone, and they like to go to special schools such as those that train actors, dancers, musicians, and artists. . . .
>
> . . . , they are more self-directed, less motivated in wanting to please than are their peers or siblings. They need and manage to find periods of isolation when they have freedom to think, to read, to write, to experiment, to paint, to play an instrument, or to explore the countryside. Sometimes this freedom can be obtained only by real or feigned illnesses; a sympathetic parent may respond to the child's need to have long free periods of concentrated effort.
>
> . . . They treasure their uniqueness and find it hard to be conforming, in dress, behavior, and other ways. . . . (pp. 336–338)

Brandwein (1955) has hypothesized that three factors are related to academic success in the sciences. These include: (a) genetic factors—high-level verbal and mathematical ability; (b) predisposing factors—persistence (willingness to spend extra time on the subject, ability to withstand discomfort, and ability to face failure and continue working) and questing, dissatisfaction with the present explanation and aspects of reality; and (c) activating factors—opportunities for advanced training and contact with an inspirational teacher.

Tannenbaum has argued that one of the characteristics of giftedness is that the individual is a *producer,* not simply a *consumer* of culture. It is not sufficient, he maintains, that a student get good grades, absorb information rapidly, and excel in convergent thinking activities. Giftedness involves new conceptualizations, divergent approaches, creative problem solutions and unusual problem solutions. In his view, students who simply consume information, no matter how rapidly, represent only one kind of giftedness and not the most significant.

Getzels and Csikszentmihalyi (1975) have turned around the focus of study from *problem-solving,* on which there is a rich body of literature and an abundance of conceptual and empirical studies, to *problem finding* on which there is relatively little systematic study. As they put it, "the world is . . . teeming with dilemmas. But problematic situations do not present themselves automatically as problems capable of solutions, to say nothing of creative solutions" (p. 90). Studying adult fine artists, Getzels suggested altering the paradigm of the human as "not only a *stimulus-reducing* or *problem-solving* organism but also a *stimulus-seeking* or *problem finding* organism" (Getzels & Csikszentmihalyi, 1975, p. 93). They hypothesize that problem finding seems to be a crucial component of creativity—one which has been relatively unstudied in understanding the nature of giftedness.

Asking the question, "What Makes Giftedness?" Renzulli (1978) analyzed definitions of giftedness, reviewed studies of the characteristics of gifted individuals, and proposed a new definition of giftedness which he believes is useful to school practitioners and defensible in terms of research findings. Renzulli's conception of the ingredients of giftedness include three elements. One component is *above-average ability.* A second cluster of traits "consistently found in creative/productive persons constitutes a refined or focused form of motivation known as *task commitment*" which represents energy brought to bear on a particular problem (task) or specific performance area." The third component or cluster of traits "consists of factors that have usually been lumped together under the general heading of '*creativity*'" (pp. 182–184).

Renzulli (1978) concludes with an operational definition of giftedness as follows:

> Giftedness consists of an interaction among three basic clusters of human traits—these clusters being above-average general abilities, high levels of task commitment, and high levels of creativity. Gifted and talented children are those possessing or capable of developing this composite set of traits and applying them to any potentially valuable area of human performance. Children who manifest or are capable of developing an interaction among the three clusters require a wide variety of educational opportunities and services that are not ordinarily provided through regular instructional programs. (p. 261)

What, then, can be said about the nature of giftedness and what are some of the issues raised by the fact that giftedness is usually defined operationally with some concept of its nature implicit in such definitions? Clearly, there is no widespread accepted theory of giftedness although there is a considerable body of knowledge about individual differences and their nurture. In a recent article titled, "What We Don't Know About Programming for the Gifted and Talented," Renzulli (1980) observed:

> In spite of vast amounts of research on every conceivable aspect of the learning process, we still have difficulty pinpointing the reasons for the remarkable differences in learning efficiency and creativity among persons with similar genetic backgrounds and environmental experiences. We simply don't know what factors cause only a miniscule number of Thomas Edisons or Langston Hugheses or Isadora Duncans to emerge while millions with equal "equipment" and educational advantages (or disadvantages) never rise above mediocrity. Why do some people who have not enjoyed the advantages of special educational opportunities achieve eminence while others who have gone through programs for the gifted fade into obscurity? The answer is, we simply do not know! (p. 601)

There are, of course some things we do know. The gifted and the talented come in a tremendous variety of shapes, forms, and sizes. Some gifted youngsters are only slightly above average with respect to the criteria applied while others are so unusual as to be extremely rare; some individuals are gifted/talented in a single area, while others seem to be unusually able in practically any area. Some individuals who seem to have outstanding ability have relatively little motivation or interest in developing that potential while others are both highly talented and highly motivated. Some are high achievers and quick absorbers of information while others utilize knowledge in new and different ways. Some are basically consumers of knowledge while others are potentially outstanding producers as well as consumers. Some are especially precocious, manifesting unusual potential at early ages while others are "late bloomers" and do not show unusual potential or performance until much later. There are cultural differences with respect to which talent areas are more likely to be rewarded and, consequently, which will be nurtured, Riessman (1962) has even written about "slow gifted children," individuals who may "take a long time to learn basic concepts, but when they finally do so . . . use these ideas in thoughtful, penetrating fashion" (p. 64). The gifted are clearly not a homogeneous group. As Clark (1979) put it, "the more gifted a person becomes, the more unique that person may appear" (p. 20).

There is, then, an issue as to *what* is giftedness and *who* is gifted. There are numerous lists of characteristics of gifted individuals—most of them lengthy and detailed. Obviously, not all individuals who are identified as being "gifted" possess all of the cognitive, affective, physical, or intuitive characteristics which are ascribed to gifted and talented individuals. In fact, a single characteristic in one child may actually indicate a very special gift or talent. Compilations of characteristics of gifted and talented individuals are useful only if it is remembered that individuals may not possess all of the traits and behaviors ascribed to a group of gifted/talented persons.

There are also a number of issues related to how such individuals should be identified. How does potential for outstanding performance manifest itself if it is indeed still only potential? There appears to be consensus that identification procedures cannot be limited to tests of intelligence, even when those tests are individual tests. A variety of techniques, procedures, and instruments must be used to identify gifted and talented students, to differentiate their educational experiences. Various kinds of rating and screening scales have been developed and used. Some identification approaches rely heavily on the performance, the products, the behaviors of individuals which are judged to be unusual, creative, or imaginative as evidence of giftedness.

Passow and Tannenbaum (1978) have pointed out that the definition of gifted and talented provides the direction for the selection and use of identification procedures and for the design of educational opportunities and differentiated curricula. In fact, the procedures and techniques used for identification affect the kinds of differentiated experiences to be provided and vice versa: identification is viewed as an integral part of differentiation (p. 14). Rather than viewing identification and educational differentiation as a two-step diagnostic-prescriptive model, Passow and Tannenbaum suggest that prescribed enrichment becomes a vehicle for identification as much as identification facilitates enrichment. For instance, standardized tests of language and cognition do not help identify a potential poet in the elementary school. Rather, a program of instruction and practice in creative poetic expression in different structural forms enables children with poetic talent to reveal themselves. It is the creation of pupil products which contributes to self-identification and since product development is a continuous one, identification is also seen as a continuous process, rather than a single-event test administration (p. 15). Identification of the gifted and talented is related not only to systematic observation and intelligent interpretation of test and observation data, but to the creation of the right kinds of educational opportunities which facilitate self-identification—identification by performance and product which results in the manifestation of gifted or talented behaviors.

Some other questions which might be raised follow: Is precocity necessarily a manifestation of giftedness? Is giftedness potential alone or must it be made visible through actual performance? Are "underachievers" indeed gifted or should only achievers be considered gifted? Can an individual be outstanding in some very narrow area, only mediocre or even below average in most other areas, and still be considered gifted? Is creative or productive behavior a component of all giftedness or is it a kind of giftedness in and of itself? Does an individual need to attain affective maturity to match his/her cognitive maturity to be considered gifted? Are there levels of affective maturity—personal, social, emotional maturity—which should be expected before identifying an individual as gifted?

All aspects of identification and nurturance of the gifted and talented depend on the underlying conception of the nature of giftedness and there are a good many operational conceptions extant. Program planners must be sensitive to the critical importance of clarification of an operational conception of the nature of giftedness and the many issues raised with respect to identification, curriculum differentiation, resource allocation, and other aspects of education and development of gifted and talented children and youth. The conception of the nature of giftedness and talent is at the heart of all planning efforts.

REFERENCES

Brandwein, P. F. *The gifted child as future scientist.* NYC: Harcourt, Brace, 1955.

Clark, B. *Growing up gifted.* Columbus, OH: Charles E. Merrill, 1979.

Cox, C. M. *The early mental traits of three hundred geniuses.* Volume II: Genetic studies of genius. Stanford, CA: Stanford University Press, 1926.

Durr, W. K. *The gifted student.* NYC: Oxford University Press, 1964.

Gallagher, J. J., & Weiss, P. *The education of gifted and talented students.* Washington, DC: Council for Basic Education, 1979.

Getzels, J. W., & Csikszentmihalyi, M. From problem solving to problem finding. In I. A. Taylor, & J. W. Getzels (Eds)., *Perspective in creativity.* Chicago: Aldine, 1975, 90–116.

Getzels, J. W., & Jackson, P. W. The meaning of 'giftedness'—an examination of an expanding concept. *Phi Delta Kappan,* November 1958, *40,* 275–277.

Goertzel, V., & Goertzel, M. G. *Cradles of eminence.* Boston: Little, Brown, 1962.

Goertzel, M. G., Goertzel, V., & Goertzel, T. G. *300 eminent personalities.* San Francisco: Jossey-Bass, 1978.

Henry, T. S. *Classroom problems in the education of gifted children.* 19th Yearbook, Part II. National Society for the Study of Education. Chicago: University of Chicago Press, 1920.

Lally, A., & LaBrant, L. Experiences with children talented in the arts. In P. Witty (Ed.), *The gifted child.* NYC: D. C. Heath, 1951, 243–256.

Marland, S. P., Jr. *Education of the gifted and talented.* Volume I: Report to the Congress of the United States by the U.S. Commissioner of Education. Washington, DC: U.S. Government Printing Office, 1971.

Parnes, S. J., & Harding, F. (Eds.). *A source book for creative thinking.* NYC: Scribners, 1962.

Passow, A. H., Goldberg, M. L., Tannenbaum, A. J., & French, W. *Planning for talented youth.* NYC: Teachers College Press, 1955.

Passow, A. H. & Tannenbaum, A. J. *Differentiated curriculum for the gifted and talented: A conceptual model.* A paper prepared for the Office of Projects for the gifted and talented, Montgomery County (Maryland) Public Schools. NYC: Teachers College, Columbia University, 1978.

Portland Public Schools. *The gifted child in Portland.* Portland, OR: Portland Public Schools, 1959.

Pritchard, M. C. The contribution of Leta S. Hollingworth to the study of gifted children. In P. Witty, (Ed.), *The gifted child.* NYC: D. C. Heath, 1951, 47–85.

Renzulli, J. S. What makes giftedness? Reexamining a definition. *Phi Delta Kappan,* November 1978, *60,* 180–184, 261.

Renzulli, J. S. What we don't know about programming for the gifted and talented. *Phi Delta Kapan,* May 1980, *61,* 601–602.

Riessman, F. *The culturally deprived child.* NYC: Harper, 1962.

Taylor, C. W., & Ellison, R. L. Moving toward working models in creativity: Utah creativity experience and insights. In I.A. Taylor, & J. W. Getzels (Eds.), *Perspectives in Creativity.* Chicago: Aldine, 1975, 1–36.

Taylor, I. A. A tretrspective view of creativity investigation. In I. A. Taylor & J. W. Getzels (Eds.), *Perspectives in creativity.* Chicago, Aldine, 1975, 1–36.

Terman, L. M. *Mental and physical traits of a thousand gifted children.* Volume I: Genetic studies of genius. Stanford, CA: Stanford University Press, 1925 and 1926.

Terman, L. M. & Oden, M. H. The Stanford studies of the gifted. In P. Witty (Ed.), *The gifted child.* NYC: D. C. Heath, 1951, 20–46.

Tuttle, F. B., Jr., & Becker, L. A. *Characteristics and identification of gifted and talented students.* Washington, DC: National Education Association, 1980.

Whipple, G. M. (Ed.). *The education of gifted children.* 23rd Yearbook, Part I. National Society for the Study of Education. Chicago: University of Chicago Press, 1924.

Witty, P. Who are the gifted? In N. B. Henry, *Education for the gifted.* 57th Yearbook, Part II. National Society for the Study of Education. Chicago: University of Chicago Press, 1958, 41–63.

2

What Do We Mean by Giftedness? A Pentagonal Implicit Theory

Robert J. Sternberg
Yale University

Li-fang Zhang
University of Iowa

This article presents a pentagonal implicit theory of giftedness and a set of data testing the theory. The exposition is divided into five parts. First, we discuss what an implicit theory is and why such theories are important. Second, we describe the pentagonal theory, specifying five conditions claimed to be individually necessary and jointly sufficient for a person to be labeled as gifted. These conditions help us understand not only why some people are labeled as gifted but also why some others are not. Third, we consider the relation of the pentagonal theory to explicit theories of giftedness. Fourth, we present data supporting the theory. Finally, we discuss some implications of the pentagonal theory for gifted education.

Editor's Note: From Sternberg, R.J., & Zhang, L. (1995). What do we mean by giftedness? A pentagonal implicit theory. *Gifted Child Quarterly*, *39*(2), 88-94.

Why is a child who scores in the top 1% on the Wechsler Intelligence Scale for Children much more likely to be labeled as gifted than a child whose 100-meter sprinting time places her in the top 1% of her age cohort? Why is a physicist who is considered Number 1 in the country by his peers or another panel of judges considered gifted, whereas the criminal who is Number 1 on the FBI's most wanted list is not? Why do contestants in beauty contests, such as the Miss America pageant, have to answer questions about issues perceived to be of domestic or international importance, whereas contestants in scientific competitions, such as the Westinghouse Science Talent Search, do not have to submit to judgments of their personal attractiveness? The pentagonal implicit theory of giftedness seeks to answer these and related questions.

THE NATURE OF IMPLICIT THEORIES

Implicit theories are not public or formal. Rather, they are intellectual constructions that reside in the minds of individuals (Sternberg, 1985b; Sternberg, Conway, Ketron, & Bernstein, 1981). Such theories can be discovered through questions and inference and are often revealed by behavior. Typically, however, we do not examine our implicit theories closely until questioned: we simply employ them in making our everyday judgments of the world and of those who inhabit it.

Contrasting with implicit theories are explicit theories, the constructions of psychologists or other scientists that are based or at least tested (in psychology) on data collected from people performing tasks presumed to measure psychological functioning. Explicit theories have dominated the literature on giftedness (see, e.g., Sternberg & Davidson, 1986, for a collection of such theories). Theorists specify what they believe to be the elements of giftedness and then try to verify that their claims are psychologically or educationally valid.

Why bother to study implicit theories of giftedness? What difference does it make what a layperson thinks about giftedness when there are well-informed theorists who have devoted their professional lives to studying and judging the problem? There are at least five reasons why it is worthwhile to understand people's conceptions or implicit theories of giftedness.

First, discovering such implicit theories can be useful in helping to formulate the common cultural views that dominate thinking within a society—what we mean, for example, by *giftedness*. Second, understanding implicit theories can also help us understand or provide bases for explicit theories because explicit theories derive in part from scientists or other researchers' implicit theories of the construct under investigation. Third, implicit, not explicit, theories have the most influence on actual life and practices. People's generalized implicit theories of giftedness, for example, determine how decisions about identification are made. Fourth, if we want to "change our ways"—to improve our criteria for identifying the gifted—we need to know exactly what those ways are. Fifth, and perhaps most importantly, one might argue that in the case of giftedness, implicit theories have a privileged status that they do not have in the case of other constructs, such as memory. In the case of memory, there is good evidence that the construct is based on an actual set of related biological phenomena, many of which probably take place in the hippocampus. In the case of giftedness, however, we appear to be dealing, at least in part, with a labeling phenomenon.

In one culture, the gifted individual might be a hunter; in another, a gatherer; and in a third, a student. The first two cultures might not even have any form of formal schooling. Just as cultural standards for beauty may vary (Duck, 1991), so may cultural standards for giftedness. We do not suggest that within a culture no objective criteria for giftedness can be defined. We do suggest that the criteria are determined by one's external culture rather than by one's internal physiology.

Putting the Research to Use

This article points out the importance of deciding specifically what we value as gifted before embarking on a program of identification. Too often, schools are willing and even eager to buy into existing identification instruments without deciding for themselves what they value most. Moreover, it is important that the program itself and the way performance in it is assessed reflect the values expressed in the means of identification.

In sum, implicit theories of giftedness are important because they provide a dimension of understanding that cannot be obtained through the study of explicit theories. Our supposition does not mean that explicit theories are unimportant. Rather, both kinds of theories are needed and should be studied in conjunction with one another. Implicit theories provide the form or structure by which we define giftedness; explicit theories provide the content that is embedded within that form or structure.

THE PENTAGONAL IMPLICIT THEORY OF GIFTEDNESS

The goal of the pentagonal implicit theory of giftedness is to capture and systematize people's intuitions about what makes an individual gifted. It is an implicit theory because it has as its object people's conception of giftedness rather than giftedness itself. It is important to state that, in general, implicit theories need not be "correct" in any ultimate sense. At one time, most people believed that the sun revolved around the earth. Their implicit theory was wrong. To the extent that giftedness is like beauty, however, there is no right

Figure 1 The Five Individually Necessary and Jointly Sufficient Criteria of the Pentagonal Implicit Theory of Giftedness

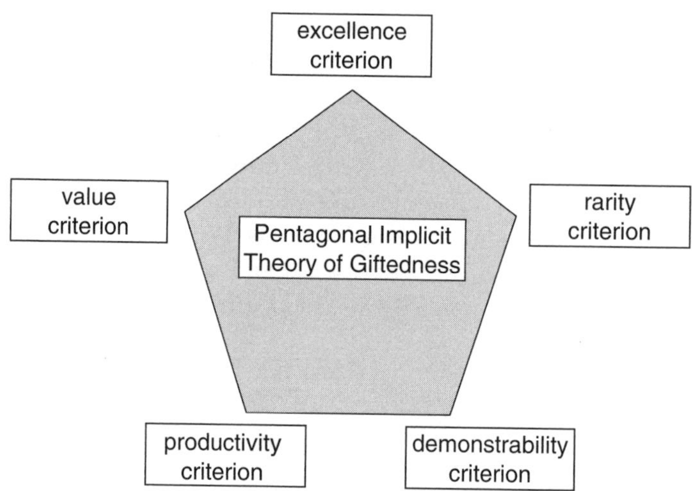

and wrong, only what people perceive to be better and worse or higher and lower on some scale. The theory, summarized in Figure 1, states that in order to be judged as gifted, a person needs to meet five criteria: (a) the excellence criterion, (b) the rarity criterion, (c) the productivity criterion, (d) the demonstrability criterion, and (e) the value criterion. These five criteria were derived by assessing intuitively a large number of people considered to be either gifted or not gifted by others and by judging what complete set of attributes the gifted people had in common. The criteria are thus proposed to be individually necessary and jointly sufficient in the identification of giftedness. Our criteria are related to those in other theories of giftedness (see Sternberg & Davidson, 1986), such as that of Tannenbaum (1986).

The Excellence Criterion

The excellence criterion states that the individual is *superior in some dimension or set of dimensions relative to peers*. To be gifted, one has to be extremely good at something—in psychological terminology, high in a judged dimension or dimensions. How high is "extremely high" may vary from one context to another, but the gifted person is always perceived to be abundant in something, whether it be creativity, wisdom, or another skill or construct. In the present view, excellence relative to peers is a necessary condition for an individual to be labeled as gifted.

The qualification "relative to peers" is necessary because the designation of excellence depends upon the skills of those against whom one is judged. A 10-year-old's raw score on an intelligence test might convert into a very high score relative to age peers but would seem unexceptional relative to children 5 years older. Similarly, a musical performance that would be exceptional for an 8-year-old taking weekly music lessons at school might be quite undistinguished for an 8-year-old who has been trained at a conservatory since age 4.

The Rarity Criterion

The rarity criterion states that in order to be labeled as gifted, an individual must possess a *high level of an attribute that is rare relative to peers*. The rarity criterion is needed to supplement the excellence criterion because a person may show an abundance of a given attribute, but if a high evaluation of that attribute is not judged to be rare, the person is not viewed as gifted. Suppose we give a test of mastery of the basics of the English language to a class of college seniors at a good university. They should all score very high on the test because all are proficient in the basics of English. But even if all received perfect scores, we would not say they are all therefore gifted. Thus, one may display excellence, but unless such excellence is rare, one is not likely to be viewed as gifted.

The Productivity Criterion

The productivity criterion states that *the dimension(s) along which the individual is evaluated as superior must lead to or potentially lead to productivity*. Consider again the contestants in the beauty contest. Why must they answer questions about issues of the day rather than rely solely on their appearance? In fact, appearance is probably the major determinant in the contest, so why is it not sufficient? Despite the fact that the contest is about beauty, beauty in itself is not perceived as productive or potentially productive. The contestant needs to demonstrate that she can *do* something. In contrast, the contestant in a scientific competition is not judged on other dimensions, such as personal appearance, because the scientific work itself—the basis of the contest—is viewed as productive.

The productivity criterion generates disagreements over exactly who should be labeled as gifted. Some, for example, believe that a high score on an intelligence test is not sufficient grounds for labeling a person as gifted. These people see the tests as meaningless (e.g., Gardner, 1983) because the high-scoring person has not shown that he or she can do anything. Others view getting a high score on the test as doing something in and of itself. At worst, the high score shows the person's potential for productivity.

In childhood, of course, it is possible to be labeled as gifted without having been productive. In fact, children are typically judged largely on potential rather than actual productivity. As people get older, however, the relative weights of potential and actualized potential change, and more emphasis is placed on actual productivity. Any number of gifted children become adults whom people do not think of as exceptional. Renzulli (1986) has referred to such adults as "school-house gifted."

People who do not realize their potential through some kind of productive work may still be labeled as gifted, but with qualifications. They are called gifted individuals whose gifts somehow failed to materialize. To earn the label "gifted" without qualification, a person must accomplish something.

The Demonstrability Criterion

The demonstrability criterion states that the *superiority of the individual on the dimension(s) which determine giftedness must be demonstrable through one or more tests that are valid assessments*. The individual needs to be able to demonstrate, in one way or another, that he or she really has the abilities or achievements which led to the judgment of giftedness. Simply claiming giftedness is not enough. Thus, a person who scores poorly on all measures used in assessment and who is unable to demonstrate in any compelling alternative way that he or she does indeed have special abilities will not be viewed as gifted.

The assessment instrument(s) used, however, must be valid. Validity means that each instrument is believed to measure what it is supposed to measure. If, for example, a child presents a high score on a new intelligence test that requires only that the child dot *i*'s, the result will not be valid. Dotting *i*'s is not an acceptable measure of intelligence. Or suppose that a job candidate gives a persuasive talk, suggesting unusual gifts both in research and in presentation. But when asked about the content of the talk, he is unable even to answer the simplest of questions. Gradually, members of the audience conclude that the job candidate was somehow programmed, probably by his advisor. In fact, he has no idea of what he was talking about. The job talk would then be invalid as a measure of the candidate because it did not actually reflect his gifts (or lack thereof).

The validity issue has become extremely important in recent years in the identification of intellectually gifted school-children. In the past, many schools were content to use standardized intelligence tests, and perhaps grades in school and scores on achievement tests, as bases for identifying children as intellectually gifted. As the focus of testing has shifted more and more toward an emphasis on performance- and product-based assessment, however, some have questioned the validity of the traditional measures (e.g., Gardner, 1983; Renzulli, 1986). Someone who would have been labeled as gifted under traditional measures might not now be so labeled. The implicit theory of giftedness may not have changed, but what is considered valid as a demonstration of giftedness may have.

The Value Criterion

The value criterion states that for a person to be labeled as gifted, *the person must show superior performance in a dimension that is valued for that person by his or her society*. The value criterion restricts the label of giftedness to those who have attributes that are valued as relevant to giftedness. The individual who is Number 1 on the FBI's most wanted list might be superior in one or more dimensions, rare in his ability to perform certain malevolent acts, and able to demonstrate his skills upon demand. He may even be highly productive, if in a criminal way. But because what he is so good at is not valued by society at large, he is not likely to be labeled as gifted by the American populace. Still, it is quite possible that he would be labeled as gifted by a pack of thieves; the pentagonal theory allows that what is prized as a basis for giftedness may differ from one culture or even subculture to another.

Who is qualified to judge giftedness, anyway? Anyone, although not all implicit theories are good ones. The pentagonal theory allows us to say that people of another place or time have erred in their evaluations of a person's gifts. If we do so, it is true that we are claiming a privileged position with regard to the identification of someone as gifted. We are arguing that our values are right because those of certain others were wrong, or because these others did not have access to information we now have. In either of these cases, we are claiming the privilege of being in a superior position to judge. What we must realize, of course, is that others may do the same with respect to us in some other time or place.

Implicit theories by nature are relativistic; there is never any guarantee that people's personal values will match across time and space. But implicit theories, as noted above, provide the best practical form or structure by which to identify the gifted. For a judgment to occur according to strict standards, one needs to add content to implicit theories. This is the role of explicit theories.

THE ROLE OF EXPLICIT THEORIES

Implicit theories are necessarily relativistic because what is perceived as gifted is based on the values of one particular time or place. In fact, what is perceived at all may be time- and culture-dependent. Explicit theories specify the content of the scales on which excellence, rarity, productivity, demonstrability, and societal valuing take place. They thus fill in the content of what it means to be gifted.

Consider, for example, intelligence. We know from studies of implicit theories that what people consider to be intelligent differs across time and place (Berry, 1984; Serpell, 1974; Wober, 1974). Thus, whether a given person is *labeled* as intelligent will depend upon time and place.

Explicit theories of intelligence attempt to specify just what intelligence is, so that whether a given person is *actually* intelligent (according to a given explicit theory) will depend upon the person's standing as measured by that theory. Note the importance of the qualifier, "according to a given explicit theory." The judgment made is still relative to an explicit theory, and as we know, such theories differ.

Consider, for example, two contemporary theories of intelligence, those of Gardner (1983) and of Sternberg (1985a). According to Gardner, a person of extraordinarily high musical ability is intellectually gifted by virtue of the superiority of the musical ability. According to Sternberg, such a person is musically talented, or, if one wishes to use the term *giftedness* for specific abilities, musically gifted; the person is not intellectually gifted by virtue of the superior musical ability, although that individual might well be intellectually gifted based on further information.

In short, explicit theories provide definitions of content. However, we are still left with the judgments from which the explicit theory is derived. The problem is that in the science of understanding human gifts, we do not have certainties. There are no explicit theories known to be totally and absolutely correct, nor are there likely to be any in the foreseeable future.

Although we have no certainties, the combination of implicit and explicit theories can help us understand both the structure people instinctively use for labeling others as gifted and the more objective content (or specific scales) they use to give force to these labels. These content scales, by the way, are not necessarily only ones of ability. Renzulli (1986) and Feldhusen (1986), for example, both include motivation in their conceptions of giftedness.

DATA

Does the pentagonal implicit theory actually capture people's intuitions about giftedness? Do people really use these criteria in making their evaluations of others? We decided to find out. Our approach was to test our pentagonal conception of people's implicit theories on two types of subjects. Other implicit-theories studies (such as Sternberg et al., 1981) do not test a prior conception but rather are wholly inductive, asking subjects to generate their own categories. There is no one right approach but rather various alternatives for eliciting people's implicit theories.

Subjects in the study described here were asked to rate the extent to which each of the variables of the implicit theory contributed to their judgment, and to their perception of the judgment of various schools, in identifying children as gifted. Subjects received case-study descriptions of children and provided ratings of the putative giftedness of these children. The study evaluated only the weights people assigned to variables in the pentagonal implicit theory and did not assess other variables that might be posited by alternative implicit theories. The pentagonal implicit theory predicts that all criteria will be given significant weights in identifying individuals as gifted.

METHOD

Two groups of subjects were surveyed. First, 24 students at Yale University—themselves highly selected for intellectual ability—participated in the study, conducted in the spring of 1992. Half of the subjects were male and half were female. Half of each gender group were given instructions requiring them to evaluate boys; the other half evaluated girls. Second, 39 parents of gifted children in Connecticut were surveyed via mail. Twenty-one evaluated girls, and 18 evaluated boys. They were presented with the following directions:

> This study looks at how people make judgments regarding which students are gifted. Imagine that a national program for gifted students is going to be conducted and that each school is selecting students for participating in this program. The schools use different tests and have different feelings about how good the tests are that they use. They also vary in how much they value independent projects that students submit. The following brief descriptions are about female [male] students in the same grade in different high schools. Each description contains six pieces of information.
>
> Each girl [boy] has taken a nationally standardized test. Nationally, their scores on these tests are described as "good," "excellent," "mediocre," and so on. However, notice that the second piece of information concerns each student's standing relative to students within her [his] own school only. Thus, one test score might place a student in the top 10% of students from her [his] own school but only in the top 50% nationally. You will also be given information about each student's accomplishment(s). Students were invited to submit independent projects. These independent projects were prescreened for quality so that only those of high quality were submitted. The number submitted varied from 0 to 5. After you have read each description, please select a number from the scale described below and write it within the parentheses given. Two sets of parentheses follow each description.
>
> In the first set of parentheses, following the words "SCHOOL'S JUDGMENT," write the number which rates **how likely** you think it is that the **school** would identify that student as gifted. In the second set of parentheses, following the words "MY JUDGMENT," write the number which rates **how likely** it is that **you personally** would identify that student as gifted. Your judgment may or may not agree with the school's since your evaluation of which criteria are important may or may not correspond with the school's.
>
> **SCALE:** 1 = almost certainly not
> 2 = probably not
> 3 = possibly not
> 4 = possibly yes
> 5 = probably yes
> 6 = almost certainly yes

Here is a sample item:

1. Bernadine's score on the Bader Creativity Test was good.
2. This score was in the top 20% of her school.

3. The Bader Creativity Test has been found to be accurate in predicting gifted performance for 40% of students.
4. The school considers the Bader Creativity Test to be a mediocre measure of giftedness.
5. Bernadine submitted 4 independent projects.
6. The school believes that independent projects are an excellent measure of giftedness.

School's judgment (**4**) My judgment (**6**)

Note that each student provided an evaluation both from the school's point of view and from his or her own point of view. Note also that items were identical for the descriptions of boys and girls, except for the substitution of names appropriate to one gender or the other. For example, "Bernadine" was "Seth" in the boys' condition. There were 60 descriptions in all, presented in three different orders across subjects to minimize order effects.

Not all items involved the Bader Creativity Test. In fact, each item involved a different test. Although the names of the tests were different, only six constructs were involved, balanced equally across items: creativity, intelligence (e.g., the Hunter Intelligence Test), social skills (e.g., the Perkins Social-Skills Test), motivation (e.g., the Bradley Motivation Test), and achievement (e.g., the Swanson Achievement Test). All test names were inventions (i.e., did not correspond to genuine tests).

The experiment was designed to allow use of multiple regressions to predict ratings of likelihood of students being identified as gifted (the dependent variable) from the six independent variables in each description. The six independent variables, based on the pentagonal implicit theory, were (a) excellence (Statement l), (b) rarity (Statement 2), (c) productivity (Statement 5), (d) demonstrability (i.e., validity) (Statement 3), (e) value (Statements 4, 6). Thus, a significant regression weight for any criterion would indicate its use in judgments of giftedness.

RESULTS

Overall mean ratings on the 6-point scale for the 24 student subjects were 4.26 for girls—school rating, 4.13 for girls—self-rating, 4.15 for boys—school rating, and 4.07 for boys—self-rating. Mean ratings of boys and girls did not differ significantly. For the 39 parent subjects, comparable means were 3.99, 4.18, 3.85, and 4.08, respectively. Of greater interest here, though, are the results of the multiple regressions, which are summarized in Tables 1 and 2. The results are practically identical for the two samples.

Multiple regressions provide a test of the fit of the pentagonal model to the data. Support for the model is indicated to the extent that (a) values of R^2 (the

Table 1 Summary of Multiple Regression Analyses: Student Sample

	β (standardized regression coefficient)			
Rating (statement)	*Girls-School*	*Girls-Self*	*Boys-School*	*Boys-Self*
Excellence (1)	.32***	.73***	.28***	.55***
Rarity (2)	.45***	.38***	.25**	.23***
Productivity (5)	.37***	.22***	.44***	.58***
Demonstrability (3)	.00	.13**	.03	.28***
Value (4)	.49***	.26***	.50***	.19***
Value (6)	.26***	.10*	.28***	.07
R^2	.78***	.91**	.68***	.87***
Root-mean-square error	.46	.33	.60	.38

*$p < .05$. **$p < .01$. ***$p < .001$.
($N = 24$ students evaluating 21 girls and 18 boys)

Table 2 Summary of Multiple Regression Analyses: Parent Sample

	β (standardized regression coefficient)			
Rating (statement)	*Girls-School*	*Girls-Self*	*Boys-School*	*Boys-Self*
Excellence (1)	.33***	.53***	.34***	.49***
Rarity (2)	.29***	.35***	.24**	.37***
Productivity (5)	.34***	.50***	.44***	.67***
Demonstrability (3)	.02	.25***	.00	.11**
Value (4)	.50***	.28***	.43***	.18***
Value (6)	.44***	.20***	.35***	.13**
R^2	.76***	.90***	.68***	.91***
Root-mean-square error	.49	.24	.66	.26

*$p < .05$. **$p < .01$. ***$p < .001$.
($N = 39$ parents evaluating 21 girls and 18 boys)

squared multiple correlation of the ratings of giftedness with each of the independent variables of the pentagonal implicit theory) is high in magnitude (the range is 0 to 1) and statistically significant, and (b) values of the regression beta weights corresponding to each of the independent variables are statistically significant. Nonsignificant beta weights indicate that, contrary to the pentagonal implicit theory, a variable was not counted in making judgments.

Excellence, rarity, productivity, and value of the test showed statistically significant regressive weights in all of the multiple regressions. The weight value for the independent projects was statistically significant in all but one regression. Patterns of weights were similar for evaluations of boys and girls. Interestingly, our subjects believed that they would take validity (demonstrability) into account in their evaluations but that the school would not. Subjects also believed that they took excellence into account more than would the school, whereas the school's system of values was clearly seen as more important to the school than it was to the subjects doing the ratings.

Overall levels of prediction were quite high, with R^2 values varying from .68 (corresponding to a multiple correlation of .82) to .91 (corresponding to a multiple correlation of .95). These levels were somewhat higher for the self-ratings than for the school ratings, which makes sense since subjects are more likely to believe they know their own implicit theory than that they know the implicit theory of the school.

These results are generally consistent with the pentagonal implicit theory. They suggest that people take into account the five points of the theory in making evaluations and believe that the school takes into account all of the points except instrument validity (demonstrability). Of course, our population of subjects was a limited one, and we plan to do subsequent research with other populations.

IMPLICATIONS FOR EDUCATIONAL PRACTICE

Consider how the pentagonal theory, in combination with explicit theories, helps us address the standard questions of identification and instruction that arise about gifted education. The pentagonal theory does not directly answer these questions but rather suggests the directions answers might take. Those who wish to use the pentagonal implicit theory in conjunction with particular explicit theories are encouraged to do so, though recommendations for precisely which approaches to take are not the goal of this paper. A wide array of explicit theories about giftedness exists, from Gardner's (1983) theory of multiple intelligences to Sternberg's (1985a) triarchic theory, and from Stanley's (1976) acceleration model to Renzulli's (1977) enrichment model. Some of these, and others, are discussed further in Sternberg and Davidson (1986).

What Percentage of Children Should Be Identified as Gifted?

This question is often asked as though there is a single right answer. Of course, there is not. But the pentagonal theory helps us address this question by separating two often confounded concepts that ought to be distinguished: excellence and rarity.

Our use of norm-based measurement, which practically equates the two, leads us into confusion. All of us who have taught know that one year we may have an excellent class, in which many or even most of the students perform at a very high level, and another year we may have a weak class in which few people perform well. Criterion-based measurement helps us avoid confounding excellence with rarity. We need to think in criterion-based terms to answer the question regarding the "right" percentage to be identified.

One way of using the pentagonal theory is to suggest that we identify as gifted that percentage of students whose performance on some set of standards meets a preset criterion of excellence and for whom we have the resources to provide special services. We will thereby acknowledge that our limitations in identification reflect not only students' abilities but also our ability to serve such students.

We need to consider excellence independently of rarity and to realize that we seek out rarity in part because of our inability to serve all students who may truly have very impressive potentials.

What Constructs or Measures Should We Use to Identify the Gifted?

The pentagonal theory makes clear that there is no one right construct or measure, or even set of constructs or measures, that we ought to use. Rather than simply doing what we do because it has always been done that way, we need to take responsibility for stating explicitly just what it is that we value and why. If we care about the potential of an individual to contribute to him/herself, others, and society in a productive way, then we need to justify why the measures we use will help identify such potentially productive individuals.

The least metacognitively aware formulators of programs for the gifted simply use whatever measures have been used in the past to identify the gifted in a way that is almost wholly lacking in reflection and self-awareness. Call them Stage I programmers. Stage II programmers, somewhat more aware of thinking theories and processes, may latch onto a particular explicit theory of giftedness and use that, citing the theorist as their authority. These programmers have considered some alternatives. Stage III programmers are still more metacognitively aware and will be able to defend why they use a particular theory or traditional techniques not clearly based in any theory. But the most thoughtful programmers, those of Stage IV, will not simply latch onto whatever happens to be around, with or without justification, but will have a conception of what it is that they value and will then seek an explicit theory, or a combination of such theories, to help realize this system of values. Stage IV programmers realize that the use of an explicit theory to help identify the gifted automatically makes a statement not only about the construct(s) with which the theory or theories deal (such as intelligence or creativity) but also about what is valued by those who will make identification decisions.

What Kind of Educational Program Is Ideal for Gifted Children?

Debates about the best program for gifted children take on a different character when viewed from the standpoint of the pentagonal theory. There is no right answer to the question of what kind of program is best. Rather, we again need to ask ourselves what we value. If we value rapid learning and believe that rapid learners will be in an enhanced position to contribute to our society, then acceleration makes sense. If we believe that what matters is the depth or care students take in probing into what they learn, enrichment will be preferable. If both are prized, we might use a combination. Whatever we do, we should ensure that the values expressed in the instructional program are the same as those expressed in the identification program. If we select for rapid learners, we ought to teach in kind. Once we clarify what we value, we should then act accordingly.

In conclusion, the pentagonal implicit theory provides a basis for understanding how people assign the label of giftedness to some individuals but not to others. It suggests the framework supporting such judgments; explicit theories fill in possible and alternative contents. By understanding implicit as well as explicit theories, we obtain a better grasp of what giftedness might mean, not only as specified by psychological or educational theorists but also as understood by the people who day-to-day make decisions about giftedness. Educators are theorists too, and those who most affect the lives of us and our children.

REFERENCES

Berry, J. W. (1984). Towards a universal psychology of cognitive competence. In P. S. Fry (Ed.). *Changing conceptions of intelligence and intellectual functioning* (pp. 35–61). Amsterdam: North-Holland.

Duck, S. (1991). *Understanding relationships*. New York: Guilford.

Feldhusen, J. F. (1986). *A conception of giftedness*. In R. J. Sternberg & J. E. Davidson (Eds.). *Conceptions of giftedness* (pp. 112–127). New York: Cambridge University Press.

Gardner, H. (1983). *Frames of mind: The theory of multiple intelligences*. New York: Basic Books.

Renzulli, J. S. (1977). The enrichment triad model: A guide for developing defensible programs for the gifted and talented. Mansfield Center. CT: Creative Learning Press.

Renzulli, J. S. (1986). The three-ring conception of giftedness: A developmental model for creative productivity. In R. J. Sternberg & J. E. Davidson (Eds.), *Conceptions of giftedness* (pp. 53–92). New York: Cambridge University Press.

Serpell, R. (1974). Aspects of intelligence in a developing country. *African Social Research, 17*, 576–596.

Stanley, J. C. (1976). The case for extreme educational acceleration of intellectually brilliant youth. *Gifted Child Quarterly, 20*, 66–75.

Sternberg, R. J. (1985a). *Beyond IQ: A triarchic theory of human intelligence*. New York: Cambridge University Press.

Sternberg, R. J. (1985b). Implicit theories of intelligence, creativity, and wisdom. *Journal of Personality and Social Psychology, 49*, 607–627.

Sternberg, R. J., Conway, B. E., Ketron, J. L., & Bernstein, M. (1981). People's conception of intelligence. *Journal of Personality and Social Psychology, 41*, 37–55.

Sternberg, R. J., & Davidson, J. E. (Eds.). (1986). *Conceptions of giftedness*. New York: Cambridge University Press.

Tannenbaum, A. J. (1986). Giftedness: A psychosocial approach. In R. J. Sternberg & J. E. Davidson (Eds.), *Conceptions of giftedness* (pp. 21–52). New York: Cambridge University Press.

Wober, M. (1974). Towards an understanding of the Kiganda concept of intelligence. In J. W. Berry & P. R. Dasen (Eds.), *Culture and cognition: Readings in cross-cultural psychology* (pp. 261–280). London: Methuen.

3

Moving into the Mainstream? Reflections on the Study of Giftedness

Nancy Ewald Jackson

University of Iowa

This position paper is a call for efforts to increase connections between studies of giftedness and mainstream psychological and educational research. Most mainstream researchers have paid scant attention to the literature on giftedness and have ignored the field's journals. However, studies of giftedness have contributed to mainstream theory and may play some special roles in theory development. Strategies for overcoming barriers to further integration with mainstream research are proposed.

Those of us who have studied giftedness for many years have reason to be pleased with a broadening interest in our work. The American

Editor's Note: From Jackson, N.E. (1993). Moving into the mainstream? Reflections on the study of giftedness. *Gifted Child Quarterly, 37*(1), 46-50. © 1993 National Association for Gifted Children. Reprinted with permission.

Psychological Association has sponsored a book (Horowitz & O'Brien, 1985) and a series of conferences on giftedness. A section of a recent (1990) issue of the *Journal of Educational Psychology* was devoted to studies in our field. We also have attracted some distinguished colleagues. Following a pattern set by Julian Stanley in the early 1970s, researchers who have earned prominence in other fields have crossed over into the study of giftedness. The work of scholars such as Robert Sternberg (Sternberg & Davidson, 1986), Frances Horowitz (Horowitz & O'Brien, 1985), and John Borkowski (Borkowski & Day, 1987) has been a great boon to our field, not only because of the quality of the work, but also because the national and international prominence of these scholars has given us voices in mainstream psychological and educational journals and organizations (e.g., Horowitz & O'Brien, 1989; Sternberg & Davidson, 1983). However, our field is still a marginal one relative to the larger scientific communities in which we operate as researchers, scholars, and academicians. The purpose of this article is to propose that greater integration of our work into the mainstream is desirable and to examine ways that we can work to overcome barriers to that integration.

ARE WE STILL IN A BACKWATER?

The low status of psychological and educational research on giftedness relative to research on mental retardation or learning disabilities was evident in two books edited by John Borkowski and Jeanne Day that were intended as integrative reviews of the literature in these three areas (Borkowski & Day, 1987; Day & Borkowski, 1987; Jackson, 1988). Most of the chapter authors were experts in either mental retardation or learning disabilities, but all contributors were charged by the editors with synthesizing the literature in all three areas. Of those authors who had not written previously about giftedness, most gave only cursory coverage to this topic. The extensive reference lists for the 14 chapters in the two volumes cited only 11 articles from journals on giftedness such as the *Gifted Child Quarterly*. In contrast, focused journals such as the *American Journal on Mental Retardation* (formerly the *American Journal of Mental Deficiency*) and the *Journal of Learning Disabilities* were cited far too often for me to count.

Citations of the journals on giftedness are also infrequent in comparative empirical studies that have been published recently in mainstream journals. For example, Swanson's (1990) comparison of gifted and average ability students' metacognitive knowledge and problem-solving skills lists no citations from journals or other literature on giftedness. Geary and Brown's (1991) study of cognitive addition in gifted, normal, and mathematically disabled children includes three references to chapters in Horowitz and O'Brien (1985) and Sternberg and Davidson (1986) but none to journals on giftedness.

Another sign of our still marginal status as a subdiscipline is that some individuals whom we easily perceive as working within our field do not publish in our journals and may not perceive themselves as interested in giftedness. At a recent conference devoted to research on giftedness, one of the speakers, Dean

Simonton, introduced himself as an outsider who studies eminence, not giftedness (Simonton, 1992). Consistent with this self-perception, the list of 68 references for Simonton's paper, which was titled "The Child Parents the Adult: On Getting Genius from Giftedness," included only 1 citation of an article (his own) from the *Gifted Child Quarterly* and 3 (2 his own) from the *Journal of Creative Behavior.* Perhaps Simonton has found that his work reaches a broader and more supportive audience if he emphasizes its connections to mainstream psychological research rather than its role as excellent research on the development of giftedness.

Some kinds of studies of giftedness may be easier than others for mainstream scholars to accept. Research like Simonton's work on the development of eminence has broad appeal because phenomena such as the career productivity of eminent scientists and artists are intrinsically interesting. It may be harder to win acceptance for the more fundamental argument that Borkowski and Day were trying to make in their integrative review volumes (Borkowski & Day, 1987; Day & Borkowski, 1987). They proposed, as have others (Jackson & Butterfield, 1986; VanTassel-Baska, 1991), that studies of children with special gifts should be considered an intrinsic part of a literature on diverse special populations from which comprehensive theories can be generated.

Arguments that we can learn about general principles or other special populations from the study of giftedness seem to encounter considerable skepticism. For example, a colleague and I recently received a thoughtful and constructive review of a case study of a precocious reader (Jackson & Henderson, 1991) that we had submitted for publication in *Exceptional Children.* The anonymous reviewer doubted our assertion that studies of exceptionally gifted learners can contribute to our understanding of general principles accounting for the full range of individual differences in learning. Rather, this reviewer argued that "[t]here are many . . . systematic studies of children who are precocious in their development of math, music, or athletic abilities, and few generalizations have emerged about development in general, or abilities in these domains specifically . . . The sad fact is that studies of precocity, . . . while reinforcing our appreciation for the subtlety and complexity of human development and intelligence, have revealed precious little about the general phenomena of interest." Similarly, a reviewer for a mainstream developmental journal rejected the argument that understanding differences between precocious and average readers will help us understand poor and disabled readers. "If one wants to understand poor readers, then one should study poor readers."

WHAT WE HAVE CONTRIBUTED

Basic and applied researchers who fail to see the potential broad relevance of studies of giftedness are missing important connections by adopting the kind of narrow perspective that threatens the vitality of the behavioral sciences (Bevan,

1991). Studies of gifted performances and gifted persons are always appropriate as individual differences tests of theories that purport to account for all human behavior. As Cronbach (1975) and Underwood (1975) have argued so eloquently, we can have much more confidence in our understanding of a psychological phenomenon if we show that our theories account both for average patterns of behavior and for individual differences, Some researchers studying intelligence and achievement have been responsive to this argument. For example, Sternberg (1985), Gardner (1983), and Csikszentmihalyi and Robinson (1986) have proposed general theories of intelligence and motivation that draw heavily on analyses of giftedness.

Studies of giftedness offer more to mainstream theory than just another way to increase the diversity of the population in which the theory is tested. The special characteristics of gifted performance and gifted populations give researchers who study giftedness certain unique opportunities.

Gifted populations and performances are well-documented and accessible. Simonton's (1992) studies of the career trajectories of eminent men illustrate one important advantage of working with gifted populations, even when a phenomenon of interest, such as life-span career productivity, has relevance for the population as a whole. The accomplishments of gifted individuals are likely to be documented in public records, biographies, and autobiographies. Therefore, one can answer questions about the lives of eminent individuals that could not be answered in similarly cost-effective retrospective studies of less extraordinarily successful men and women. Theories about career development generated from studies of the eminent require further testing before they can be generalized to people in general, but the savings accrued from beginning theory development in a population with well-documented lives may be enormous.

Even those gifted individuals who have not achieved eminence are likely to be cooperative, faithful and traceable research participants. Therefore, data collected from long-term longitudinal studies of gifted populations are likely to have special value because they are relatively undistorted by loss of participants. For example, studies following Terman's sample into early (Terman & Oden, 1947) and late adulthood (e.g., Tomlinson-Keasey & Little, 1990) have suggested relationships between early family environment and later productivity that could be tested for generality in other populations.

Some phenomena occur only, or most dramatically, in gifted populations. Studies of gender differences in achievement motivation done by Dweck and her colleagues (1986) provide one of many possible examples of how a phenomenon of general theoretical and practical interest, such as maladaptive attribution patterns, may be most dramatically apparent in a gifted population. The tendency of gifted girls to show a pattern of learned helplessness in achievement situations is a compelling phenomenon in itself, but it also is a phenomenon that must be accounted for in any comprehensive theory of giftedness. Reports that gifted girls may lack confidence in future success despite high past achievement have called widespread attention to the importance of social feedback and cognitive factors in the development of achievement motivation. Similarly, Benbow's (1988) studies of gender differences in the mathematics achievement of gifted boys and girls have demonstrated that it is not always boys who are at greater risk for dropping out of academic programs.

Studies of giftedness can test hypotheses about conditions necessary for successful performance. Because giftedness in childhood often means precocious achievement, studies of gifted children have played a special role in the developmental psychology literature by demonstrating the existence of achievements that are incompatible with hypotheses about maturational limits or experiential prerequisites. One such study, Chi's (1978) comparison of memory for chess positions in child chess prodigies and adults who were novice chess players, is cited in virtually every textbook in developmental and educational psychology. Chi showed that it is not necessary to be grown up to recall information well: one simply needs to know a great deal about the kind of information that one is asked to remember. Her study is integral to theories of memory and comprehension that, in turn, have facilitated the education of learners at all levels of ability.

Research on the development of precocious reading also provides examples of how studies of giftedness can contribute to comprehensive theories that involve hypotheses about prerequisites or necessary relations between skills. Although evidence to the contrary is scattered throughout several literatures (e.g., Healy, 1982; Scarborough, 1990), reading and oral language proficiency often have been presented as global abilities that are closely linked with one another (e.g., Smith, 1971). However, Crain-Thoreson and Dale (1992) found that preschoolers identified for extreme precocity in oral language development at age 2 are not likely to have become precocious readers by age 4. Similarly, children who begin reading at extremely early ages sometimes have modest or even below-average verbal intelligence (Jackson, 1992; in press).

Contrasts between gifted and average performers clarify the meaning of differences between average and poor performers. Studies of individual differences in child development often have focused on contrasts between average and poor performers. However, identifying differences only at the lower end of the ability continuum leaves open many questions about the origin and nature of those differences. Extending studies of individual differences into the upper range of ability is especially useful because the factors that distinguish poor from moderately successful performance may be either the same as or different from the factors that distinguish moderately successful from gifted performance. Knowing which pattern holds can be important for understanding disability as well as giftedness.

One such question that has been asked by several investigators (Jackson, in press) is how precocious readers' special strengths are related to weaknesses identified in disabled readers (e.g., Rack, Snowling, & Olson, 1992; Scarborough, 1990). Are the strengths of precocious readers a mirror image of disabled readers' deficits, or is the pattern of individual differences across the full range of ability more complex? Whichever pattern holds, considering reading disability in a broader context helps clarify the meaning and likely causes of disabled readers' deficits. For example, poor readers often are found to read especially slowly (Breznitz, 1987). Is this skill deficit something that makes disabled readers qualitatively distinct from all other readers (Stanovich, Nathan, & Zolman, 1988)? Is it a result of the kinds of reading instruction disabled readers have been given? How much does exceptionally slow reading contribute to disabled readers' problems in comprehension? Questions like these can't be answered directly by studies of precocious readers. However, they are cast in a different light if one knows that precocious readers read at exceptionally *rapid* rates (Jackson, in press). The results of studies of precocious readers suggest that text-reading speed is an important correlate of progress in reading across the full range of individual differences, indirectly supporting arguments (Breznitz, 1987) that both poor and average readers should be taught in ways that help them improve their reading speed.

REMOVING BARRIERS TO STRONGER CONNECTIONS

The counter-examples discussed above should discount the assertion that studies of giftedness have revealed "precious little" about general phenomena. Nonetheless and to my regret, a negative appraisal of the impact of our work on general theory development does not seem far off base. We can fault our potential audiences for being unreceptive to the messages we are sending, but if we feel our message is important, we should try harder to make ourselves heard.

Accept the challenge. A friend who often reviews for the *Gifted Child Quarterly* once said that she tended to reject articles in which the investigator had used gifted children as "a population" with which to address some general question about development or cognition. She seemed to feel that studying gifted children in this way somehow demeaned their specialness. Many who work with gifted populations feel that they still need to struggle to gain recognition for the special needs of children with intellectual and other gifts. In contrast, researchers studying persons with mental retardation have a long history of working with a dual perspective, studying the population's special characteristics and needs while also including persons with mental retardation in comparative research designed to study the nature of intelligence and of individual differences in learning and cognition (e.g., Butterfield & Ferretti, 1987).

Perhaps our field has reached a point where we can acknowledge both the need to focus on the special characteristics of children or adults who have various gifts and the need to change our thinking and language to acknowledge that persons with gifts are persons first. By doing so, we would remind ourselves and the potential readers of our work that there should be commonalities between what we learn from our studies of children and adults who have special gifts or talents and what others have learned from their studies of other populations.

Attitudes are reflected in language. Researchers and practitioners working with other special populations have rejected terms that emphasize a characteristic rather than the whole person who has that particular characteristic. We now speak and write of "persons with mental retardation" or "children with physical disabilities" rather than of "the retarded" or "disabled children." The point of this style of nomenclature is to emphasize the common humanity of individuals with special characteristics, and it is required for anyone who publishes in journals such as the *American Journal on Mental Retardation.* In contrast, we rarely write about "youth with mathematical talent," and a phrase such as "children with general intellectual giftedness" does not even sound like acceptable English. Perhaps it also is time to "put the person first" when that person is exceptionally *enabled* rather than disabled.

Ground studies of giftedness in current mainstream theory. Studies of children and adults with special gifts are more likely to influence mainstream theory if they are conceptualized, conducted, and reported so that their potential relevance for understanding other populations and general principles is apparent. Chi's report of chess prodigies' recall performance and the other influential studies mentioned above had relevance for mainstream researchers because they grew out of theoretical frameworks or addressed issues that were important in mainstream thinking. Recent issues of the *Gifted Child Quarterly* and other journals on giftedness have included some studies that are similarly grounded in current theories of general interest. The mainstream literature is especially evident in review articles. However, an analysis of citations in the 1989 issues of the *Gifted Child Quarterly* and the *Journal of Creative Behavior* revealed a heavy reliance on publications within the field of gifted education and on older, rather than current, mainstream literature (Vockell & Canard, 1992). Much of our own theory is minimally connected to current theories of development, education, or cognition. It is healthy for theorists to ground their ideas in the phenomena they are studying (Bevan, 1991). However, theories about the nature of gifted performance, the development of giftedness, or the socio-emotional and educational needs of children with intellectual gifts are likely to be strengthened if they also are embedded in current mainstream theory and research.

Those of us who teach courses on giftedness and review for journals in the field can help keep our colleagues up to-date. We might make it a policy to include relevant recent articles from the mainstream literature in the required readings for our graduate courses. Some of these articles may be reports of studies of gifted populations, but others are likely to be theoretical or empirical papers that provide background for understanding some aspect of giftedness. In advising students who are earning graduate degrees in gifted education, we can insist on recent coursework in rapidly changing fields such as cognitive development and the psychology of learning and motivation. We also can make a special effort to consider whether authors of the papers we review for publication have made appropriate use of current mainstream theories and empirical findings.

Clarify the roles of journals on giftedness. Communicating the results of our research so that it will reach both those colleagues who share our interest in giftedness and a broader scholarly community poses some strategic problems. At present, citation patterns in the mainstream literature suggest that outsiders seeking information about giftedness are likely to look no further than edited books such as those by Horowitz and O'Brien (1985) and Sternberg and Davidson (1986). These books and others have helped us reach broader audiences, but books cannot substitute for refereed journals of record as a repository of basic research findings.

The *Gifted Child Quarterly* has some edge over the competition for status as the primary journal in our field. Original research is published here, and some of it is solid, important, and both theoretically and technically sophisticated. However, a mainstream researcher who regularly reads journals such as the *Journal of Educational Psychology* is not likely to be attracted by an assortment of reviews, program descriptions, and empirical papers assembled to appeal to both scholars and practitioners in gifted education.

All of our journals are written for diverse audiences. Perhaps because the various journals are published by competing organizations, we haven't made the clear divisions in purpose and target audiences that characterize publications in other fields. Therefore, none of our journal editors can assume the level of methodological or theoretical sophistication that often is required of readers of mainstream journals. Complex research articles are balanced with articles written primarily for practitioners. Efforts to strengthen the research content of the *Gifted Child Quarterly* appear to have aroused some opposition (Feldhusen, 1991). Focusing our journals more distinctly might help both insiders and outsiders use our literature more productively.

CONCLUSION

Science is a communal enterprise, and the value of an individual's research rests on the extent to which it contributes to a scholarly community. While the small community of scholars interested in giftedness is important to all of us, our research is likely to be stronger if it also is embedded in the work of larger communities of psychologists and educators. Cultivating a broader audience for our scholarly work may also enhance our credibility when we seek support for gifted education (VanTassel-Baska, 1991). Therefore, we should not be willing to accept an appraisal of our work as contributing little to generalizations about basic psychological and educational principles, and we should work to make such appraisals both unsupportable and unlikely.

REFERENCES

Benbow, C. P. (1988). Sex differences in mathematical reasoning ability in intellectually talented preadolescents: Their nature, effects, and possible causes. *Behavioral and Brain Sciences, 11,* 169–183.

Bevan, W. (1991). Contemporary psychology: A tour inside the onion. *American, Psychologist, 46,* 475–483.

Borkowski, J. G., & Day. J. D. (Eds.). (1987). *Cognition in special children. Comparative approaches.* Norwood, NJ: Ablex.

Breznitz, Z. (1987). Increasing first graders' reading accuracy and comprehension by accelerating their reading rates. *Journal of Educational Psychology, 79,* 236–242.

Butterfield, E. C., & Ferretti, R. P. (1987). Toward a theoretical integration of cognitive hypotheses about intellectual differences among children. In J. G. Borkowski & J. B. Day (Eds.), *Cognition in special children: Comparative approaches* (pp. 195–234). Norwood, NJ: Ablex.

Crain-Thoreson, C., & Dale, P. S. (1992). Do early talkers become early readers? Linguistic precocity, preschool language, and emergent literacy. *Developmental Psychology, 28,* 421–429.

Chi, M. T. H. (1978). Knowledge structures and memory development. In R. S. Siegler (Ed.), *Children's thinking: What develops?* (pp. 73–96). Hillsdale, NJ: Erlbaum.

Cronbach, L. J. (1975). Beyond the two disciplines of scientific psychology. *American Psychologist, 30,* 116–127.

Csikszentmihalyi, M., & Robinson, R. E. (1986). Culture, time, and the development of talent. In R. J. Sternberg & J. E. Davidson (Eds.). *Conceptions of giftedness* (pp. 264–284). New York: Cambridge University Press.

Day, J. D., & Borkowski, J. G. (Eds.), (1987). *Intelligence and exceptionality: New directions for theory, assessment, and instructional practices.* Norwood. NJ: Ablex.

Dweck, C. (1986). Motivational processes affecting learning. *American Psychologist, 41,* 1040–1048.

Feldhusen, J. (1991). From the editor: Gifted education needs reform. *Gifted Child Quarterly, 35,* 115.

Gardner, H. (1983). *Frames of mind.* New York: Basic Books.

Geary, D. C., & Brown, S. C. (1991). Cognitive addition: Strategy choice and speed-of-processing differences in gifted, normal, and mathematically disabled children. *Developmental Psychology, 27,* 398–406.

Healy, J. (1982). The enigma of hyperlexia. *Reading Research Quarterly, 17,* 319–338.

Horowitz, F. D., & O'Brien, M. (Eds.). (1985). *The gifted and talented: Developmental perspectives.* Washington, DC: American Psychological Association.

Horowitz, F. D., & O'Brien, M. (1989). In the interest of the nation. A reflective essay on the state of our knowledge and the challenges before us. *American Psychologist, 44,* 441–445.

Jackson, N. E. (1988). An exceptional approach to exceptionality. *Contemporary Psychology, 33,* 976–977.

Jackson, N. E. (1992). Understanding giftedness in young children: Lessons from the study of precocious reading. In N. Colangelo, S. G. Assouline, & D. L. Ambroson (Eds.). *Talent development: Proceedings from the 1991 Henry B. and Jocelyn Wallace National Research Symposium on Talent Development* (pp. 163–179). Unionville, NY: Trillium Press.

Jackson, N. E. (in press). Precocious reading of English: Sources, structure, and predictive significance. In P. Klein & A. J. Tannenbaum (Eds.), *To be young and gifted.* Norwood, NJ: Ablex.

Jackson, N. E., & Butterfield, E. C. (1986). A conception of giftedness designed to promote research. In R. J. Sternberg & J. E. Davidson (Eds.), *Conceptions of giftedness* (pp. 151–181). New York: Cambridge University Press.

Jackson, N. E., & Henderson, S. (1991, April). *Early development of language and literacy skills of an extremely precocious reader.* Paper presented at the biennial meeting of the Society for Research in Child Development, Seattle, WA.

Rack, J. R., Snowling, M. J., & Olson, R. K. (1992). The nonword deficit in developmental dyslexia: A review. *Reading Research Quarterly, 27,* 28–53.

Scarborough, H. (1990). Very early language deficits in dyslexic children. *Child Development, 61,* 1718–1743.

Simonton, D. K. (1992). The child parents the adult: On getting genius from giftedness. In N. Colangelo, S. G. Assouline, & D. L. Ambroson (Eds.), *Talent development: Proceedings from the 1991 Henry B. and Jocelyn Wallace Research Symposium on Talent Development* (pp. 267–286). Unionville, NY: Trillium Press.

Smith, F. (1971). *Understanding reading.* New York: Holt.

Stanovich, K. E., Nathan, R. G., & Zolman, J. E. (1988). The developmental lag hypothesis in reading: Longitudinal and matched reading-level comparisons. *Child Development, 59,* 71–86.

Sternberg, R. J. (1985). *Beyond IQ.* New York: Cambridge University Press.

Sternberg, R. J., & Davidson, J. E. (1983). Insight in the gifted. *Educational Psychologist, 18,* 51–57.

Sternberg, R. J., & Davidson, J. E. (Eds.). (1986). *Conceptions of giftedness.* New York: Cambridge University Press.

Swanson, H. L. (1990). Influence of metacognitive knowledge and aptitude on problem solving. *Journal of Educational Psychology, 82,* 306–314.

Terman, L. M. & Oden, M. H. (1947). *The gifted child grows up. Genetic studies of genius* (Vol. 4). Palo Alto, CA: Stanford University Press.

Tomlinson-Keasey, C., & Little, T. D. (1990). Predicting educational attainment, occupational achievement, intellectual skill, and personal adjustment among gifted men and women. *Journal of Educational Psychology, 82,* 442–455.

Underwood, B. J. (1975). Individual differences as a crucible in theory construction. *American Psychologist, 30,* 128–134.

VanTassel-Baska, J. (1991). Gifted education in the balance: Building relationships with general education. *Gifted Child Quarterly, 35,* 20–25.

Vockell, E. L., & Canard, R. (1992). Sources of information in gifted education literature. *Gifted Child Quarterly, 36,* 17–18.

4

Metacognition, Intelligence and Giftedness

Bruce M. Shore

Arlene C. Dover

McGill University

The contribution of metacognition to the better understanding of giftedness is explored in the context of the "triarchic" of intelligence and its subtheory of insight proposed by Sternberg and his colleagues at Yale University, and in relation to research into the interaction between availability and flexibility of cognitive style on one hand, and metacognitive knowledge and skill on the other. Support is offered for the importance of interactions among the elements (meta-components, performance components, and knowledge-acquisition components) of the triarchic theory to better explain giftedness. Finally, rather than regarding a theory of giftedness to be a subtheory of one of intelligence, might there be merit in considering the opposite order?

Editor's Note: From Shore, B.M., & Dover, A.C. (1987). Metacognition, intelligence and giftedness. *Gifted Child Quarterly, 31*(1), 37-39.

Metacognition is the knowledge and awareness of one's own cognitive processes (Flavell, 1976) and the ability to monitor, regulate and evaluate one's thinking (Brown, 1978). Though the term remains somewhat imprecise (cf. Bracewell, 1983), it provides a potentially useful framework for examining qualitative differences between the thinking of gifted and other persons.

Metacognitive processes enable individuals to better control their thinking and thereby become more efficient and flexible learners. Research on metacognition has become popular among both developmental and process-oriented psychologists, providing a bridge between cognitive behavior modification (Meichenbaum, 1980), educational technology (Gagné, 1980), and theories of intelligence (e.g., Sternberg, 1979).

Two types of behavior are commonly characterized as comprising metacognition: knowledge and skill. Metacognitive knowledge is generally assessed through verbalizations about one's learning characteristics, state of knowledge, or understanding of task features which may influence one's performance. A variety of criteria have been used to operationalize the concept of metacognitive skill. These include checking, planning, selecting and monitoring (Brown & Campione, 1980), self-questioning and introspection (Brown, 1978), and monitoring or interpreting ongoing experience (Flavell & Wellman, 1977). Bracewell (1983) argues that the distinction between metacognitive knowledge and skill may not be entirely necessary or particularly useful.

Insofar as metacognition implies control over mental activities and strategies which enhance learning, the overall concept is especially relevant to education. Presumably, the more knowledge students have about their abilities and learning strategies, the more apt they are to acquire new knowledge and skills. Recently, researchers have begun to explore differences between the thinking and learning of gifted and other students including what knowledge students have about themselves as thinkers and how they apply that knowledge in learning situations.

THEORETICAL BACKGROUND

There appear to be two research teams exploring the relation of metacognition to giftedness while attempting to fit their observations into a suitable theoretical context. At Yale University, Sternberg (1980, 1984a, 1984b, 1985) and his colleagues have developed an original theory of intelligence which they call "triarchic." It includes three types of intellectual elements: (a) Metacomponents—executive processes used in planning, monitoring and evaluating one's information processing, (b) Performance components—processes used in the actual execution or set of tasks, and (c) Knowledge-acquisition components—those abilities related to achievement and, perhaps, to the current interest in expert versus novice performance. Sternberg proposes that tasks involving these three components "will measure intelligence to the extent that they involve coping with novelty or automatization of task performance" (1984, p. 10), a generalization which he conceptualizes as a two-facet subtheory of the triarchic theory. According to this model, giftedness is characterized by the ability to cope with novelty across all three types of intellectual processes (Sternberg & Davidson, 1983), and is termed "insight" (not necessarily to be confused with "aha" types of insight used in other contexts). More specifically, insight comprises three principal selective processes: selective encoding, combination, and comparison.

Sternberg and his coworkers have dealt with three principal themes over the past five or six years, leading to the present theorizing. The first was an expression of dissatisfaction with the adequacy of intelligence tests. The second described the development of the triarchic theory which better explained exceptionally high ability. The third thrust has dealt with insight and giftedness. In the spring of 1984, however, in a symposium at Teachers College, Columbia University, Sternberg summarized his work to that point and, at the conclusion of several examples, made an interesting final statement to the effect that gifted, successful people shape their environments; they do not necessarily have high IQs, nor do they necessarily completely adapt or change their environment. The ring of Piagetian adaptation and accommodation is present in the choice of words, and it is not merely a coincidence that Flavell (1976), a key interpreter of Piaget, was also one of the first to write about metacognition. This provides a good connection to our research on metacognition and giftedness.

We have come to compatible conclusions from a different theoretical base. Rather than theories of intelligence, our interest in the last decade has been on learning style, on the match between instruction and instructional need. The points of contact with Sternberg's work came from several studies (summarized by Shore, 1982) which suggested that not a single cognitive style, but flexibility or adaptability of style, was an essential ingredient of successful university or other high-level learning.

We developed a general hypothesis (not broad enough to be regarded as a theory, but it might have a place within Sternberg's model) that the interaction between level of metacognition and the availability and flexibility of cognitive styles is an important characteristic of giftedness. If the distinction should prove important, we are probably talking more specifically about metacognitive knowledge rather than skill in the first instance, and whether or not metacognitive skill is a substantially different concept from an articulated cognitive style remains to be determined in the second. This refinement is about to be explored. In our work to date it was simply proposed that gifted persons would be distinguished by a high level of metacognition in combination with flexibility and adaptability from a large repertoire of cognitive styles. To illustrate, someone with no repertoire of approaches to, say, a learning task, and who normally does not monitor performance on it, would not likely be regarded as gifted. As the number of approaches or styles increases, and as awareness of processing strategies improves, so should performance in a greater "variety of situations." The highest levels are attained when alternate strategies are available and metacognitive processes govern not only performance within individual strategies, but the switching process as well. (An intriguing subquestion which we soon hope to explore is the application of these notions to at least some gifted learning-disabled individuals.) Some recent research has lent support to these ideas.

RECENT RESEARCH ON METACOGNITION AND GIFTEDNESS

Hannafen and J. O. Carey (1981) found that high achieving students were better able to describe their learning strategies. While this may have been due to superior verbal skills or motivation rather than to their metacognitive abilities, it is also possible that low achievers could not describe their learning strategies because they may not have been using any systematically. Chatman and Williford (1982) studied gifted grade-four students' awareness and use of cognitive strategies while solving problems. Using an unstructured interview to assess awareness, they found that none of their subjects could verbalize their thought processes. In a second experiment with the same sample, they asked the children whether particular strategies could have been helpful in solving the problems. Although many of the students understood how specific strategies could have helped, few actually reported using them. Chatman and Williford's research suggests that while gifted students possess some metacognitive knowledge, they will not necessarily utilize it appropriately.

A few years ago we reported that scores on a purportedly spatial task, the portable rod-and-frame apparatus used to assess field independence dependence, loaded on a spatial factor for particularly spatially able adolescents, and on a verbal factor for more verbally capable individuals (Shore, Hymovitch, & Lajoie, 1982). The former happened to be mostly boys and the latter girls, but these gender differences were not our interest. These results are consistent with those of Maccoby and Jacklin (1974) on sex differences in verbal and spatial abilities. Most interestingly, performance on the rod-and-frame task was best correlated with spatial abilities among the spatially capable and with verbal abilities among the more verbally capable; this connection was strongest for the most able among both groups. Sternberg and Weil (1980) have reported aptitude-strategy interactions on cognitive tasks, and Mathews, Hunt, and MacLeod (1980) reported such effects on a verbal-pictorial task.

We then undertook to test the hypothesis that the verbally able subjects redefined the task as a verbal one so as to be better able to perform it. This was done by asking samples of verbally and spatially capable subjects to verbalize as they performed the task (Shore & Carey, 1984). Conscious control over the solution process was suggested by the subject's verbal reports which indicated that they were actively monitoring their own knowledge and repertoire of strategies in order to perform the task at hand. The more verbally able subjects, as expected, less often reported using visual images and referents, and the verbally able more often "talked their way" through the problem using verbal strategies to control their decision making in the task. Similarly, subjects with equal or superior spatial ability used spatial strategies more often.

In another study, Dover (1983) found support for the contention that academically gifted children may be differentiated according to their metacognitive abilities. Twenty-five gifted and twenty-five nongifted grades five and six children performed Luchins's (1942) Einstellung water-jar task. The groups were compared on flexibility, accuracy and speed, and on a measure of metacognitive knowledge assessed by a structured interview about their solution processes. Gifted students performed the task more quickly, as expected, but they also more often gave the alternative solution when it was available. They demonstrated superior problem-solving skill, greater awareness of their solution processes, and more efficient monitoring skills.

THEORETICAL IMPLICATIONS

These two lines of research are addressing the same issues, and a useful exercise is to try to bring them together. At first glance, our work seems to fit within the general heading of Sternberg's metacomponents, but it bears as well upon performance and knowledge acquisition. With regard to the two-facet subtheory, it is certainly related to the novelty element in that it is the novelty in a situation that determines the need for adaptive behavior. One possibility, then, is that we are simply elaborating the idea of novelty or insight as a part of the subtheoretical level where Sternberg has placed it. If that is our contribution, then it may be a useful addition to a theory which has left some conceptual vacancies available (Sternberg, 1984a, includes several commentaries by other theorists on this matter).

We must also face the possibility that our approach is redundant. Does Sternberg's (or another) theory account for all we are trying to describe? While there is considerable compatibility, itself an endorsement of both approaches, it seems that one element of our proposition does extend our understanding of the triarchic theory and giftedness, namely, by providing evidence that the combination of metacognition with availability and alternation of strategies contributes to giftedness. This is an extension of the major elements of the triarchic theory: Not only do the three components exist, but they also interact with each other. These interactions are anticipated in Sternberg's work (1980, 1985), but so far they have played a relatively lesser role in the development of the theory. Our research may be regarded as exploring the interactions between metacomponents and performance components and, to a lesser extent, between metacomponents and learning acquisition, and leading to the suggestion that these interactions should perhaps be given greater weight.

This leaves us with a question: Is it possible that insight is not merely a subelement, part of a sub-theory, but an element at a more general level of a theory of intelligence and one which adds the interactions we are examining? Is the constellation of abilities, skills and knowledge we call giftedness a subset of that which we call intelligence, or vice-versa? By the very nature of their interests, researchers of creativity might ask the same question. Should the nature of intelligence not be found within a good theory of giftedness? Beginning with Sternberg's triarchic theory of intelligence and his identification of novelty and insight as distinguishing characteristics of giftedness, perhaps the next step should be toward macro- rather than micro-extensions of the theory in order to find the place of giftedness. Finally, if there is any truth in this speculation, then a major responsibility falls to those who study giftedness to exert themselves more than ever to work from a strong theoretical base in planning research and considering implications for action.

REFERENCES

Bracewell, R. J. (1983). Investigating the control of writing skills. In Mosenthal, P., Tamor, L., & Walmsley, S. A.(Eds.). *Research on writing: Principles and methods.* New York: Longman.

Brown, A. L. (1978). Knowing when, where, and how to remember: A problem of metacognition. In R. Glaser (Ed.), *Advances in Instructional psychology,* Vol. 1. Hillsdale, NJ: Erlbaum.

Brown, A. L., & Campione, J. C. (1980). *Inducing flexible thinking: A problem of access.* University of Illinois, Urbana, Center for the Study of Reading Technical Report No. 189. Cambridge, MA: Bolt, Beranek & Newman.

Chatman, S. P., & Williford, J. N. (1982). The gifted student's awareness and use of cognitive strategies in academic tasks: An exploratory study. Paper presented at the annual meeting of the National Association for Gifted Children, New Orleans.

Dover, A. C., (1983). *Metacognition and problem solving in gifted children.* Unpublished master's thesis in Educational Psychology, McGill University, Montreal.

Flavell, J. H. (1976). Metacognitive aspects of problem solving. In L. B. Resnick (Ed.), *The nature of intelligence.* Hillsdale, NJ: Erlbaum.

Flavell, J. H., & Wellman, H. M. (1977). Metamemory. In R.V. Kail & J. W. Hagen (Eds.), *Perspectives on the development of memory and cognition.* Hillsdale, NJ: Erlbaum.

Gagné, R. M. (1980). Is educational technology in phase? *Educational Technology, 20* (2), 7–14.

Hannafen, M. J., & Carey, J. O. (1981). Research in progress: Toward a procedure to identify the spontaneous memory strategies of children. Paper presented at the annual meeting of the Association for Educational Communication and Technology, Philadelphia.

Luchins, A. S. (1942). Mechanization in problem solving. *Psychological Monographs, 54* (6) (Whole No. 248).

Maccoby, E. E., & Jacklin, C. (1974). *The psychology of sex differences.* Stanford, CA: Stanford University Press.

Mathews, N. N., Hunt, E. B., & MacLeod, C. M. (1980). Strategy choice and strategy training in sentence-picture verification. *Journal of Verbal Learning and Verbal Behavior, 19,* 531–548.

Meichenbaum, D. A. (1980). A cognitive-behavioral perspective on intelligence. *Intelligence, 4* (4), 271–283.

Shore, B. M. (1982). Developing a framework for the study of learning style in high level learning. In J. W. Keefe (Ed.), *Student learning styles and brain behavior: Programs, instrumentation, research.* Reston, VA: National Association of Secondary School Principals.

Shore, B. M., & Carey, S. M. (1984). Verbal ability and spatial task. *Perceptual and Motor Skills, 59,* 255–259.

Shore, B. M., Hymovitch, J., & Lajoie, S. P. (1982). Processing differences in relations between ability and field independence. *Psychological Reports, 50,* 391–395.

Sternberg, R. J. (1979). The nature of mental abilities. *American Psychologist, 34* (3), 214–230.

Sternberg, R. J. (1980). Sketch of a componential subtheory of human intelligence. *Behavioral and Brain Sciences, 3,* 573–584.

Sternberg, R. J. (1984a). Toward a triarchic theory of human intelligence. *Behavioral and Brain Sciences, 7,* 269–315.

Sternberg, R. J. (1984b). What should intelligence tests test? Implications for a triarchic theory of intelligence for intelligence testing. *Educational Researcher, 13*(1), 5–15.

Sternberg, R. J. (1985). *Beyond IQ: A triarchic theory of human intelligence.* Cambridge, MA: Cambridge University Press.

Sternberg, R. J., & Davidson, J. E. (1983). Insight in the gifted. *Educational Psychologist, 18* (1), 51–57.

Sternberg, R. J., & Weil, E. M. (1980). An aptitude-strategy interaction in linear syllogistic reasoning. *Journal of Educational Psychology, 72,* 226–234.

5

Divergent Thinking, Creativity, and Giftedness

Mark A. Runco

California State University, Fullerton

Creativity is an important facet of giftedness. Creativity is, however, very difficult to define and measure. Divergent thinking tests are often used, though of course they really just *estimate* the *potential* for creative thought. In the past few years, the technologies for the assessment and enhancement of divergent thinking have changed dramatically. This article reviews the most recent research on divergent thinking. Several new assessment techniques are reviewed, including those using either lenient or stringent solution standards, those relying on ideational pools (examinees' total output of ideas), and those involving qualitative aspects of ideation. Recent research showing moderately high predictive validity coefficients is also reviewed. The role played by evaluation and valuation in the divergent thinking process is outlined, as is the role of problem definition and problem identification. Special considerations for the creativity of gifted children are noted throughout the article, and specific directions for future research on the divergent thinking of gifted children are presented in the conclusion.

Editor's Note: From Runco, M.A. (1993). Divergent thinking, creativity, and giftedness. *Gifted Child Quarterly, 37*(1), 16-22.

DIVERGENT THINKING, CREATIVITY, AND GIFTEDNESS

In a recent debate concerning metaphors, scientific investments, and creativity, Runco (1991a) and Sternberg and Lubart (1991) found one point on which to agree: There is value in the continued study of divergent thinking. This is an important point, for many individuals studying creativity have been highly critical of the research on divergent thinking (e.g., Weisberg, 1986). Criticisms usually focus on the only moderate predictive validity of divergent thinking tests and ambiguous connection to creative performances occurring in the natural environment.

These criticisms have proven to be quite helpful for those still conducting research on divergent thinking. They have, for example, uncovered the areas which are in need of additional study. They have also helped to qualify and delimit the role of divergent thinking in the creative process. Divergent thinking is not synonymous with creative thinking, and divergent thinking tests are not as valid as we might hope. In fact, the predictive validity coefficients reported 10, 15, and 20 years ago were just marginal. Still, divergent thinking does seem to be an important component in some creative performances, and recent research has reported quite respectable predictive validity coefficients (Okuda, Runco. & Berger, 1991; Sawyers & Canestaro, 1989). That research will be reviewed below.

Theorists who dismiss divergent thinking as entirely unimportant have ignored recent empirical research. This is apparent when reading their work, for they do not cite research from the 1980s and 1990s. Additionally, some critics seem to expect too much from divergent thinking. Again, divergent thinking is not synonymous with creativity. Divergent thinking tests are, however, very useful *estimates* of the *potential* for creative thought. Although a high score on a divergent thinking *test does not guarantee outstanding performance in the natural* environment, these tests do lead to useful predictions about who is capable of such performances. As Hong and Milgram (1991) described it, divergent thinking is a predictor of original thought, not a criterion of creative ability.

Divergent Thinking and Gifted Children

The research on divergent thinking is particularly important for those interested in gifted children. Creativity is a vital component of giftedness (Albert & Runco, 1986, 1989; Feldhusen & Treffinger, 1990; Renzulli, 1978; Runco & Okuda, in press), and for many years the creativity of children has been more often than not estimated with divergent thinking tests. Divergent thinking is also an important topic because it seems to contribute to academic success (Feldhusen, Bahlke, & Treffinger, 1969), and it may be tied to psychological health (Runco, Ebersole, & Mraz, 1991; Schotte & Clum, 1987).

Putting the Research to Use

When faced with a divergent thinking task, gifted children typically give ideas reflecting exceptional fluency, originality, and flexibility; but those working with the gifted should also consider other, more recently identified, ideational idiosyncracies. These may be qualitative and manifest in the actual contents of the ideas, for example, gifted children thinking about unusual topics or following unique themes when solving open-ended tasks. Problem identification and problem-definition skills should also be considered when working with the gifted. Both can be exercised and assessed with modified divergent thinking tasks, tasks which allow children to identify and define a specific "problem" before solving it. Such problem finding seems to be distinct from problem solving and seems to elicit intrinsically motivated patterns of thought. It may also be critical for performance in the natural environment.

The ability to evaluate the originality and usefulness of ideas should also be recognized by those working with the gifted. Gifted children should, then, be given opportunities to practice selecting original and useful ideas. Moreover, adults should monitor *their* evaluations in order to avoid prejudging the ideas which are given by children. Research suggests that judgments given by adults are often inaccurate, and these may contribute to the slumps found in the creative thinking of certain age groups. With this in mind, *valuation*—the effort toward appreciation—may be more important than critical evaluations, both for the gifted child and for his or her parents and teachers.

Runco (1991b, 1992a) reviewed the research on divergent thinking. However, because of publication lags and the recent surge in the number of investigations of creativity, his reviews do not contain some very important research. The present article is, then, an addendum to the earlier reviews. Several new assessment techniques are reviewed, including those using either lenient or stringent solution standards, those relying on ideational pools (examinees' total output of ideas), and those involving qualitative aspects of ideation. Recent research showing moderately high predictive validity coefficients is also reviewed. The role played by evaluation and valuation in the divergent thinking process is outlined, as is the role of problem definition and problem identification, importantly, this is not intended as a comprehensive review, nor as an exposition of a new theory about the role of creativity in giftedness. As noted above, this is an addendum (cf. Runco, 1991b, 1992a). The connection between creativity and giftedness is discussed in detail by Albert and Runco (1986), Feldhusen and Treffinger (1990), Milgram (1990), and Renzulli (1978). Special considerations for the creativity of gifted children are noted throughout the present article, and specific expectations for the creativity of gifted children are presented in the conclusion, along with directions for future research on divergent thinking.

Divergent Thinking Tests

In an effort to improve the validity of divergent thinking assessments, the tests themselves have been changed over the past few years. This is the *technology for ideational assessment* to which Runco (1991b) referred. In one example of this, Milgram (1990; Hong & Milgram, 1991) demonstrated the important difference between tests with *lenient* solution standards (in which virtually any stimulus can be interpreted as a problem, and virtually any response can be viewed as a potential solution) and tests with stringent solution standards (in which both solutions and problems are clearly defined). Most of the divergent thinking tests developed in the 1960s and 1970s relied on lenient solution standards. Hong and Milgram (1991) suggested that tests with stringent standards might be more useful—at least for school children.

Hong and Milgram (1991) compared popular and original responses elicited by lenient solution standards to those elicited by tests with stringent standards. In their work with preschool children, they used "the Chair" and "Oranges" lenient tests. In the former, children were told.

> You want to join your classmates sitting at the table drawing but the only chair left is broken and only has three legs [examiner shows subject a three-legged chair]. What can you do with the chair so that you can sit at the table?

Children were given materials along with these instructions, including a vase filled with soil, a waste basket, poles and stakes, and play dough.

Children can offer numerous ideas about and solutions to "the Chair" and "Oranges." Hong and Milgram defined these as either *popular* (given by a large proportion of the sample) or *original* (given by a small proportion). This scoring system is itself notable since it uses clearly distinct indices, unlike the older scoring systems which relied on overlapping fluency and originality scores (cf. Hocevar, 1979; Runco & Albert, 1985). In most scoring systems, one idea can contribute to both fluency and originality scores. This is not the case for popular and originality scores.

Hong and Milgram (1991) also administered several stringent solution standard tests, including "the Cylinder in the Can" and "Box." In these it was possible to determine whether or not each solution actually solved the problem. Comparisons indicated that both lenient and stringent solution standard responses were unrelated to IQ. This confirms that the ideational tests are not simply tapping general intellectual ability. A second finding was that original responses from lenient tests were only moderately correlated with original responses from stringent tests; and popular responses from lenient tests were only moderately correlated with popular responses from stringent tests (coefficients approximately .3 for preschool children and .5 for school-aged children). Although these associations were statistically significant, they do not reflect much shared variance (9% and 25%, respectively). Thus performance on the two types of tests seems to be relatively independent. In behavioral terms, the skills required by the two types of tests probably differ. The stringent tests are probably more like problems which will be encountered in the natural environment (Hong & Milgram, 1991).

This brings us to the renewed interest in real-world performances. Like Hong and Milgram (1991), Okuda et al. (1991) suggested that divergent thinking tests would be more predictive of real-world performances if they contained problems children might encounter in school and at home. Granted, this argument is not entirely new (e.g., Renzulli, 1982), but Okuda et al. empirically compared typical divergent thinking tests with those containing real-world questions. They also compared *presented* and *discovered* divergent thinking tests.

Okuda et al. (1991) administered the real-world divergent thinking tests to 77 fourth-, fifth-, and sixth-grade children—many with very high intellectual abilities. In one presented problem the children were told

> Your friend Teddy sits next to you in class. Teddy likes to talk and often bothers you while you are doing your work. Sometimes the teacher scolds you for talking, and many times you do not finish your work because Teddy is bothering you. What are you going to do?

The discovered problems allowed the children to define a problem before they generated ideas. One of these read

> Now I would like you to think of different problems in school [or at home] which are important to you. You may write down problems about school, teachers, rules, or classmates [or parents, brothers or sisters, chores, or rules]. Take your time and think of as many problems as you can.

Okuda et al. found that responses from the real-world discovered problems were the best predictors of creative activity and accomplishment in the real world (activity and accomplishment having been assessed with a self-report check list[1]). As a matter of fact, the predictive validity coefficients for these tests are among the highest in the literature on divergent thinking. Moreover, hierarchical multiple regression analyses indicated that scores from the real-world discovered problems contributed to the prediction of creative activity and accomplishment above and beyond the prediction of more typical divergent thinking. This work highlights the need to distinguish between artificial tests (e.g., name all of the things you can think of which are square) and more realistic problems. It also highlights the difference between problem discovery and problem solving (Runco, in press-b). This distinction will be discussed further below.

Sawyers and Canestaro (1989) reported similarly high predictive validities for ideational tests. They administered the *Multidimensional Stimulus Fluency Measure* (MSFM) to students enrolled in an interior design course and gathered data on course grades and the creativity of the final course project. The MSFM is an adaptation of the Wallach and Kogan (1965) tests. Although Sawyers and Canestaro (1989) worked with college students, the MSFM can be used with children of nearly any age (e.g., Goble, Moran, & Bomba, 1991; Tegano & Moran, 1989). The work of Sawyers and Canestaro (1989) is very important because it demonstrates domain specificity—in this case, within the domain of interior design—as well as highly respectable validity coefficients (approximately .45). Runco (1987) described the relevance of domain specificity for those studying gifted children (also see Csikszentmihalyi, 1990).

Tegano and Moran (1989) used the MSFM with children in preschool and the first and third grades and uncovered interesting sex differences. No sex differences were found for preschool children, but in the third grade boys had higher originality and popular scores. Tegano and Moran suggested that conformity, assimilative strategies, and socialization each contributed to the different levels of performance by boys and girls in the third grade.

Ideational Indices

Other innovations in the assessment of divergent thinking involve scoring techniques. One innovation was mentioned above, namely the use of popular and original scores (Goble et al., 1991; Hong & Milgram, 1991; Sawyers & Canestaro, 1989; Tegano & Moran, 1989). A second was described by Runco and Mraz (1992). They suggested that divergent thinking tests could be scored more accurately—and with less effort—by focusing on one score for each examinee's entire ideational output.

Too often, children's responses to divergent thinking tests are separated, and each idea is compared to other ideas to determine originality, flexibility, and so on. When this method is used, a score for an individual child is based on the sum of ratings given to each idea. Hence a child who gives 10 ideas, 5 of which are unique, will probably be given a fluency score of 10 and an originality score of 5. (Originality may be scored in terms of unusual rather than unique ideas, but the emphasis is still on single ideas.) Runco and Mraz (1992) took a different approach and had raters judge *ideational pools*. Here, an examinee's ideas are not separated from one another. Rather, they are given to raters just as they were produced by the examinee—that is, in a set or list (after verbatim transcription). Judges simply award one score (e.g., a "creativity" score) to each pool of ideas. In other words, judges are asked to make their decisions based on the entire set of ideas rather than on idea-to-idea basis.

The scoring of ideational pools is useful because it retains the actual associative pattern used by examinees. Ideas can be scored just as they were produced by children. The use of ideational pools is also justified by the work of Rossman and Gollob (1975). They used different tests but demonstrated that examiners and raters are most accurate when given a great deal of information. This is the reason Runco and Mraz (1992) gave judges all of the ideas given by each examinee. Judges can look at an ideational pool and know how many ideas were given by that one child, how many ideas were unusual which associative patterns or strategies were used, and so on. Runco and Mraz found that scores based on examinees' entire ideational output were highly reliable. The interjudge reliability coefficients were quite high—*in excess of .90. Interitem* reliability coefficients were also high—approximately .62.

Practically speaking, the technique involving ideational pools is attractive because it is less time-consuming than traditional techniques. In the new scoring system, there is no need to compare and classify ideas (which takes time and may require subjective discriminations). Admittedly, future research on this technique is needed. For example, Runco and Mraz (1992) did not have performance criteria for their subjects and were therefore unable to examine the predictive validity of their scoring method. Also, they obtained ratings about *creativity* rather than *originality.* They did this because previous research suggested that judges can give accurate ratings specifically for creativity (cf. Amabile, 1990; Runco, 1989). Unfortunately, Runco and Mraz (1992) found that ratings of creativity were correlated with ratings of "intelligence" (which were also based on ideational pools). Judges were not, then, discriminating when asked which children were creative and which were intelligent. This problem of discriminant validity has a long history in the creativity research (e.g., Getzels & Jackson, 1962) but might be avoided if judges are asked to give ratings of something relevant but more easily defined—like originality.

Problem Identification

Chand and Runco (in press) extended the work of Okuda et al. (1991) and further developed problem discovery tests. They used the presented and discovered problems from Runco and Okuda (1988) and one new test. The new *discovery and solution* test allowed examinees to select one of the problems they had themselves thought of and then think of solutions to it. Chand and Runco argued that the discovered problem tests were best viewed as *problem generation* tests, and they suggested that allowing examinees to select one of their own problems allows intrinsically motivated performances. This is important because intrinsic motivation seems to maximize creativity (Amabile, 1990; Hennessey, 1989; MacKinnon, 1983) and because it is another of the important facets of giftedness (Renzulli, 1978).

In addition to developing the new discovery and solution divergent thinking test, one of the most important aspects of this investigation—especially for those interested in gifted education—was the demonstration that explicit instructions had different effects on various tests. Explicit instructions are often used to maximize performance and to insure that all examinees have the same perception of the task at hand (Harrington, 1975). They typically contain very specific information about how to do well on a test. For example, examinees might be told to "give ideas that no one else will think of" in an effort to maximize originality scores. Such explicit instructions seem to guarantee that each examinee has the same objective (original ideas) and is aware of appropriate strategies (i.e., looking to ideas which will be thought of by no one else). In earlier research, Runco (1986) reported that the originality of both gifted and nongifted students improved after they received explicit instructions, and Runco and Okuda (in press) found much the same using instructions to enhance flexibility scores. The instructions used by Chand and Runco (in press) were designed to enhance originality.

Chand and Runco (in press) found an interaction between instructional condition (i.e., explicit vs. standard) and the type of problem or test (i.e., presented problems, problem generation, or the discovery and solution test). The explicit instructions led to high scores on the presented problems and the discovery and solution test but had no effect on the problem generation task. These findings suggest that explicit instructions can be used to teach ideational strategies—strategies which can lead to improved originality and flexibility, of thought (Runco & Okuda, in press)—but they, are only useful with certain tests. Using the terminology of cognitive psychology, explicit instructions seem to strengthen the metacognitive abilities of children. Recall here that gifted children have idiosyncratic metacognitive abilities (Davidson & Sternberg, 1984; Runco, 1986).

Evaluative Skill

Runco (1992b) argued that *evaluative* and *valuative skills* are both involved in divergent and creative thinking. In his view, evaluations occur when an individual selects ideas and tries to find the best, most creative, or most useful solution or response. Ideas are probably not randomly generated (Runco, 1992b; Simonton, 1988) but are only recorded, applied, or even considered after an evaluation. To be realistic, ideas might be selected after a valuation rather than an evaluation. *Valuation* is the most appropriate label for a specific attempt to find the value or fit of ideas. *Evaluation* is its critical counterpart, where children (or their parents or teachers) look for what's wrong rather than what's right.

Runco (1992b) confirmed that some children recognize a creative idea when they see one, but some children do not. He also found that evaluative skill was moderately correlated with the ability to generate ideas, that is, with divergent thinking test scores. This correlation might reflect an overlap of skills, with the production of ideas dependent on evaluation. This might in turn reflect a developmental interaction, for those children who are good divergent thinkers probably will have more practice evaluating ideas than other children. Practically speaking, valuation and evaluation should probably be assessed whenever divergent thinking is assessed.

Runco and Vega (1990) reported that parents and teachers also differ in their evaluative abilities. In this investigation, some parents and teachers knew which ideas were creative and which were not. Surprisingly, parents and teachers did not differ from one another in terms of the accuracy of their evaluations. This was contrary to expectations, for parents and teachers do have significantly different experiences, and these could quite easily lead to discrepant evaluative tendencies. However, the only hint of an effect for experience was that parents with several children were more accurate at identifying creative ideas than parents with few children.

This work on evaluative skill has important educational implications. For example, it might be that the pressure placed on children to think in a conventional manner would be applied more selectively and appropriately if parents and teachers improve their evaluative and valuative skills. It is even feasible that this type of improvement would minimize the "fourth-grade slump" in children's creativity (Torrance, 1968). This slump will be discussed further below. For now the point is that valuation and evaluation might be treated as important educational objectives. More research on evaluative skill is needed.

Research on the training of evaluative strategies should be considered (cf. Runco & Basadur, 1990), as should comparisons of *interpersonal* and *intrapersonal* evaluations. Runco and Smith (1991) uncovered significant differences between interpersonal evaluative accuracy and intrapersonal evaluative accuracy, but they did not have children or parents and teachers in their sample. Interpersonal skills should be examined further because they are used when parents or teachers evaluate ideas given by their children or their students, and intrapersonal skills should be studied because they are used when children evaluate their own ideas.

Higher Order and Qualitative Divergent Thinking Factors

The research on problem discovery and evaluative skills is consistent with claims that creative thinking is multidimensional. The multidimensionality issue was empirically addressed by Michael and Bachelor (1990) in their reanalysis of one of Guilford's data bases. Michael and Bachelor were particularly interested in higher order divergent production factors among Guilford's structure of intellect (SOI) tests. They tested a variety of factor models and reported that the best fit (in terms of variance accounted for) was a model containing nine oblique factors. They did find a model with higher order factors which had almost as good a fit and went so far as to say that "divergent thinking tests designed to portray creativity can be conceptualized meaningfully and parsimoniously within the framework of a higher-order factor structure" (1990, p. 71). The most important aspect of their findings may be that they "cast some doubt upon the orthogonally derived solution of Guilford" (1990, p. 71). In other words, there may be more overlap among the various divergent thinking tests than is suggested by Guilford's well-known model. A comprehensive reexamination of Guilford's model was presented by Bachelor and Michael (in press).

Another extension of traditional views of divergent thinking involves qualitative interpretations of ideation. Dudek and Verreault (1989) and Urban

(1991), for example, reported that divergent thinking tests elicit information about children's affective states. Dudek and Verreault (1989) compared highly creative children with uncreative children in terms of the quantity and quality of ideas given to the *Torrance Tests of Creative Thinking*. Dudek and Verreault were especially interested in the quality scores which they felt reflected primary process content. They wrote:

> It is our contention that the child who develops a capacity for high divergent thinking has retained contact with the chaotic primary process that follows no rules and no conventions. It is *perversely divergent*. (1989, p. 80)

Dudek and Verreault operationalized "defense demand," "defense effectiveness," and "regression in the service of the ego" ideational scores and found several significant differences between the highly creative and the uncreative children. For example, the creative children gave responses containing significantly more evidence of regression and significantly more defense demand (e.g., "crudity of the response").

The notion that divergent thinking has meaningful qualitative aspects is especially important because of the increased appreciation for the affective components of creativity (e.g., Shaw & Runco, in press). Creativity requires more than cognitive skill; it also requires particular affective tendencies and sensitivities. This is reason why creativity cannot be equated with problem solving skill. Creativity may reflect a *need* or *feeling* (e.g., self expression) as much as a facility with ideas or ability to solve problems. This is another reason why motivation should be included in operational definitions of giftedness (Albert & Runco, 1986; Feldhusen & Treffinger, 1990; Milgram, 1990; Renzulli, 1978).

Practically speaking, the research of Dudek and Verreault (1989) suggests that we should no longer look only at quantitative aspects of ideation, like fluency. We may encounter a child who is ungifted and unexceptional in terms of the number of his or her responses, but if we look closely at the specific characteristics of the responses, we may see some indication of exceptional talent.[2] In the words of Dudek and Verreault (1989), "low fluency might . . . reflect conscious resistance to testing low motivation, situational blocking due to anxiety, or depression" (p. 81). This implies that we might overlook a creative or gifted child with notable potential because he or she is uninterested or otherwise unmotivated to produce ideas, original or otherwise. It may also be the case that if we look more closely at the qualitative aspects of divergent thinking, we might find children who are gifted in specific domains (Gruber, 1985; Runco, 1987). Gruber raised the intriguing idea of giftedness in the moral domain.

A second qualitative scheme was described by Urban (1991). His assessment was developed in German and called the *Test zum schopferischen Denken—Zeichnerisch*, or the Test for Creative Thinking—Drawing Production. But here I shall refer to it (in somewhat easier English) as the Drawing Production Test of

Creative Thinking, or DPTCT. When describing the development of the DPTCT, Urban (1991) wrote:

> The German term *schopferisch* describes the shaping, the production, and the final gestalt of the creative end product. The objective was to consider not only divergent, quantitative aspects of thought, but also aspects of quality, content, "gestalt," and elaboration. (p. 179).

Clearly, like Dudek and Verreault (1989), Urban was interested in assessing qualitative aspects of children's creative thought. In the DPTCT, children are asked to complete a figure or drawing using line fragments. The test is scored for certain production tendencies (e.g., New Elements, Connections to Make a Theme, Humor, Unconventionality).

In his research using these qualitative indices, Urban (1991) uncovered a "breakdown" or slump in creativity of 6 year old children. This parallels the *fourth-grade slump* noted by Torrance (1968), the *literal stage* noted by Gardner (1982), and the conventional artistic proclivities of school-aged children noted by Rosenblatt and Winner (1988). This is an important conceptual convergence to note, and one with utility for those interested in the creativity of gifted children. Parents and teachers, for example, should be aware of the tendency for children to experience a slump or breakdown in the elementary school years. Parents and teachers should also be aware of the connection between a slump and literal thinking. If they encourage, reinforce, and model nonliteral thinking, parents and teachers may minimize breakdowns in divergent thought. Moreover, parents and educators should be aware that the literal thinking which contributes to the fourth-grade slump also allows children to learn conventional and appropriate behaviors and rules. Like the hypothetical thinking skills of adolescents (Elkind, 1980), there are costs and benefits to literal thinking, and adults should be aware of both. Literal thinking may inhibit divergent thought, but it simultaneously allows children to use language and a variety of other symbols in an efficient manner.

CONCLUSIONS

The research reviewed in this article suggests that our understanding of divergent thinking—and creative potential—has continued to evolve. This area of study is far from stagnant. The evolution of the divergent thinking paradigm is very important for those interested in giftedness, given the role of creativity in gifted performances (Albert & Runco, 1986; Feldhusen & Treffinger, 1990; Milgram, 1990; Renzulli, 1978). The recent research indicates that it is no longer sufficient to look to general divergent thinking when attempting to identify gifted children. *Divergent thinking* might even be considered a misnomer given that divergence per se is not the concern. Gifted children can be expected to stand out in their fluency, originality, and flexibility, but educators should also consider (a) the qualitative aspect of ideation, including the affective contents; (b) children's capabilities for finding and defining problems; and (c) their valuative and evaluative skills.

Although the research on divergent thinking has continued to evolve, theoretical advances have lagged behind. For example, most descriptions of divergent thinking seem to assume that the individual uses passive associative processes. The problem is that thinking is not a passive process. Information processing is a selective process, with individuals actively directing their attention and deciding which information to remember and manipulate (Runco, in press-a). Selectivity is implied by the work on evaluative skill, problem definition, and strategies. A new model of ideation which emphasizes active and directed cognition seems to be needed.

There is also a need for tests which involve skills like those actually required in the natural environment. As suggested earlier in this article, progress has been made in this direction (Hong & Milgram, 1991; Okuda et al., 1991). Progress has also been made toward the identification of more efficient quantitative methods (Michael & Bachelor, 1990; Runco & Mraz, 1992) and toward the understanding of qualitative aspects of ideation (Dudek & Verreault, 1989; Urban, 1991). Clearly, divergent thinking involves more than productivity and ideational fluency. If we know how fluent a child is with ideas, what do we really know? Just that the child can be fluent with ideas. To understand creative children we need to know many other things—about domains of interest and affective tendencies, to name just two examples. This may be particularly true of the creatively gifted child (Runco & Okuda, in press).

Readers interested in other overviews of divergent thinking should consult Cropley (1992), Khire (in press), and Runco (1991b; Runco & Okuda, in press). Runco (1991b, chap. 20; Runco & Okuda, in press) and Cropley (1992) focused specifically on the educational implications of the research on divergent thinking. There are also fairly recent empirical investigations specifically on the effectiveness of the Parnes-Osborn enhancement techniques with middle school children (Baer, 1988); the relationships between parental separation (Jenkins, Hedlund, & Ripple, 1988) and age-interval between siblings (Radio Gaynor & Runco, 1992) and divergent thinking; and the relationships among verbal loquacity, social competence, and divergent thinking (Kagan, 1988).

Some of the research reported in the present review involved nongifted individuals. However, if creative potential is normally distributed (Milgram, 1990; Nicholls, 1983), what we find with other children may help us to understand gifted children. There is a tradition of research which empirically determines whether or not findings from nongifted populations generalize to the gifted (e.g., Albert & Runco, 1989; Milgram & Milgram, 1976; Moran & Lion, 1982; Runco, 1985, 1986, 1987; Runco & Albert, 1985, 1986), and the findings reviewed herein concerning lenient versus stringent tests, real-world tests, evaluative and valuative thinking, and qualitative scoring should be replicated and cross-validated with samples of gifted children. Indeed, the present review may be used as an outline of specific directions for future research on creative giftedness.

NOTES

1. Something should be said about this check list. It was similar to the criterion, used by Wallach and Wing (1969) and contained a list of activities and accomplishments from several domains (art, crafts, music, mathematics). Children simply indicated how often they had done each activity, Runco (1987) argued that this type of check list is useful (a) because children know more about their activities than anyone else and (b) because it samples several domains. As a self report, honesty and memory biases can influence scores. On the other hand, Runco, Noble, and Luptak (1990) found agreement between reports given by children and their mothers, suggesting a type of interjudge reliability.

2. This is, in a sense, another way of looking at the quality quantity issue (cf. Hong & Milgram, 1991; Runco, 1987).

REFERENCES

Albert, R. S., & Runco, M. A. (1986). The achievement of eminence: A model of exceptionally gifted boys and their families. In R. J. Sternberg & J. E. Davidson (Eds.), *Conceptions of giftedness* (pp. 332–357). New York: Cambridge University Press.

Albert, R. S., & Runco, M. A. (1989). Independence and cognitive ability in gifted and exceptionally gifted boys. *Journal of Youth and Adolescence, 18,* 221–230.

Amabile, T. M. (1990). Within you, without you: A social psychology of creativity and beyond. In M. A. Runco & R. S. Albert (Eds.). *Theories of creativity,* (pp. 61–91). Newbury Park, CA: Sage.

Bachelor, P. A., & Michael, W. B. (in press). The structure of intellect model revisited. In M. A. Runco (Ed.), *Creativity, research handbook.* Cresskill, NJ: Hampton.

Baer, J. M. (1988), Long-term effects of creativity training with middle school students. *Journal of Early Adolescence, 8,* 183–193.

Chand, I., & Runco, M. A. (in press). Problem finding skills as components in the creative process. *Personality and Individual Differences.*

Cropley, A. J. (1992). *More ways than one: Foresting creativity.* Norwood. NJ: Ablex.

Csikszentmihalyi, M. (1990). The domain of creativity. In M. A. Runco & R. S. Albert (Eds.). *Theories of creativity* (pp. 190–212). Newbury Park, CA: Sage.

Davidson, J. E., & Sternberg R. J., (1984). The role of insight in intellectual giftedness. *Gifted Child Quarterly, 28,* 58–64.

Dudek, S. Z., & Verreault, R. (1989). The creative thinking and ego functioning of children. *Creativity Research Journal, 2,* 64–86.

Elkind, D. (1980). *Children and adolescents.* New York: Oxford University Press.

Feldhusen, J. F., Bahlke, S. J., & Treffinger, D. J. (1969). Teaching creative thinking. *Elementary School Journal, 70,* 48–53.

Feldhusen, J., & Treffinger, D. (1990). *Creative thinking and problem solving in gifted education* (3rd ed.). Dubuque, IA: Kendall-Hunt.

Gardner, H. (1982). *Art, mind, and brain: A cognitive approach to creativity.* New York: Basic Books.

Getzels, J. W., & Jackson, P. W. (1962). *Creativity and intelligence: Explorations with gifted students.* New York: Wiley.

Goble, C., Moran, J. D., & Bomba, A. K. (1991). Maternal teaching techniques and preschool children's ideational fluency. *Creativity Research Journal, 4,* 278–280.
Gruber, H. E. (1985). Giftedness and moral responsibility: Creative thinking and human survival. In F. D. Horowitz & M. O'Brien (Eds.). *The gifted and talented: Developmental perspectives* (pp. 301–330). Washington, DC: American Psychological Association.
Harrington, D. M. (1975). Effects of explicit instructions to "be creative" on the psychological meaning of divergent thinking test scores. *Journal of Personality, 43,* 434–454.
Hennessey, B. (1989). The effect of extrinsic constraint on children's creativity while using a computer. *Creativity Research Journal, 2,* 151–158.
Hocevar, D. (1979). Ideational fluency as a confounding factor in the measurement of originality. *Journal of Educational Psychology, 71,* 191–196.
Hong, E., & Milgram, R. M. (1991). Original thinking in preschool children: A validation of ideational fluency measures. *Creativity Research Journal, 5,* 253–260.
Jenkins, J. E., Hedlund, D. E., & Ripple, R. E. (1988). Parental separation effects on children's divergent thinking abilities and creative potential. *Child Study Journal, 18,* 149–159.
Kagan, D. N. (1988). Measurements of divergent and complex thinking. *Educational and Psychological Measurement, 48,* 873–884.
Khire, U. (in press). Guilford's SOI model and behavioral intelligence with special reference to creative behavioral abilities. In S. G. Isaksen, M.C. Murdock, R. L. Firestine, & D. J. Treffinger (Eds.). *Understanding and recognizing creativity.* Norwood. NJ: Ablex.
MacKinnon, D. W. (1983). The highly effective individual. In R. S. Albert (Ed.). *Genius and eminence: The social psychology of creativity and exceptional achievement* (pp. 114–127). Oxford, UK: Pergamon. (Original work published 1960.)
Michael, W. B., & Bachelor, P. A. (1990). Higher order structure-of-intellect creativity factors in divergent production tests: Reanalysis of a Guilford data base. *Creativity Research Journal, 3,* 58–74.
Milgram, R. M. (1990). Creativity: An idea whose time has come and gone? In M. A. Runco & R. S. Albert (Eds.). *Theories of creativity* (pp. 215–233). Newbury Park, CA: Sage.
Milgram, R. M., & Milgram, N. A. (1976). Group versus individual administration in the measurement of creative thinking in gifted and nongifted children. *Child Development, 47,* 563–565.
Moran, J. D., & Lion, E. Y. Y. (1982). Effects of reward on creativity in college students of two levels of ability. *Perceptual and Motor Skills, 54,* 43–48.
Nicholls, J. G. (1983). Creativity in the person who will never produce anything original or useful. In R. S. Albert (Ed.). *Genius and eminence: The social psychology of creativity and exceptional achievement* (pp. 265–279). Oxford, UK: Pergamon.
Okuda, S. M., Runco, M. A., & Bergel, D. E. (1991). Creativity and the finding and solving of real world problems. *Journal of Psychoeducational Assessment, 9,* 45–53.
Radio Gaynor, J. I., & Runco M. A. (1992). Family size, birth order, age-interval, and the creativity of children. *Journal of Creative Behavior, 26,* 108–118.
Renzulli, J. S. (1978). What makes giftedness? Re-examining a definition. *Phi Delta Kappan, 60,* 180–184.
Renzulli, J. S. (1982). What makes a problem real: Stalking the illusive meaning of qualitative differences in gifted education. *Gifted Child Quarterly, 26,* 147–156.
Rosenblatt, E., & Winner, E. (1988). The art of children's drawing. In H. Gardner & D. Perkins (Eds.). *Art, mind, and education* (pp. 3–16). Urbana, IL: University of Chicago Press.

Rossman, B. B., & Gollob, H. F. (1975). Comparison of social judgments of creativity and intelligence. *Journal of Personality and Social Psychology, 31,* 271–281.

Runco, M. A. (1985). Reliability and convergent validity of ideational flexibility as a function of academic achievement. *Perceptual and Motor Skills, 61,* 1075–1081.

Runco, M. A. (1986). Maximal performance on divergent thinking tests by gifted, talented, and nongifted children. *Psychology in the Schools, 23,* 308–315.

Runco, M. A. (1987). The generality of creative performance in gifted and nongifted children. *Gifted Child Quarterly, 31,* 121–125.

Runco, M. A. (1989). The creativity of children's art. *Child Study Journal, 19,* 177–189.

Runco, M. A. (1991a). Comment on investment and economic theories of creativity: A reply to Sternberg and Lubart. *Creativity Research Journal, 4,* 202–205.

Runco, M. A. (1991b). *Divergent thinking.* Norwood, NJ: Ablex.

Runco, M. A. (1992a). Children's divergent thinking and creative ideation. *Developmental Review, 12,* 233–264.

Runco, M. A. (1992b). The evaluative, valuative, and divergent thinking of children. *Journal of Creative Behavior, 25,* 311–319.

Runco, M. A. (in press-a). Creativity, cognition, and their educational implications. In J. C. Houtz (Ed.), *The educational psychology of creativity.* New York: Fordham University Press.

Runco, M. A. (Ed.). (in press-b). *Problem finding, problem solving, and creativity.* Norwood. NJ: Ablex.

Runco, M. A., & Albert, R. S. (1985). The reliability and validity of ideational originality in the divergent thinking of academically gifted and nongifted children. *Educational and Psychological Measurement, 45,* 483–501.

Runco, M. A., & Albert, R. S. (1986). Exceptional giftedness in early adolescence and intrafamilial divergent thinking. *Journal of Youth and Adolescence, 15,* 333–342.

Runco, M. A., & Basadur, M. (1990). *Assessing ideational and evaluative skills and creative styles and attitudes.* Paper presented at the International Engineering Management Conference, San Jose, CA.

Runco, M. A., Ebersole, P., & Mraz, W. (1991). Self-actualization and creativity. *Journal of Social Behavior and Personality, 6,* 161–167.

Runco, M. A., & Mraz, W. (1992). Scoring divergent thinking tests using total ideational output and a creativity index. *Educational and Psychological Measurement, 52,* 213–221.

Runco, M. A., Noble, E. P., & Luptak, Y. (1990). Agreement between mothers and sons on ratings of creative activity. *Educational and Psychological Measurement, 50,* 673–680.

Runco, M. A., & Okuda, S. M. (1988). Problem discovery, divergent thinking, and the creative process. *Journal of Youth and Adolescence, 17,* 211–220.

Runco, M. A., & Okuda, S. M. (in press). Reaching creatively gifted children through their learning styles. In R. M. Milgram & R. Dunn (Eds.), *Teaching the gifted and talented through their learning styles.* New York: Praeger.

Runco, M. A., & Smith, W. R. (1991). Interpersonal and intrapersonal evaluations of ideas. *Personality and Individual Differences, 13,* 295–302.

Runco, M. A., & Vega, L. (1990). Evaluating the creativity of children's ideas. *Journal of Social Behavior and Personality, 5,* 439–452.

Sawyers, J. K., & Canestaro, N. C. (1989). Creativity and achievement in design coursework. *Creativity Research Journal, 2,* 126–133.

Schotte, D. E., & Clum, G. A. (1987). Problem-solving skills in suicidal psychiatric patients. *Journal of Consulting and Clinical Psychology, 55,* 49–54.

Shaw, M., & Runco, M. A. (Eds.). (in press). *Creativity and affect.* Norwood, NJ: Ablex.
Simonton, D. K. (1988). *Scientific genius: A psychology of science.* New York: Cambridge University Press.
Sternberg, R. J., & Lubart, T. I. (1991). Short selling the investment theory of creativity: A reply to Runco. *Creativity Research Journal, 4,* 200–202.
Tegano, D. W. & Moran, J. D. (1989). Sex differences in the originality of preschool and elementary school children. *Creativity Research Journal, 2,* 102–110.
Torrance, E. P. (1968). A longitudinal examination of the fourth-grade slump in creativity. *Gifted Child Quarterly, 12,* 195–199.
Urban, K. K. (1991). On the development of creativity in children. *Creativity Research Journal, 4,* 177–191.
Wallach, M. A., & Kogan, N. (1965). *Modes of thinking in children.* New York: Holt. Rinehart & Winston.
Wallach, M. A., & Wing, C. (1969). *The talented student.* New York: Holt, Rinehart & Winston.
Weisberg, R. W. (1986). *Creativity, genius, and other myths.* New York: Freeman.

6

Wisdom as a Form of Giftedness

Robert J. Sternberg

Yale University

This article describes an important, yet largely neglected, kind of giftedness, namely, wisdom. First, the article discusses how giftedness is identified currently. Second, the article is an alternative view based on a balance theory of wisdom. The theory is described, and it is shown why the theory offers a useful way of conceptualizing wisdom. Finally, the article concludes that, given the state of the world, we should have a strong incentive to identify and develop wisdom as a form of giftedness.

If we ask what distinguishes four extremely gifted individuals of the 20th century—Mahatma Gandhi, Mother Theresa, Martin Luther King, Jr. and Nelson Mandela—we could safely conclude that it is not the kind of giftedness measured by conventional tests of intelligence. The kind of giftedness these individuals share is not even captured by broader theories of intelligence. For example, these individuals may all have been high in interpersonal intelligence (Gardner, 1983), but so was Adolf Hitler. Hitler was certainly able to understand crowds and was

Editor's Note: From Sternberg, R. J. (2000). Wisdom as a form of giftedness. *Gifted Child Quarterly, 44*(4), 252–260.

masterful at imposing his will on people. The giftedness these individuals share is also different from social intelligence (Cantor & Kihlstrom, 1987) and emotional intelligence (Goleman, 1995; Salovey & Mayer 1990). Like practical intelligence, these kinds of intelligence may be used to further one's own interests to the exclusion of, or even systematically against, the interests of others.

My own triarchic theory of intelligence and intellectual giftedness (Sternberg, 1984, 1985, 1997, 1999b) also fails to capture what distinguishes the four individuals. They all may have been analytically gifted, but probably they would hardly compare in IQ with analytical geniuses like Sir Isaac Newton, John Stuart Mill, or Albert Einstein. They all may have been creative (showing signs of what Renzulli [1984] has called "creative-productive giftedness"). But, there is, again, no sign that they would compare with Geoffrey Chaucer and Victor Hugo in literature, Ludwig von Beethoven and Peter Tchaikovsky in music, or Louis Pasteur and Charles Darwin in science. They did not leave behind stunning works of literature, music, science, philosophy, or similar achievements. They were enormously, practically gifted, but so have been Saddam Hussein and Mobutu Sese Seku, wily men who devised ways to stay in power and maintain absolute control in the face of enormous odds. These examples point out that practical intelligence can be used exclusively to further one's own ends or the ends of those with whom one is intimately connected. Wisdom never can be used in this way. High-level practical intelligence may lead to success in life according to traditional standards, but wisdom may be a key to satisfaction and contentment in life according to one's own standards.

Putting the Research to Use

A major goal of education is to prepare students to lead successful and satisfying lives. Too often, though, the emphasis seems to be more on "successful" than "satisfying." Students learn the routes to success without learning the routes to satisfaction. Teaching for wisdom can help students lead happier, as well as more productive, lives. Moreover, it is probably the single best route to the molding of better citizens. For example, students need to learn how to think dialogically, understanding points of view other than their own, and to think not only in terms of their own interests, but in terms of the interests of others and of the society, as well. These issues become especially important in a highly individualistic society such as the United States, which tends to deemphasize the importance of caring for others and of collective responsibility. Unless students are specifically taught to focus upon the common good, rather than only upon the good of themselves and those close to them, they may simply never learn how to think in such a fashion. They also may become citizens, who like so many others, emphasize short-term interests over long-term goals. Our current research on teaching for wisdom, funded by the W. T. Giant Foundation, seeks to teach middle-school children how to put into practice the principles described in the accompanying article.

The kind of giftedness people like Mahatma Gandhi, Mother Theresa, Martin Luther King, Jr. and Nelson Mandela have in common, then, appears to be one of wisdom, rather than of intelligence either as traditionally defined or as defined in more modern theories. Human intelligence has, to some extent, brought the world to the brink. It may take wisdom to find our way around it.

THE NATURE OF WISDOM

Wisdom can be defined as the "power of judging rightly and following the soundest course of action, based on knowledge, experience, understanding, etc." (Neufeldt & Guralnik, 1997, p. 1533), but dictionary definitions usually do not suffice for psychological understanding. A number of scholars have attempted to approach wisdom in different ways, both philosophical (see Robinson, 1990) and psychological. Alternative approaches are summarized in Sternberg (1990, 1998) and in Baltes & Staudinger (in press). Some theorists of intelligence and learning, such as Guilford (1967) and Bloom (1985), have discussed the importance of evaluative skills in high or gifted levels of intelligence, and these skills may provide one kind of link between intelligence and wisdom.

The approach to wisdom proposed here is taken by Sternberg (1998). This notion of wisdom starts with the construct of tacit knowledge (Polanyi, 1976) about oneself, others, and situational contexts. Tacit knowledge comprises the lessons of life that are not explicitly taught and that often are not even verbalized (Sternberg, Wagner, Williams, & Horvath, 1995). Thus, tacit knowledge has three main features: (a) it is procedural; (b) it is relevant to the attainment of goals people value; and (c) it typically is acquired through experience or mentoring, rather than through direct classroom or textbook instruction. An example of tacit knowledge is knowing how to write and present an article to ensure publication.

Tacit knowledge forms an essential component of practical intelligence. Indeed, the particular notion of tacit knowledge used here derives from the triarchic theory of intelligence (Sternberg, 1985, 1997). An advantage of the proposed theory is that it is linked to a theory of intelligence (the triarchic one) at the same time that it makes explicit how wisdom is different from the triarchic (analytical, creative, and practical) aspects of intelligence as they typically are encountered.

Although tacit knowledge is acquired within a domain, it more typically applies to a field—a distinction made by Csikszentmihalyi (1988, 1996). Csikszentmihalyi refers to the domain as the formal knowledge of a socially defined field. So, for example, knowing how to construct, conduct, or analyze the results of experiments would be knowledge important to the *domain* of experimental psychology. But, knowing how to speak about the results persuasively, how to get the results published, or knowing how to turn the results into the next grant proposal would constitute knowledge of the *field*. Thus, academic intelligence would seem to apply primarily in the domain, whereas practical intelligence, in general, and wisdom, in particular, would seem to apply primarily in the field. Because the field represents the social organization of the domain, it is primarily in the field that intrapersonal, interpersonal, and extrapersonal interactions take place.

The much greater importance of the field, rather than of the domain, to wisdom helps to clarify why tacit informal knowledge, rather than explicit formal knowledge, is the basis of wisdom. Formal knowledge about the subject matter of a discipline is certainly essential to expertise in that discipline (Chi, Glaser, & Farr, 1988; Hoffman, 1992); but, domain-based expertise is neither necessary nor sufficient for wisdom. All of us know domain-based experts who seem unwise. At least some of us also know wise individuals who have little formal education. Their education is in the "school of life," which is in the acquisition of tacit (informal) knowledge.

The argument, then, is that intelligence is important for giftedness, but so is wisdom. One needs creative abilities to come up with ideas; one needs analytical abilities to decide whether one's own ideas (and those of others) are good ideas; one needs practical abilities to make ideas functional and to persuade other people of the value of these ideas. But, one needs wisdom to balance the effects of one's ideas, not just on oneself, but on others and on institutions, as well, both in the short and the long terms.

THE BALANCE THEORY OF WISDOM

Wisdom as Tacit Knowledge Used for Balancing Interests

The definition of wisdom proposed here (see Figure 1) draws both upon the notion of tacit knowledge, as described above, and on the notion of balance. In particular, wisdom is defined as the application of tacit knowledge as mediated by values toward the goal of achieving a common good through a balance among multiple *interests*—(a) intrapersonal, (b) interpersonal, and (c) extrapersonal—in order to achieve a balance among *responses to environmental contexts*—(a) adaptation to existing environmental contexts, (b) shaping of existing environmental contexts, and (c) selection of new environmental contexts, over the (a) short- and (b) long-terms.

In this theory, a common good refers to what is good in common for all, not just for those with whom one identifies, such as family, friends, or members of one's preferred group. Thus, dictators who seek to maximize their own gain or those of a particular group at the expense of others—whatever their own view of themselves may be—are not maximizing a common good.

Thus, whereas practical intelligence can be applied toward the maximization of any set of interests—whether of an individual or a collective—wisdom is applied in particular to *a balance of intrapersonal, interpersonal, and extrapersonal interests.* Practical intelligence may or may not involve a balancing of interests, but wisdom must. Its output is typically in the form of advice, usually to another person, but sometimes for oneself. The individual gifted in wisdom is exceptionally good at giving the best advice.

Figure 1 A Balance Theory of Wisdom

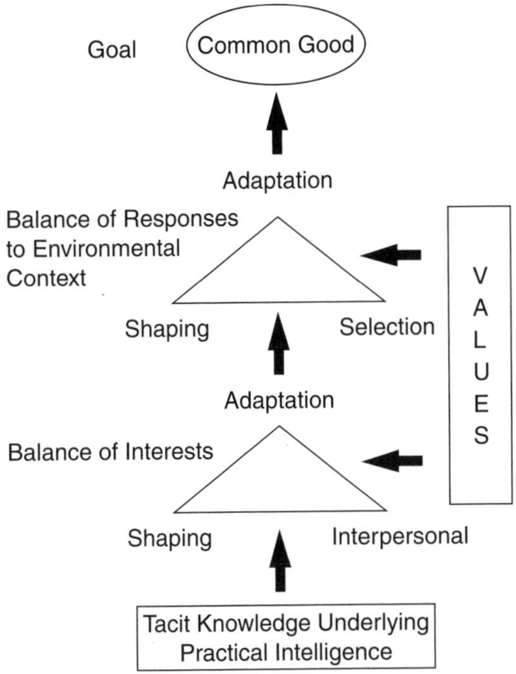

Note. Tacit knowledge underlying practical intelligence is applied to balance intrapersonal, interpersonal, and extrapersonal interests to achieve a balance of the responses to the environmental context of adaptation to, shaping of, and selection of environments in order to achieve a common good. Values mediate how people use their tacit knowledge in balancing interests and responses.

We now can understand better why cruel despots may be practically intelligent, but not wise. An implication of the present view is that, when one applies practical intelligence, one deliberately may seek outcomes that are good for oneself or one's family and friends that may, at the same time, be bad for a common good. For example, despots exhibit practical intelligence by managing to control an entire country largely for their own benefit. Hitler or Stalin may have balanced factors in their judgments, but *not* for a common good.

One also may apply practical intelligence to maximize someone else's benefit, as does a lawyer. In the subset of practical intelligence that is wisdom, one certainly may seek good ends for oneself (intrapersonal interests), but one also seeks to balance them with good outcomes for others (interpersonal interests) and with the contextual factors (extrapersonal interests) involved. The balance among interests determines the adapting, shaping, and selecting of environments.

Problems requiring wise solutions always involve at least some element of intrapersonal, interpersonal, and extrapersonal interests, although the weights may be different in different instances, just as they may be different for adaptation, shaping, and selection. The gifted individual weighs interests especially well. Thus, whereas traditional concepts of giftedness emphasize amounts on one or more scales, the concept of giftedness in wisdom emphasizes balance in judgment. For example, one might decide that it is wise to go to college, a problem that seemingly involves only one person. Yet, many people are affected by an individual's decision to go to college: parents, friends, significant others, children, and the like. The decision always has to be made in the context of the whole range of available options.

In making the decision, one selects a future environment and, in doing so, adapts to and shapes one's current environment as well as the environments of others. Similarly, a decision about whether to have an abortion requires wisdom because it involves not only oneself, but also the fetus that will not be born, others to whom one is close such as the father, and the rules and customs of the society. In the case of abortion, one is profoundly adapting to, shaping, and selecting the environment, both for oneself and for a potential infant. In each case, one might make a practically intelligent decision for oneself without balancing interests. But, for the decision to be wise, it must take into account other interests and seek a common good over the short and long terms.

The ultimate test of whether a judgment is wise is in how the judgment is made, rather than in what the judgment is. Two individuals can come to different conclusions, but both be wise if they fulfill the criteria specified by the balance theory in their judgmental information processing. For example, religious leaders of different faiths may have different belief systems and yet be comparably wise.

It is worth emphasizing that interpersonal and extrapersonal values *never* disappear in the theory. They are always weighted in the balance, no matter how difficult or stressful a situation may be. The balance is part of why people give their lives for their countries, their religious beliefs, or their children. According to the balance theory, thinking is *unwise* when, due to expediency, one removes from the balance others and institutions. Once this door to removing others or institutions is opened, people quickly find reasons to consider only their self-interest.

Consider further the nature of adaptation, shaping, and selection. In adaptation, the individual tries to find ways to conform to the existing environment that forms his or her context. Sometimes, adaptation is the best course of action under a given set of circumstances. More typically, one seeks a balance between adaptation and shaping, realizing that fitting into an environment requires not only changing oneself, but changing the environment, as well. When an individual finds it impossible, or at least implausible, to attain such a fit, he or she may decide to select a new environment altogether, leaving, for example, a job, a community, or a marriage. Again, balance, rather than sheer amount of skills and values, is crucial to wisdom.

Processes Underlying Wisdom

Underlying wisdom is a series of processes. Among these processes are what I have referred to as "metacomponents" (Sternberg, 1985, 1999b), including

(a) recognizing the existence of a problem, (b) defining the nature of the problem, (c) representing information about the problem, (d) formulating strategy for solving the problem, (e) allocating resources to the solution of a problem, (f) monitoring one's solution of the problem, and (g) evaluating feedback regarding that solution. In deciding about college, for example, one first has to see both going to college and not going as viable options (problem recognition); then figure out exactly what going or not going to college would mean for one-self (defining the problem); then consider the costs and benefits to oneself and others of going or not going to college (representing information about the problem).

The use of these metacomponents is a hallmark of thinking in general (Sternberg, 1985), and they are used in all of analytical, creative, and practical thinking. What distinguishes their use in wisdom is that these processes are applied to balancing their impact on interested parties.

The balance theory suggests that wisdom is at least partially domain-specific, in that tacit knowledge is acquired within a given context or set of contexts. It typically is acquired by (a) selectively encoding new information that is relevant for one's purposes in learning about that context, (b) selectively comparing this information to old information in order to see how the new fits with the old, and (c) selectively combining pieces of information in order to make them fit together into an orderly whole (Sternberg, Wagner, & Okagaki, 1993). These processes are referred to as knowledge-acquisition components in the triarchic theory of intelligence (Sternberg, 1985). Again, the processes are used in all aspects of intelligence (analytical, creative, and practical). However, there is nothing peculiar to wisdom in the uses of these components other than that the knowledge may later be used for wise purposes.

The use of metacomponents and knowledge acquisition in wisdom or any other kind of practical intelligence points out a key relationship between wisdom and intelligence (as conceptualized by the triarchic theory). All aspects of intelligence—analytical, creative, and practical—involve utilization of metacomponents for executive processing and knowledge-acquisition components for learning. What differs is the kind of context in which they are applied. Analytical intelligence is called upon for relatively familiar decontextualized, abstract, and often academic kinds of situations. Creative intelligence is called upon for relatively unfamiliar, novel kinds of situations. Practical intelligence is called upon for highly contextualized situations encountered in the normal course of one's daily life. Wisdom applies *only* to highly contextualized situations. It does not apply to all of the kinds of abstract situations to which one might apply one's intelligence (e.g., in the context of ability-test or achievement-test problems) or one's creativity (e.g., in formulating original, high-quality, but abstract ideas).

Consider a concrete, if extreme, example of the difference between practical intelligence and wisdom. An individual becomes a government official with the hope of financial gain from his position. He quickly learns how, by accepting contributions from wealthy supporters, he can become rich, thereby achieving his goal of financial gain. He is at the edge of what is legal but, through expensive legal advice, always manages to stay within the dictates of the law. He is pleased to see how politics can be mixed with financial success. During his term in office, he shows up for the necessary meetings, but does little else. He leaves office having contributed little to his country, but a lot to his bank account. This individual has been practically intelligent in that he has found a way to manipulate the environment to achieve his own goals. But, he has not been wise because he has used his position only to advance his own interests and not those of his constituents, Thus, he has achieved his goals at the expense of their legitimate hopes that he would work for their benefit. Although he has done nothing illegal, he has deprived his constituents of representation that would have benefited them. He has looked out for his own interests, but not those of others or of his country.

People who acquire wisdom in one context may be those who would be well able to develop it in another context, but the tacit knowledge needed to be wise in different contexts may differ. For example, the wise individual in one society may be able to give useful advice in the context of that society, but the same advice might be suicidal in another society (e.g., to criticize a governmental policy as it applies to a particular individual). Thus, the ability to be wise may transfer, but the actual content of wise advice may vary. A wise person, therefore, will know not only when to give advice, but when not to (see Meacham, 1990) because the individual will know the limitations of his or her own tacit knowledge. Thus, giftedness in wisdom is a function of how one makes judgments, rather than of the particular judgments one makes.

The Role of Values

In discussing wisdom (as well as practical intelligence, in general), there is no escape from values. As shown in the model, values always play a major role—in terms of what constitutes a common good, in terms of what constitutes an acceptable balance among interests, and in terms of what constitutes an adequate balance among adaptation, shaping, and selection of environments. Anyone's examples of the exercise of wisdom or its absence will reflect his or her own values. Those individuals who wish a construct that is value-free would do best to look elsewhere. At the same time, many psychological constructs—intelligence, creativity, beauty, judgment, personality—involve a value system, whether the value system is explicit or not. The value system must be one that seeks a common good.

It truly is impossible to speak of wisdom outside the context of a set of values, which, in combination, may lead one to a moral stance or, in Kohlberg's (1969, 1983) view, stage. Behavior is viewed as wise as a function of what is valued in a societal/cultural context. Values mediate how one balances interests and responses and collectively contribute even to how one defines a common good. Wisdom is in applying processes of thought in combination with values to achieve solutions to problems that take into account a common good within a societal/cultural context, which may be as narrow as a family or as broad as the world. Although different societies may hold to different values, certain values seem to be endorsed across a whole spectrum of societies—values such as truth, honesty, sincerity, mercy, and compassion for others.

Wisdom intersects with the moral domain and the notion of moral reasoning as it applies in the two highest stages (4 and 5) of Kohlberg's (1969) theory. At the same time, wisdom is broader than moral reasoning. It applies to any human problem involving a balance of intrapersonal, interpersonal, and extrapersonal interests, whether or not moral issues are at stake.

Sources of Individual and Developmental Differences in Wisdom

The balance theory suggests a number of sources of developmental and individual differences in wisdom. These sources determine who will be gifted with wisdom and who will not be. There are two kinds of sources: those directly affecting the balance processes and those that are antecedent.

There are five sources of individual differences. Gifted people would have to master most or all of them.

1. *Goals.* People may differ in the extent to which they seek a common good and, thus, in the extent to which they aspire to wisdom. The seeking of a common good does not apply to intelligence in general, however. One could be analytically, creatively, or even practically intelligent without looking out for the interests of others.

2. *Balancing of Responses to Environmental Contexts.* People may differ in their balance of responses to environmental contexts. Responses always reflect an interaction of the individual making the judgment and the environmental context, and people can interact with contexts in myriad ways. Balancing is needed adequately to achieve one's goals.

3. *Balancing of Interests.* People may balance interests in different ways. This balancing is unique to wisdom and does not necessarily apply to analytical, creative, or common practical intelligence. Again, adequate balancing is needed to achieve one's goals.

4. *Practical Intelligence Manifested as Tacit Knowledge.* People bring different kinds and levels of tacit knowledge to judgmental situations, which are likely to affect their responses. This aspect of wisdom applies also to practical intelligence, but typically does not apply to analytical or creative intelligence.

5. *Values.* People hold different values that mediate their utilization of tacit knowledge when balancing interests and responses.

These sources of variation differentiate how well people can apply their wisdom in different kinds of situations. Wisdom is associated with greater intellectual and even physical maturity, presumably because the development of tacit knowledge and values is something that unfolds over the course of the life span and not just in childhood or even in early years of adulthood.

Although the goal of this article is to express a theory, rather than to present empirical data, the theory as it stands is testable, and we currently are testing it. For example, it suggests that judgments made about interpersonal conflicts or organizational negotiations should be rated as more wise to the extent that they take into account a common good of all stakeholders and to the extent that they balance intrapersonal, interpersonal, and extrapersonal interests. Such outcomes often are not sought, as when parties to a divorce try only to maximize their own self-interest or when management-union negotiations are between negotiators looking out for the interests only of one party to the negotiations. The theory predicts that judgments will be rated as wise by experts to the extent that they take into account these parameters of the theory.

Problems Used in Measuring Wisdom

If one looks at the kinds of problems that have been used to measure wisdom empirically, one can evaluate the degree to which they measure wisdom according to the balance theory. In our own work, we are using intrapersonal, interpersonal, and organizational-conflict situations. A life-planning task (Baltes, Staudinger, Maercker, & Smith, 1995) is also an excellent task for measuring wisdom. It involves one's own interests, but usually will take into account the interests of others about whom one cares deeply as well as the context in which one lives and in which one may live in the future. A task in which one must decide what to do when a good friend calls and says he or she wants to commit suicide (Staudinger & Baltes, 1996) would also involve the interests of the other, one's own interest in getting involved, the consequences of not being successful in persuading the individual not to commit suicide, and also the difficulty of acting in the context of an unexpected telephone call. Similarly, counseling a 14-year-old girl who is pregnant or a 16-year-old boy who wants to marry soon (Baltes & Smith, 1990) both involve balancing the interests of the individuals to be counseled, the other people in their lives, and the costs of giving the wrong advice. But, adults are not the only ones who possess wisdom. According to Harris (1998), most of the advice children receive is from other children. In their plans, children take into account other children at least as much as they take into account adults. Hence, it is all the more important for children to acquire wise ways of thinking.

Wise people recognize the limitations of plans. There is a saying that, if one wishes to make God laugh, one should tell God one's plans. People who are gifted in wisdom recognize the limitations and fallibility of their own thinking.

Perhaps the ideal problems we could pose for measuring wisdom are complex conflict-resolution problems involving the formation of judgments, given multiple competing interests and no clear resolution of how these interests can be reconciled (e.g., Sternberg & Dobson, 1987; Sternberg & Soriano, 1984). Given the relevance of such problems, it makes sense that Smith and her colleagues

(Smith, Staudinger, & Baltes, 1994) would have found that clinical psychologists would do particularly well on wisdom-related tasks. Another group who might be expected to do well would be experienced foreign-service officers and other negotiators who have helped nations reach resolutions of their disagreements.

The wisdom of problem posing and problem solving cannot be measured adequately through some kind of objective multiple-choice or short-answer test. Rather, it can be measured by people who recognize wisdom using the balance theory as a basis for judging the wisdom of how people reach judgments. Like creativity, wisdom is in the interactions among a person, a task, and a situation, not simply in the head of a person (see Csikszentmihalyi, 1996). But wisdom differs from creativity in that wisdom need not represent a novel idea, and creativity need not be directed toward a common good.

Development of Wisdom

Although wisdom may sound like a construct relevant only to adults, I would argue that we need to start developing wisdom in children. We can begin by developing a valuing and appreciation of wisdom and what it can bring to society. The devaluing of older people in many societies reflects a simultaneous devaluing of the wisdom that elders can bring to the societies. Wisdom as a form of giftedness can be developed in a number of ways. Seven of these ways are particularly important.

First, provide students with problems that require wise thinking. Such problems might require negotiations between parties, giving advice to others, or dealing with ethical or moral dilemmas. For example, such a problem might involve giving advice to another student on how to deal with a substance-abuse problem.

Second, help students think in terms of a common good in the solution of these problems. For example, what would happen if everyone had a substance-abuse problem? How would such a situation affect the moral, health-related, and even economic situation of the society? Clearly, the common good would be diminished.

Third, help students learn how to balance their own interests, the interests of others, and the interests of institutions in the solution of these problems. For example, how might the substance-abuse problem destroy the individual's life in the long term, if not the short term? What effects is it likely to have on the individual's loved ones and others who care about the individual? And, what will it do to the individual's ability to contribute to society?

Fourth, provide examples of wise thinking from the past and analyze them. Provide examples of people who have overcome substance-abuse problems and have gone on to make important contributions to society. And, provide examples of people who have not overcome such problems and who have gone on to ruin (e.g., actors and athletes who have destroyed their careers).

Fifth, model wisdom for the students. Show them examples of wise thinking you have done and perhaps not-so-wise thinking that has taught you lessons. You might take decisions you have made or now are making and show them how you do what you are asking the students to do.

Sixth, help students to think dialectically. Wisdom is probably best developed through the incorporation of dialectical thinking (Hegel, 1807/1931) into one's processing of problems (Basseches, 1984; Labouvie-Vief, 1990; Pascual-Leone, 1990; Riegel, 1973; Sternberg, 1999). The essence of dialectical thinking is that most problems in the world do not have right or wrong answers, but better or worse ones, and what is seen as a good answer can vary with time and place. With respect to time, it involves recognizing that ideas evolve over time through an ongoing, unending process of thesis followed by anti-thesis followed by synthesis, with the synthesis in turn becoming the next thesis (Hegel). When dialectical thinking occurs with respect to place (or space), it involves the recognition that, at a given point in time, people may have diverging viewpoints on problems that seem uniquely valid or at least reasonable to them. The values we espouse today or in the United States cannot immediately be applied to other times or other places without considering the context in which others live and have lived. For example, there may have been times and still may be places where the use of certain kinds of psychoactive drugs has been a legitimate part of religious worship, But, in today's world, use of such drugs may be the road to self-destruction and, moreover, is illegal.

Seventh, show your students that you value wise information processing and solutions. Without rewards for wise behavior, whatever wisdom children show may be extinguished quickly. If one wants children to act wisely, one must show them how by doing it oneself. It is essential that students feel that they are not only being told to think wisely, but also will be rewarded for doing so.

Finally, carry what you learn and encourage students to carry what they learn outside the classroom. The goal is not to teach another "subject" that will serve as the basis for an additional grade to appear on a report card. The goal is to change the way people think about and act in their lives.

CONCLUSION

The theory of giftedness in wisdom proposed here has a number of possible strengths. First, it is formulated in at least some detail. Second, the theory and, I hope, the exposition of it clarify how wisdom is both similar to and different from related constructs, such as intelligence. Third, the theory is formulated in a way that it can be tested—for example, by determining whether solutions to problems that balance intrapersonal, interpersonal, and extrapersonal interests are indeed perceived as wiser than solutions that do not. We currently are conducting such tests. Finally, the theory seems to capture intuitive conceptions of what giftedness in wisdom should be.

At the same time, there are weaknesses that will need to be corrected. First, there is a need for explicit instructional techniques to help develop wisdom. Second, the theory is new and while empirical work is under way, it is not completed. Third, there is a need to show that higher levels of wisdom as conceptualized by this theory lead to behavior in everyday life that is demonstrably wise.

There is no unique form of giftedness that a society should reward, but one could ask legitimately whether there is any more fundamentally important form of giftedness than wisdom. One also might ask whether there is any form of giftedness that societies today ignore more than wisdom. Many countries, even the United States, seem to separate themselves from the wisdom that could help individual development, societal development, and the interaction between the two.

Wisdom is not the same as intelligence. There is one source of evidence that suggests that, as individual-difference variables, wisdom and academic intelligence might be rather different "kettles of fish." We know that IQs have been rising substantially over the past several generations (Flynn, 1987; Neisser, 1998). The gains have been experienced both for fluid and for crystallized abilities, although the gains are substantially greater for the former. Yet, it is difficult for some to discern any increase in the wisdom of the peoples of the world. Levels of conflict in the world show no sign of de-escalating; rather, they have intensified in many parts of the world. So, maybe it is time that psychologists, as a profession, take more seriously the formulation of theories of wisdom and of theory-based measures of wisdom. Educators need to take seriously the identification and development of giftedness in wisdom. Although there has been some scholarship in the area, the amount is dwarfed by work on intelligence. We need to create experiences that will guide people to develop wisdom, much as we have done with respect to the development of intelligence (e.g., Perkins & Grotzer, 1997).

Ironically, Luis Alberto Machado, former Minister for the Development of Intelligence in Venezuela, argued that the key to a better society is intelligence. In the 1980s, he oversaw massive intervention programs in Venezuela to improve the intelligence of Venezuelan school children. His political party lost the next election, and with that loss went the intervention programs. Rising IQs have provided a natural experiment; intelligence as defined in the traditional sense has gone up. Yet, the conditions of the world have not improved in tandem. Perhaps the answer is not, and never was, increased intelligence, but increased wisdom.

With a world in turmoil, perhaps we need to turn our attention in schools, not only to the identification and development of knowledge bases, nor even of giftedness in intelligence, narrowly or broadly defined. Perhaps we need to turn our attention to the identification and development of giftedness in wisdom. If there is a key to a better world, this may be it.

REFERENCES

Baltes, P. B., & Staudinger, U. M. (in press). *Wisdom: The orchestration of mind and virtue.* Boston: Blackwell.

Baltes, P. B., & Smith, J. (1990). Toward a psychology of wisdom and its ontogenesis. In R .J. Sternberg (Ed.), *Wisdom: Its nature, origins, and development* (pp. 87–120). New York: Cambridge University Press.

Baltes, P. B., Staudinger, U. M., Maercker, A., & Smith, J. (1995). People nominated as wise: A comparative study of wisdom-related knowledge. *Psychology and Aging, 10,* 155–166.

Basseches, J. (1984). *Dialectical thinking and adult development.* Norwood, NJ: Ablex.

Bloom, B. S. (1985). *Developing talent in young people.* New York: Ballantine.

Cantor, N., & Kihlstrom, J. F. (1987). *Personality and social intelligence.* Englewood Cliffs, NJ: Prentice-Hall.

Chi, M. T. H., Glaser, R., & Farr, M.J. (1988). *The nature of expertise.* Hillsdale, NJ: Erbaum.

Csikszentmihalyi, M. (1988). Society, culture, and person: A systems view of creativity. In R. J. Sternberg (Ed.), *The nature of creativity* (pp. 325–339). New York: Cambridge University Press.

Csikszentmihalyi, M. (1996). *Creativity.* New York: HarperCollins.

Flynn, J. R. (1987). Massive IQ gains in 14 nations. *Psychological Bulletin, 101,*171–191.

Gardner, H. (1983). *Frames of mind: The theory of multiple intelligences.* New York: Basic Books.

Goleman, D. (1995). *Emotional intelligence.* New York: Bantam Books.

Guilford, J. P. (1967). *The nature of intelligence.* New York: McGraw-Hill.

Harris, J. R. (1998). *The nurture assumption: Why children turn out the way they do.* New York: Free Press.

Hegel, G. W. F. (1931). *The phenomenology of the mind* (2nd ed.; J. D. Baillie, Trans.). London: Allen & Unwin. (Original work published 1807)

Hoffman, R. R. (Ed.). (1992). *The psychology of expertise: Cognitive research and empirical AI.* New York: Springer-Verlag.

Kohlberg, L. (1969). Stage and sequence: The cognitive-developmental approach to socialization. In G. A. Goslin (Ed.), *Handbook of socialization theory and research* (pp. 347–380). Chicago: Rand McNally.

Kohlberg, L. (1983). *The psychology of moral development.* New York: Harper & Row.

Labouvie-Vief, G. (1990). Wisdom as integrated thought: Historical and developmental perspectives. In R. J. Sternberg (Ed.), *Wisdom: Its nature, origins, and development* (pp. 52–83). New York: Cambridge University Press.

Meacham, J. (1990). The loss of wisdom. In R. J. Sternberg (Ed.), *Wisdom: Its nature, origins, and development* (pp. 181–211). New York: Cambridge University Press.

Neisser, U. (Ed.). (1998). *The rising curve.* Washington, DC: American Psychological Association.

Neufeldt, V., & Guralnik, D. B. (Eds.). (1997). *Webster's New World College Dictionary* (3rd ed.). New York: Macmillan.

Pascual-Leone, J. (1990). An essay on wisdom: Toward organismic processes that make it possible. In R. J. Sternberg (Ed.), *Wisdom: Its nature, origins, and development* (pp. 244–278). New York: Cambridge University Press.

Perkins, D. N., & Grotzer, T. A. (1997). Teaching intelligence. *American Psychologist, 52,* 1125–1133.

Polanyi, M. (1976). Tacit knowledge. In M. Marx & F. Goodson (Eds.), *Theories in contemporary psychology* (pp. 330–344). New York: Macmillan.

Renzulli, J. S. (1984). *Technical report of research studies related to the revolving door identification model* (Rev. ed.). Storrs, CT: Bureau of Educational Research, University of Connecticut.

Riegel, K. F. (1973). Dialectical operations: The final period of cognitive development. *Human Development, 16,* 346–370.

Robinson, D. N. (1990). Wisdom through the ages. In R. J. Sternberg (Ed.), *Wisdom: Its nature, origins, and development* (pp. 13–24). New York: Cambridge University Press.

Salovey, E, & Mayer, J. D. (1990). Emotional intelligence. *Imagination, Cognition, and Personality, 9,* 185–211.

Smith, J., Staudinger, U. M., & Baltes, P. B. (1994). Occupational settings facilitating wisdom-related knowledge: The sample case of clinical psychologists. *Journal of Consulting and Clinical Psychology, 66,* 989–999.

Staudinger, U. M., & Baltes, P. M. (1996). Interactive minds: A facilitative setting for wisdom-related performance? *Journal of Personality and Social Psychology, 71,* 746–762.

Sternberg, R. J. (1984). Toward a triarchic theory of human intelligence. *Behavioral and Brain Sciences, 7,* 269–287.

Sternberg, R. J. (1985). *Beyond IQ: A triarchic theory of human intelligence.* New York: Cambridge University Press.

Sternberg, R. J. (Ed.). (1990). *Wisdom: Its nature, origins, and development.* New York: Cambridge University Press.

Sternberg, R. J. (1997). *Successful intelligence.* New York: Plume.

Sternberg, R. J. (1998). A balance theory of wisdom. *Review of General Psychology, 2,* 347–365.

Sternberg, R. J. (1999a). A dialectical basis for understanding the study of cognition. In R.J. Sternberg (Ed.), *The nature of cognition* (pp. 51–78). Cambridge, MA: MIT Press.

Sternberg, R. J. (1999b) The theory of successful intelligence. *Review of General Psychology, 3,* 292–316.

Sternberg, R. J., & Dobson, D. M. (1987). Resolving interpersonal conflicts: An analysis of stylistic consistency. *Journal of Personality and Social Psychology, 52,* 794–812.

Sternberg, R. J., & Soriano, L. J. (1984). Styles of conflict resolution. *Journal of Personality and Social Psychology, 47,* 115–126.

Sternberg, R. J., Wagner, R. K., & Okagaki, L. (1993). Practical intelligence: The nature and role of tacit knowledge in work and at school. In H. Reese & J. Puckett (Eds.), *Advances in lifespan development* (pp. 205–227). Hillsdale, NJ: Erlbaum.

Sternberg, R. J., Wagner, R. K., Williams, W. M., & Horvath, J.A. (1995). Testing common sense. *American Psychologist, 50,* 912–927.

7

Giftedness and Talent: Reexamining a Reexamination of the Definitions

Francoys Gagné

University of Quebec at Montreal

In the scientific literature, there is ambiguity in the distinction between the concepts of *giftedness* and *talent.* This paper examines several common definitions of these two terms, with particular emphasis on the models proposed by Renzulli (1979) and Cohn (1981). Our critique of these two models leads to a clear differentiation between giftedness and talent: the former is associated with domains of abilities which foster and explain exceptional performance in varied fields of activities, that is, talents. Thus, one can be gifted without necessarily being talented (as with the case of underachievers), but not vice versa. Several factors which can act as catalysts for the actualization of giftedness in specific talents are discussed, particularly motivation and environmental quality.

Editor's Note: From Gagné, F. (1985). Giftedness and talent: Reexamining a reexamination of the definitions. *Gifted Child Quarterly, 29*(3), 103–112.

In general usage, no definite distinction is made between the ideas of giftedness and talent. One will as likely say "Peter is scholastically gifted" or "he has great academic talent," "Nicole is a gifted painter" or "her work shows a lot of talent as a painter," etc. These two terms are confused not only colloquially but also in dictionary usage. For example, Webster's Dictionary defines "gifted" as "possessing natural talent" (1970, p. 162). Even the scientific literature on giftedness, principally deriving from American sources, supports this ambiguity by randomly using one or the other term in the same paragraph, thus suggesting that they are synonyms. Only a few authors have attempted to clearly distinguish between these two concepts.

This ambiguity in terminology reflects the conceptual ambiguity of giftedness and talent. After more than a half-century of research on giftedness, the concept remains subject to various and sometimes divergent definitions. Richert, Alvino and McDonnell even speak of a "labyrinth of seemingly conflicting definitions in use in the United States" (1982, p. 84). This is a disturbing situation in that the accepted definition determines both the procedures used to identify the gifted and the content of enrichment programs offered to those identified (Passow, 1981).

The object of the present essay is to demonstrate that these two concepts are in no way synonymous, but encompass completely separate ideas. We will begin this demonstration by reviewing the principal distinctions outlined in the North American literature. This descriptive and critical analysis will lead to the presentation of a model for differentiating between these two ideas.

REVIEW OF THE LITERATURE

Four major trends of opinion are presented in the literature: (a) no distinctions between giftedness and talent, (b) conceptual separation between intelligence and other abilities, (c) marginal distinctions, and, finally, (d) the recent models of Renzulli and Cohn, subsequently integrated by Foster (1981).

Nondifferentiation

Those who indicate nondifferentiation constitute by far the most important school of thought. One only has to read the recent *Gifted Child Quarterly* issue on identification (1984, 28(4)) to observe this nondifferentiation in action. We have selected only a few examples from well-known authors. In a recent article, Gallagher (1979) takes cognizance of several pressing issues in the area of giftedness, one of these being the lack of definition of this concept. Nowhere in this article does he make a distinction between giftedness and talent. These two terms are used interchangeably. Torrance (1980), considered to be one of the chief advocates of a concept of creativity dissociated from that of intelligence, begins his recent contribution to a volume of articles devoted to the education of the gifted and talented as follows: "This chapter will deal with the identification of giftedness in talents other than in the academic area" (1980, p. 43). No other particulars are given to support the interdependence of these two concepts. Is giftedness to be understood simply as excellence in an area of talent? Finally, the most "official" definition of giftedness, drafted by the Commissioner of Education of the United States (Marland, 1972), and embodied in the 1978 Gifted and Talented Children Act, begins: "Gifted and talented children are those . . ." (p. 2). Nowhere else in the course of his remarks does he specify the distinction between the two terms.

INTELLIGENCE AS SEPARATE FROM OTHER ABILITIES

Among authors who do attempt to differentiate giftedness and talent, the most frequent distinctions associate the former with intellectual abilities (often including scholastic ability), while the latter is reserved for other types of skills or aptitudes. For instance, Ward, an eminent theorist in giftedness, identified two modalities of giftedness, namely "1. *General Intelligence,* usually manifest in I.Q. scores, and 2. *Specific Aptitudes* (or talents), as measured by valid tests" (in Barbe & Renzulli, 1975, p. 62). Fleming and Hollinger (1981) clearly adopt this position in describing talents as "non-IQ test derived" (p. 188). Borthwick, Dow, Lévesque, and Banks (1980) quote a similar tandem definition adopted by the Province of Ontario. Finally, according to Zettel (1979), the State of Delaware is the only one to have inscribed in law a differential definition.[1] It reads as follows:

> "Gifted children" means children . . . who are endowed by nature with high intellectual capacity and who have a native capacity for high potential intellectual attainment and scholastic achievement . . . "Talented children" means children . . . who have demonstrated superior talents, aptitudes or abilities, outstanding leadership qualities and abilities, or consistently remarkable performance in the mechanics [sic], manipulative skills, the art of expression of ideas, oral or written, music, art, human relations or any other worthwhile line of human achievement. (p. 63)

It should be noted that these two definitions go far beyond a single contrast between intellectual and other kinds of abilities; they also imply a distinction between innate versus acquired abilities and between capacity and performance. However, the principal contrast remains between intelligence and other abilities.

Marginal Distinctions

Two authors have differentiated between giftedness and talent in a manner which has not been widely endorsed or accepted by other researchers or professionals. On the one hand, Robeck (1968) mentions a hierarchical distinction: the talented have IQ scores ranging from 130 to 145, while gifted individuals score from 145 to 160. Those who surpass this level are referred to as highly gifted. On the other hand, Gowan (1979) maintains that giftedness and talent respectively correspond to verbal and nonverbal creative potential. Owing to their limited acceptance, the above definitions will not be considered in greater detail.

The Renzulli and Cohn Models

Probably the most well-known attempt to redefine giftedness is credited to Renzulli (1978, 1979). He puts forward two major criticisms, among others, to the definition proposed by the U.S. Office of Education (Marland, 1972). First, the definition does not include any reference to motivation, even though a large body of research concerning gifted or talented adults confirms the importance of this variable in the expression of creative and productive behaviors. Second, the six categories of giftedness referred to in the definition (general intellectual ability, particular scholastic aptitude, creative and productive thinking skills, abilities in leadership, visual and expressive arts, and the psychomotor domain) are not "parallel": two of them (specific academic aptitude and visual and performing arts) call attention to fields of human endeavor or general performance areas in which talents and abilities are manifested, while the remaining four categories are brought to bear on performance areas (1979, p. 7).

Based on a detailed review of writings dealing with explanatory factors related to the exceptional performance of adults considered to be "creative/productive" or eminent in various spheres of human endeavor, Renzulli (1979) offers a redefinition of giftedness which proposes the interaction of three fundamental psychological traits: (a) greater than average (but not necessarily exceptional) ability; (b) creativity; (c) motivation, which he terms "task commitment." In order for giftedness to become manifest, these three components should be simultaneously present and must take root in some area of performance. Renzulli introduces both general and specific performance domains. The complete model is outlined in Figure 1.

Similarly, Cohn (1977, 1981) has formulated a model of giftedness which clearly dissociates the concepts of giftedness and talent. Cohn's model, presented in Figure 2, breaks down giftedness into three major categories of abilities—intellectual, artistic, and social—each one further divisible into more specific subcategories of talents.

Recently, Foster (1981) has attempted to integrate the models of Renzulli and Cohn. As illustrated in Figure 3, the synthesis undertaken by Foster is, in effect, quite simple: he inserts Cohn's model in between the left and right hand sides of the Renzulli model. Both Cohn's major categories of abilities and the components of Renzulli's two performance levels (general and specific) are respectively arranged hierarchically. Figure 3 demonstrates this integration applied to the particular example of talent in leadership.

Foster appropriately comments that an examination of this integrated model clearly brings to mind career decision making models similar to those devised by Holland or Roe (Osipow, 1973, cited by Foster, 1981). The left hand side, which serves to isolate exceptional from average performance, is the only sharply dissimilar component.

CRITICAL EXAMINATION OF THE PROPOSED DISTINCTIONS

Our interest in this problem began with a query on the applicability of Renzulli's model to the case of underachieving gifted children or adolescents. Underachievement is generally revealed by a marked disparity between intellectual ability and academic performance in one or more subjects (Whitmore, 1980). Can one say that a child who obtains an IQ score of 130 or more is not gifted because he is not sufficiently motivated (for one reason or another) to succeed in class? Is there not a need to make a distinction between the potential indicated by psychometric instruments and its manifestation in a field of performance, in this case, academic work? Moreover, the same problem presents itself with respect to other abilities. For example, Bloom (1982), in reporting the preliminary results of an important study on the process of accession to prominence in six distinct talent areas (concert pianists and sculptors in the arts, mathematicians and research neurologists in the cognitive domain, olympic swimmers and tennis players in the psychomotor domain) notes a similar problem:

> In homes where other children were also interested in the talent area, the parents sometimes mentioned that one of the other children had even greater "gifts" than the individual in the sample, but that the other child was not willing to put in the time and effort that the parents or the teacher expected and required. (pp. 512–513)

Critique of Renzulli's Model

The factor that makes Renzulli's model inapplicable to underachievers is the presence of motivation as an essential component of giftedness. If one accepts the premise that gifted underachievers are really gifted, it is necessary to redefine giftedness in such a way that motivation plays a different role. However, it remains necessary to reserve a central role for this construct since, as Renzulli's literature review strongly demonstrates, exceptional performance in a field of endeavor largely stems from an intense and prolonged investment of energy in tasks pertinent to that field.

Renzulli's model presents a second problem, similar to the first, namely the identification of creativity as an essential component of giftedness. Surely, the literature which Renzulli cites to justify this inclusion appears convincing, at first glance. However, the apparent primacy of creativity stems, in our opinion,

Figure 1 Graphic representation of the definition of giftedness according to Renzulli

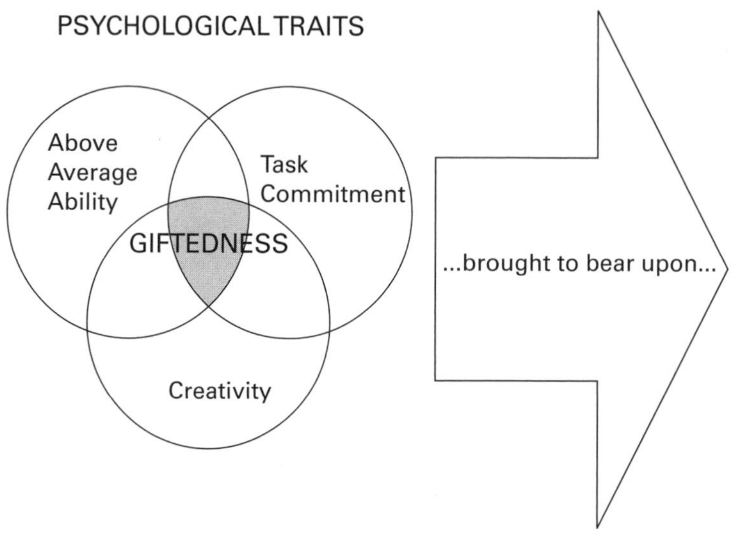

Note. From *What makes giftedness: A reexamination of the definition of the gifted and talented* (p. 24) by J. S. Renzulli, 1979. Ventura, CA: Ventura County Superintendent of Schools Office. Copyright 1979 by Joseph S. Renzulli. Reprinted by permission.

from a bias in the selection of fields of study (architecture, arts, sciences) and in the types of eminence researched. For example, Renzulli extensively cites MacKinnon's (1964) study in which a panel of judges identified a group of prominent architects on the basis of the following criteria: originality of thought, ingenuity, rejection of established convention, etc. It is hardly surprising that with criteria such as these, creative individuals were identified. It is true that "it is usually the originality, novelty, or uniqueness of a person's contribution that brings him or her to the attention of the public" (Renzulli, 1979, p. 15). However, this statement refers to individuals who can be considered agents of change, transformers, inventors, and the like. What, then, can we say of celebrated athletes whose accomplishments make international headlines, musicians of international repute, teachers or professors who have positively influenced their students, and many others who have attained a certain prominence, if not absolute renown, by means of interpretive performance or other skills, and not primarily creative ability? Creativity may be regarded as a major determinant of exceptional performance in certain fields of endeavor, but not in all. It therefore should be considered as one ability domain, among others, in which giftedness can express itself.

This leads to the third and final criticism of Renzulli's model. It does not differentiate above average ability into separate ability domains. In fact, Renzulli's text leaves the distinct impression that these abilities are intellectual; all the studies which he cites examine the role of IQ (or its manifestation in academic

Figure 2 Graphic representation of Cohn's model of giftedness

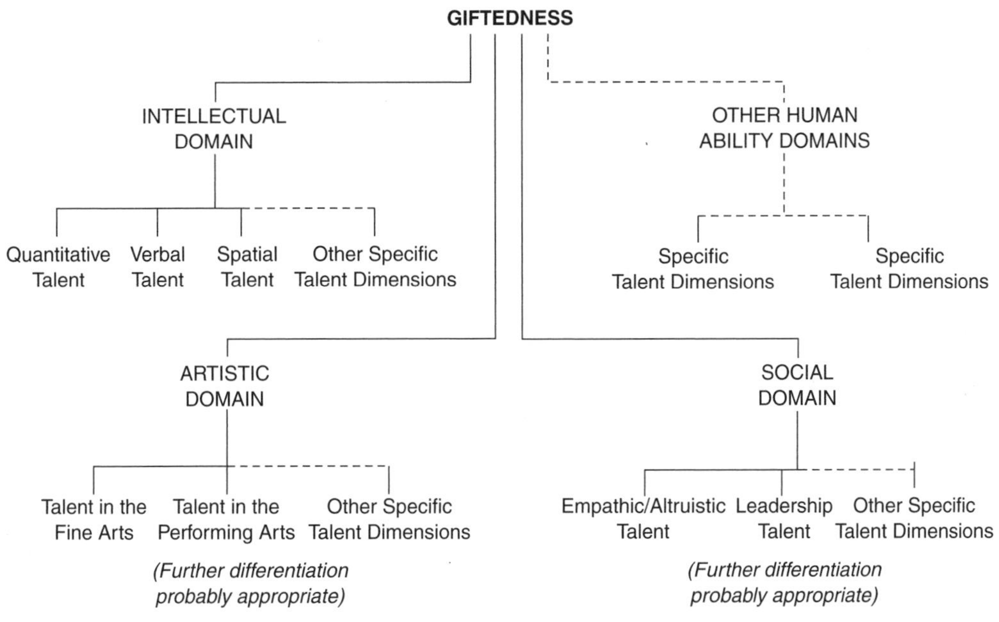

Note. From "What is giftedness? A multidimensional approach" by S. J. Cohn, 1981, in A. H. Kramer (Ed.), *Gifted children: Challenging their potential* (p. 37). New York: Trillium Press. Copyright 1981 by Third International Conference on Gifted Children—Organizing Committee (1979) and World Council for Gifted and Talented Children. Reprinted by permission.

performance) as a precursor to exceptional performance at an adult age. Do domains of ability, other than intellectual ones, not exist as well? Cohn identifies two others: social and artistic abilities. With reference to social abilities, recent work (see notably Ford & Tisak, 1983) appears to confirm the construct validity of measurement instruments intended as indicators of these abilities. Even though we are dealing with a still nascent field of research, the existence of such a domain of abilities seems to be both recognized and accepted by many. With reference to artistic abilities which Cohn divides into various subcategories of talent (see Figure 2), disagreement must be expressed. Indeed, the arts constitute several fields of talent to which no specific "artistic" abilities correspond Moreover, no taxonomy of human abilities ever included artistic ability (on this subject see Anastasi, 1982, chap. 13). The skills capable of explaining various artistic talents which are strongly heterogeneous must be sought out in other domains.

Other areas of ability can be added to this list: one suggestion is creative ability, already pointed out above, without entering into the debate on whether or not it belongs to the domain of intellectual abilities. Then there is psychomotor ability, of great importance in athletics and sports. Concerning this category of skills, one wonders why the U.S. Office of Education decided in 1978

Figure 3 The Renzulli/Cohn integrated model illustrating the particular case of talent in leadership

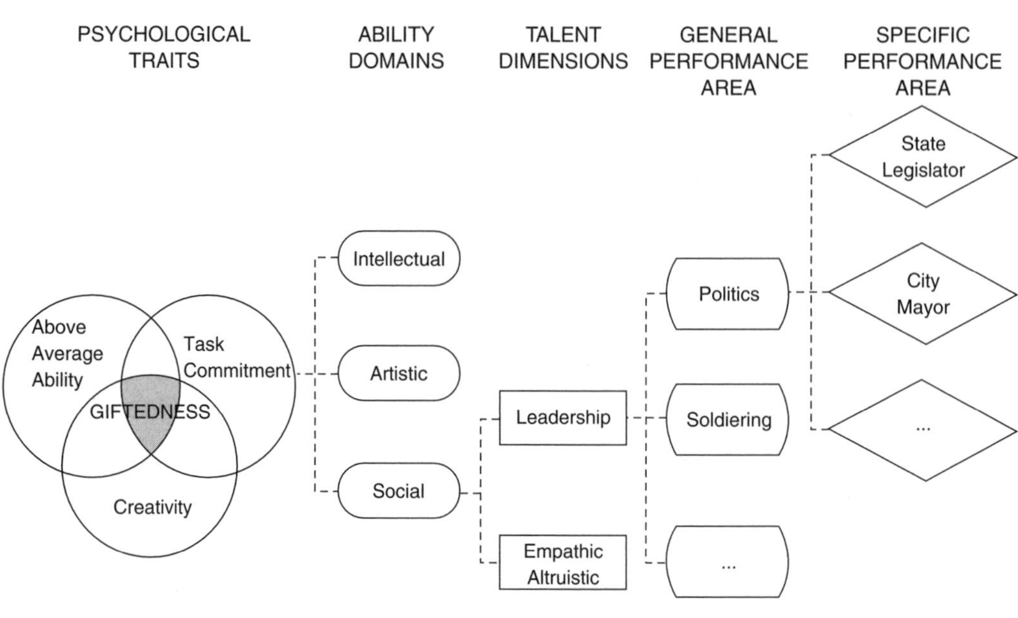

Note. From "Leadership: A conceptual framework for recognizing and educating" by W. Foster, 1981, *Gifted Child Quarterly, 25,* p. 20. Copyright 1981 by the National Association for Gifted Children. Reprinted by permission.

(Passow, 1981, p. 5) to eliminate these abilities from the original definition put forward by Commissioner Marland in 1972. This resulted in the excision of a domain of abilities whose importance was evident not only in sports but also in the arts (sculpture, music, dance, cabinet-making, drawing) and in many other fields (surgery, gem-cutting, construction trades, etc.).

In short, an adequate model for giftedness should introduce a parsimonious taxonomy of human abilities. Renzulli's model does not posit any taxonomy of this type, since he clearly dissociates creativity and superior ability, the latter corresponding only (it seems) to intellectual skills.

Critique of Cohn's Model

Cohn's model answers partly this criticism, since it breaks down the general concept of giftedness into several ability domains. However, it poses a major problem of its own due to its hierarchical structure, namely the insertion of diverse subcategories of talent into one or another of the identified ability domains. The implication of this hierarchical structure is clear: Excellence in one subcategory of talent can only be related to abilities in a single domain. This model of one-to-one relations between abilities and talents tallies poorly with reality in two respects. First, it contradicts a good number of studies cited by Renzulli which indicate that emergence in certain fields of talent involves several abilities, for example intellectual and creative. In addition, in the particular case of teaching, research has clearly demonstrated (see notably Doyle, 1975, p. 49) that excellence is due to a combination of factors: cognitive (clarity, structure, competence in the subject matter), creative (interest, stimulation of thinking) and social (friendliness, sensitivity to the reactions of the group, tactfulness). Second, even within one domain of talent, if it is not too restrictively defined, success can take diverse forms reflected by distinct profiles of abilities. Next to a surgeon, whose dexterity and sureness of movement are the envy of his profession, can be found a colleague renowned for the creation of a new technique or piece of equipment, such as an artificial heart. The same situation occurs in the world of the circus where trapeze artists work alongside clowns and animal trainers.

In short, an adequate model of giftedness and talent must allow for multidirectional and not merely bidirectional connections between abilities and talents. The expression "multidirectional connections" means, on the one hand, that a given ability can contribute to excellence in several fields of talent and, on the other hand, that a particular talent can be accounted for by a profile of diverse abilities.

PROPOSAL FOR A DIFFERENTIATED MODEL OF GIFTEDNESS AND TALENT

The essence of the differentiated model that we are about to present in response to the various criticisms of existing models discussed above is a dichotomy between *domains of ability* and *fields of performance,* respectively corresponding to *giftedness* and *talent.* This dichotomy is not in itself new. The distinction between abilities or aptitudes and performance can be found frequently in the literature (cited earlier) and also serves as a principle of differentiation between the left and the right parts of the diagram presented by Renzulli to illustrate his model (see Figure 1). The contribution of our model is its association of giftedness with domains of ability, and talent with fields of performance.

Definitions of Giftedness and Talent

These connections engender the following definitions of giftedness and talent:

Giftedness corresponds to competence which is distinctly above average in one or more domains of ability.

Talent refers to performance which is distinctly above average in one or more fields of human performance.

Several elaborations of these two definitions follow:

1. The terms competence and performance are important to understanding the differences between giftedness and talent. Talent, which is defined in the context of a large or narrow field of human activity, expresses itself through a set of behaviors linked to this field of activity. The talented shooter of clay pigeons shows his expertise by the high proportion of pigeons struck; the talent of the mathematician may be revealed by the rapidity and ease with which he solves mathematical problems; the talented painter will be judged so by the quality of his works. Giftedness is somewhat different in that abilities are generally identified using more unidimensional and standardized measures so as to connect together in the purest form possible those individual characteristics which "explain" the observed performance. Strictly speaking, it is true that responses to standardized measures constitute a "performance"; as a matter of fact, they must be observable or, in other words, operational. However, precisely because of the antecedence of abilities with respect to talented behavior and their explicative power with respect to observed performance in fields of talent, we have retained the use of the two separate terms, competence and performance.

2. This distinction is also intended to reduce the ambiguity between the two concepts as much as possible by adopting definitions which do not include the same words. It is this guideline which determined the choice of the terms *domain* (in the case of abilities) and *field* (to refer to "domains" of talent). It implies that to every field of talent corresponds a characteristic profile of abilities which would explain exceptional individual performance. In the course of the last 50 years, psychometric research concerned with scholastic activity has clearly demonstrated the existence of necessary, although not sufficient, ties between different intellectual abilities and varying scholastic performance (Carroll, 1982). The body of research dealing with other ability domains or fields of talent is still in an embryonic state.

3. This distinction implies, as a corollary, that every talented individual is necessarily gifted, although the inverse is not true; a gifted individual is not necessarily talented. Since it is a manifestation of giftedness in a particular field of activity, talent necessarily implies the presence of underlying abilities capable of explaining it. However, it can certainly happen, as is well illustrated in the case of underachieving children, that an individual shows himself to be gifted, that is the possessor of exceptional abilities, without having manifested his giftedness in any academic talent. In this regard, let us remember Bloom's anecdote cited above. Our distinction thus permits an elegant solution to the impasse generated by Renzulli's model which forced us to exclude underachievers from the category of gifted individuals. Our model allows us, in fact, to define these people as gifted intellectually, but not talented academically.

4. In light of these two definitions, we can infer that the six categories mentioned in the Marland definition overlap the concepts of giftedness and talent. Three of them (general intellectual ability, creative and productive thinking skills, and the psychomotor domain) identify domains of giftedness, while the other three (scholastic aptitude, leadership, and visual and expressive arts) refer to fields of talent.

Figure 4 Graphic representation of a differentiated model of giftedness and talent

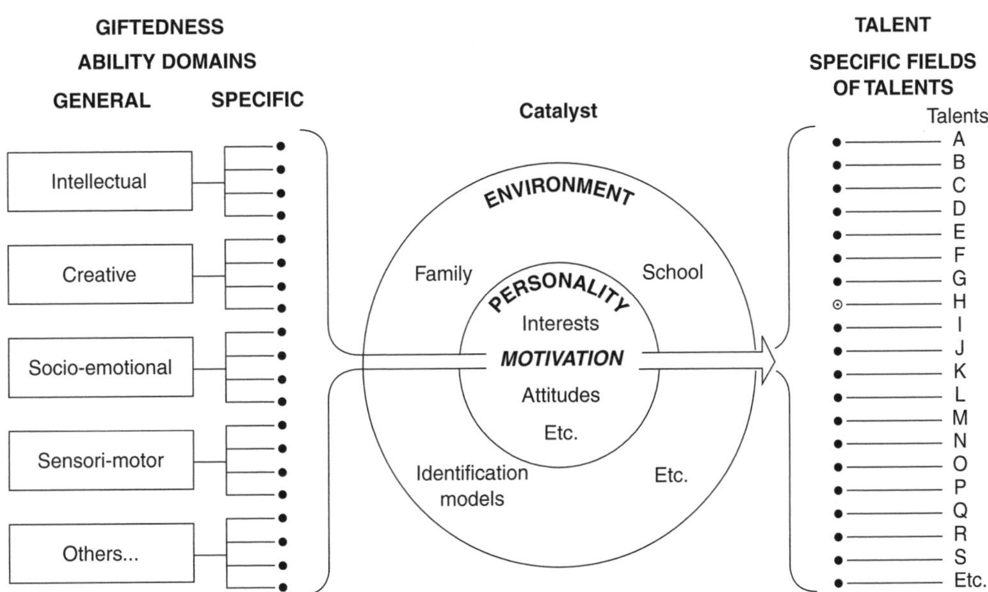

The Model

As we have already pointed out, the difficulty created by Renzulli's model stems essentially from the presence of motivation as an essential component of giftedness. What happens to this construct in the presently proposed model? Its fate is illustrated in Figure 4 which visually explains the various components with their reciprocal connections. It can be observed that motivation has lost little of its importance, since it has become one of the essential prerequisites for transforming giftedness into talent. Several comments related to this diagram follow. They explain various beliefs and observations concerning the connections between giftedness and talent.

1. Four major domains of human ability are suggested: intellectual, creative, socioaffective, and sensorimotor. Since we have not made detailed inventory on this subject, the door is being left open for the identification or differentiation of other general domains of ability. It should be noted that the term sensorimotor ability is given preference over psychomotor, in order to underscore the important role of the various senses in many spheres of talent (e.g., marksmanship, wine tasting, perfume analysis).

2. Owing to important differences among authors and to insufficient research, the particular domains of ability are not specified. For example, in the intellectual domain alone, subcategories can vary considerably. In opposition to upholders of the g factor who vigorously defend the general IQ, a fair number of researchers have tried to identify relatively independent groups and subgroups

of abilities through factor analysis. Work by Thurstone, Kelly, Guilford, Vernon, and many others, aptly synthesized by Anastasi (1982, chapter 13), suggests a large variety of abilities: verbal, numerical, spatial, perceptual, mechanical, mnemonic, etc. Some systems (e.g., Thurstone) place these in parallel, others (e.g., Vernon), create a hierarchy of major, minor, and specific factors. For his part, Guilford has proposed a tridimensional model of the structure of intellect whose 120 cells stem from the junction of six operations, four contents, and five different products.

As if the problem was not already sufficiently complex and in dire need of some synthesis, specialists in cognitive psychology have also brought forth taxonomies of cognitive abilities. For example, consider the recent proposal by Sternberg (1981, 1984) of a triarchic theory of intelligence encompassing three distinct subtheories: a *componential* subtheory that posits three kinds of information-processing abilities (metacomponents, performance components, and knowledge-acquisition components), a *two-facet* subtheory which relates the above components to performance in coping with either novelty or automatization and, finally, a *contextual* subtheory comprised of three hierarchically related processes (adaptation, selection, shaping) which attempts to achieve the best possible fit between the individual and his sociocultural environment.

Finally, in a most interesting effort to synthesize available knowledge from psychometrics, cognitive psychology, and neuropsychology, Gardner (1982a, 1982b) has presented in much detail a theory of multiple intelligences in which six distinct "intelligences" are isolated: linguistic, musical, logical-mathematical, spatial, bodily-kinesthetic, and personal. This last one is subdivided into an intrapersonal component (access to one's own feeling life) and an interpersonal component (the ability to notice—and make distinctions among—other individuals' moods, temperaments, motivations, and intentions).

3. Contrary to the position taken by Renzulli, the importance of creativity, now one of several general domains of ability, is diminished. In this new position, it is no longer an essential factor of giftedness or of talent. Unquestionably, it contributes to several talents, notably in the artistic field. However, it is also possible to identify numerous fields of talent in which abilities of a more technical nature have overtaken the importance of creativity: the interpretation of a musical score in contradistinction to its composition, expertise in microphotography, diagnosis in internal medicine or automobile repair, and athletics.

4. On the right hand side of the diagram, talents have been purposely isolated rather than regrouped into general and specific fields. The decision is based on several factors. First, the inventory of general fields proposed by Renzulli does not seem to be sufficiently exhaustive. Where are the talented sales representative, the architect, the mechanic, the electrician, the cabinet-maker, the stamp collector, the diamond-cutter to be placed? Second, Cohn's system contradicts the multidirectionality of the relations between abilities and talents in this model, or, in other words, the fact that a particular talent is subtended by a profile of abilities that can derive from different general domains. Third, the same principle of

hierarchization of talents into general and specific domains runs into a major confounding fact, namely, the interrelatedness of fields of human activity. For example, the inventor of a new artificial heart works in the medical domain, applying to it principles and techniques of the physical or biological sciences and of engineering. Where is this talent to be placed? Similarly, in the domain of computer science, extremely varied talents come together. What becomes of the designer of hardware, of intricate microcircuitry, of print-out screens, of programming languages, or of sophisticated software? Where does one place the chemist who has specialized in the techniques of treating silicone in the making of "chips," in chemistry or in computer sciences? In short, the codification of talents poses problems which are best deferred to future work.

5. The two brackets that border the specific ability domains on one side, and the specific talent fields on the other, represent the *multidirectionality* of the relations between giftedness and talent. Each specific talent is expressed by a particular profile of abilities differing somewhat from the profile characteristic of another talent.

6. The variables placed in the center act as catalysts for the expression of talent. On the one hand, interests, varying personality traits, and environment should fix the orientation of the individual toward a particular field of talent, while motivation will contribute mostly to the intensity of the talent, obviously in conjunction with ability level. This last remark raises the question of the stability of talents. If a child of five or six does not develop his or her special talent in swimming, for example, through rigorous practice and with the constant support of parents and teachers, he or she will probably not be considered talented 10 years later. He or she might still remain more talented than the average but, at age 15, only those who emerge at the local, state, or national level will be judged exceptionally talented. As clearly demonstrated by the SMPY project (Stanley, 1977) levels of talent are no less spread out than levels of giftedness.

7. The model shown in Figure 4 indicates that the environment has a greater influence on talent than on giftedness. The presence of the catalysts in the central section of the model bespeaks this difference. But, beyond this comparative statement, one should be very prudent when it comes to quantifying the respective impact of "nature" and "nurture," as witnessed by the acrimonious debate over the hereditary (or environmental) basis of intelligence (Eysenk & Kamin, 1981). All the more so, since such a debate appears to be irrelevant when discussing the specific educational needs of gifted or talented children. Whatever the origins of these gifts or talents, their presence in an individual creates needs which demand differentiated educational curricula (Massé & Gagné, 1983). It would thus be unfortunate for a strictly heuristic question to contaminate and inflame an otherwise very simple problem, that of the right of this special population to a maximum development of their abilities or talents.

8. A few words about the implications of this distinction for identification and programming purposes. Let us recall first an often forgotten principle that the specific objectives of the program must guide the definition of the appropriate

clientele (Feldhusen, Asher, & Hoover, 1984). Thus, a program whose purpose is the development of reasoning or thinking skills should be primarily offered to children gifted in these ability domains. On the other hand, if the program promotes the development of mathematical talent, it will screen its candidates, as the SMPY does so effectively, with instruments specifically tailored for this field of talent. It would be eminently unjust to deny a manifestly talented youth access to a program in his or her field of talent under the pretext, for example, that his or her IQ falls somewhat below the arbitrary cut-off score established at the state or local level. Even though the identification of numerous talents calls for what are often subjective judgments instead of more standardized measures, it remains preferable "to have imprecise answers to the right questions than precise answers to the wrong questions" (Renzulli, 1984, p. 164).

9. Finally, our distinction leads to a substitution of the expression "gifted *and* talented" for "gifted *or* talented."

CONCLUSION

Having critically analyzed various proposals aimed at distinguishing between giftedness and talent, we have advanced a model differentiating between these two constructs. The model presents giftedness as exceptional competence in one or more domains of ability, and defines talent as exceptional performance in one or more fields of human activity. Motivation, a major component of giftedness in Renzulli's model, becomes one of the principal catalysts of the actualization of giftedness into talent, more particularly, of the emergence of exceptional talent. Creativity, another of the three essential components of giftedness according to Renzulli, is relegated to a less central role as one of the general ability domains. This reordering permits the accommodation of many talents such as sports and athletics, musical or theatrical interpretation, trades, and leadership in which divergent thinking does not appear to play a primary role.

In concluding this essay on a redefinition of giftedness and talent, the author is conscious of the multitude of questions left unanswered. Some of these have already been formulated by Foster (1981) in respect to Cohn's and Renzulli's models and they apply as well to ours. Essentially, Foster questions the explanatory power of such models.

> It does not shed any light on why someone comes to express the appropriate mix of above average ability, task commitment and creativity or why such a person expresses those traits in the social domain as opposed to the intellectual or the artistic domain. At a more detailed level it gives no hint as to why a person expresses a talent for initiating and carrying through political and social movements. (1981, p. 19)

In fact, each component of our model raises questions as yet not clearly addressed and answered by research. For example, the codification of general and specific domains of ability as well as fields of talent are areas of research worthy of further study. With respect to the latter, it would be particularly interesting to further explore the potential contributions of Holland's model which provided the analytical framework for structuring the domains of interest listed in the Strong-Campbell Interest Inventory (Campbell, 1977). The central zone of our model occupied by the catalysts is also in need of elaboration, perhaps by calling upon such work as that of Atkinson, O'Malley and Lens (1976).

Independently of the numerous clarifications that should be made to this model, it is our firm belief that these two constructs are not synonymous, that they are not distinguishable as a function of the opposition between intellectual and other types of ability, but rather according to a dichotomy between domains of ability and fields of performance, and finally that motivation serves as a catalyst in the actualization of exceptional gifts into exceptional talents.

NOTE

1. According to Wells (1981), it was the State of Louisiana that took this initiative. However, the adopted definition is not cited.

REFERENCES

Anastasi, A. (1982). *Psychological testing* (5th ed.). New York: Macmillan.

Atkinson, J. W., O'Malley, P. M., & Lens, W. (1976). Motivation and ability: Interactive psychological determinants of intellective performance, educational achievement, and each other. In W. H. Sewell, R. M. Mauser, & D. L. Featherman (Eds.), *Schooling and achievement in American society* (pp. 29–60). New York: Academic Press.

Bloom, B. S. (1982). The role of gifts and markers in the development of talent. *Exceptional Children 48*, 510–522.

Borthwick, B., Dow, I., Lévesque, D., & Banks, R. (1980). *The gifted and talented student in Canada: Results of a CEA survey.* Toronto: The Canadian Education Association.

Campbell, D. P. (1977). *Manual for the SVIB-SCII.* Stanford, CA: Stanford University Press.

Carroll, J. B. (1982). The measurement of intelligence. In R. J. Sternberg (Ed.), *Handbook of human intelligence* (pp. 29–120). Cambridge, MA: Cambridge University Press.

Cohn, S. J. (1977). *A model for a pluralistic view of giftedness and talent.* Unpublished paper prepared for the United States Office of Education.

Cohn, S. J. (1981). What is giftedness? A multidimensional approach. In A. H. Kramer (Ed.), *Gifted children: Challenging their potential* (pp. 33–45). New York: Trillium Press.

Doyle, K. O. (1975). *Student evaluation of instruction.* Lexington, MA: D. C. Heath.

Eysenck, H. J., & Kamin, L. (1981). The intelligence controversy. New York: Wiley.

Feldhusen, J. F., Asher, J. W., & Hoover, S. M. (1984). Problems in the identification of giftedness, talent, or ability. *Gifted Child Quarterly, 28*, 149–151.

Fleming, E. S., & Hollinger, C. L. (1981). The multidimensionality of talent in adolescent young women. *Journal for the Education of the Gifted, 4*, 188–198.

Ford, M. E., & Tisak, M. S. (1983). A further search for social intelligence. *Journal of Educational Psychology, 75*, 196–206.

Foster, W. (1981). Leadership: A conceptual framework for recognizing and educating. *Gifted Child Quarterly, 25,* 17–25.

Gallagher, J. J. (1979). Issues in education for the gifted. In A. H. Passow (Ed.), *The gifted and the talented: Their education and development.* (78th Yearbook of the National Society for the Study of Education, Part I) (pp. 28–44). Chicago: University of Chicago Press.

Gardner, H. (1982a). Giftedness: Speculations from a biological perspective. In D. H. Feldman (Ed.), *Developmental approaches to giftedness and creativity* (New directions for child development, volume 17, pp. 47–60). San Francisco: Jossey-Bass.

Gardner, H. (1982b). *Frames of mind.* New York: Basic Books.

Gowan, J. C. (1979). The use of developmental stage theory in helping gifted children become creative. In J. J. Gallagher, J. C. Gowan, A. H. Passow, & E. P. Torrance (Eds.), *Issues in gifted education* (pp. 47–78). Ventura, CA: Ventura County Superintendent of Schools Office.

In search of identification. (1984). *Gifted Child Quarterly, 28* (4).

MacKinnon, D. W. (1964). The creativity of architects. In C. W. Taylor (Ed.), *Widening horizons in creativity* (pp. 359–378). New York: Wiley.

Marland, S. P. (1972). *Education of the gifted and talented: Report to the Congress of the United States by the U.S. commissioner of education.* Washington, D.C.: U.S. Government Printing Office.

Massé, P., & Gagné, F. (1983). Observations on enrichment and acceleration. In B. M. Shore, F. Gagné, S. Larivée, R. H. Tali, & R. E. Tremblay (Eds.), *Face to face with giftedness* (pp. 395–413). New York: Trillium Press.

Passow, A. H. (1981). The nature of giftedness. *Gifted Child Quarterly, 25,* 5–10.

Renzulli, J. S. (1978, November). What makes giftedness? Reexamining a definition. *Phi Delta Kappan, 60,* 180–185, 261.

Renzulli, J. S. (1979). *What makes giftedness: A reexamination of the definition of the gifted and talented.* Ventura, CA: Ventura County Superintendent of Schools Office.

Renzulli, J. S. (1984). The triad/revolving door system: A research-based approach to identification and programming for the gifted and talented. *Gifted Child Quarterly, 28,* 163–171.

Richert, S. E., Alvino, J. J., & McDonnell, R. C. (1982). *National report on identification.* Sewell, NJ: Educational Improvement Center-South.

Robeck, M. C. (1968). *Special class programs for intellectually gifted pupils.* Sacramento, CA: California State Department of Education. (ERIC Document Reproduction Service No. ED 042 271).

Stanley, J. C. (1977). Rationale of the study of mathematically precocious youth (SMPY) during its first five years of promoting educational acceleration. In J. C. Stanley, W. C. George, & C. H. Solano (Eds.). *The gifted and the creative: A fifty-year perspective* (pp. 75–112). Baltimore, MD: Johns Hopkins University Press.

Sternberg, R. J. (1981). A componential theory of intellectual giftedness. *Gifted Child Quarterly, 25,* 86–93.

Sternberg, R. J. (1984). What should intelligence tests test? Implications of a triarchic theory of intelligence for intelligence testing. *Educational Researcher, 13(1),* 5–15.

Torrance, E. P. (1980). Extending the identification of giftedness: Other talents, minority and handicapped groups. In National/State Leadership Training Institute on the Gifted and Talented (Ed.), *Educating the preschool/primary gifted and talented* (pp. 43–58). Ventura, CA: Ventura County Superintendent of Schools Office.

Ward, V. S. (1975). Basic concepts. In W. B. Barbe & J. S. Renzulli (Eds.), *Psychology and education of the gifted* (pp. 61–71). New York: lrvington Publishers.

Webster, D. (1970). Webster's New World Dictionary (College ed.). Toronto: Nelson, Foster & Scott.

Wells, D. (1981). Definitions of gifted and talented used in the United States. *Journal for the Education of the Gifted, 5,* 283–293.

Whitmore, J. R. (1980). *Giftedness, conflict, and underachievement.* Boston: Allyn & Bacon.

Zettel, J. (1979). State provisions for educating the gifted and talented. In A. H. Passow (Ed.), *The gifted and the talented: Their education and development* (78th yearbook of the National Society for the Study of Education) (pp. 63–74). Chicago: University of Chicago Press.

8

Profiles of the Gifted and Talented

George T. Betts
Maureen Neihart

University of Northern Colorado

After several years of observations, interviews, and reviews of literature, the authors have developed six profiles of gifted and talented children and youth. These profiles help educators and parents to look closely at the feelings, behaviors, and needs of the gifted and talented. Also, tips on identification of each profile are included as well as information on facilitating the gifted and talented in the school and home.

Gifted children are usually discussed as an undifferentiated group. When they are differentiated, it tends to be on the basis of differences in intellectual abilities, talents, or interests rather than from a total or "gestalt" point of view in terms of behavior, feelings, and needs. For example, creatively gifted,

Editor's Note: From Betts, G.T., & Neihart, M. (1988). Profiles of the gifted and talented. *Gifted Child Quarterly*, 32(2), 248–253. © 1988 National Association for Gifted Children. Reprinted with permission.

intellectually gifted, learning disabled gifted, and artistically gifted are among the different categories that have been reported. The purpose of this article is to describe a theoretical model to profile the gifted and talented that differentiates gifted individuals on the basis of behavior, feelings, and needs. The matrix describes and compares the needs, feelings and behaviors of six different profiles of gifted children. This model serves to increase awareness among educators and parents of differences among gifted children and provides guidelines for identifying gifted children. It can also be used to develop appropriate educational goals for the gifted. These types are offered as a generalization to facilitate the task of identifying and guiding gifted children in all aspects of development. They are not intended to describe any one child completely.

Personality is the result of life experiences and genetic makeup. All gifted children are not affected by their special abilities in the same way. Gifted children interact with and are influenced by their families, their education, their relationships, and their personal development. Experience with gifted children in a variety of settings has served to increase awareness that the gifted cannot be seen as one group (Strang, 1965).

Little has been done, however, to distinguish among groups of gifted children. Roeper (1982) proposed five types of gifted children based strictly on the approaches gifted children use to cope with their emotions. She identified the perfectionist, the child/adult, the winner of the competition, the self-critic, and the well-integrated child. She focused on the development of coping styles and the ways in which gifted children experience and express feelings,

Few studies focus on a holistic perspective of the gifted child. Most address one aspect of development or an area of achievement or interest. (Colangelo & Parker, 1981; Delisle, J.R., 1982; Gregory & Stevens-Long, 1986; Kaiser, Berndt, & Stanley, 1987; Schwolinski & Reynolds, 1985). The development of the whole child must be addressed, taking into account the interaction of emotional, social, cognitive, and physical factors. It is essential to remember that "A child is a total entity; a combination of many characteristics. Emotions cannot be treated separately from intellectual awareness or physical development; all intertwine and influence each other" (Roeper, 1982, p. 21). Giftedness should not be defined by separate categories; every aspect of personality and development influences and interacts with every other aspect. Giftedness should be examined as a construct that impacts on personality.

PROFILES OF THE GIFTED AND TALENTED

The following presentation of six different profiles of gifted and talented students can provide information for educators and parents about the behavior, feelings, and needs of gifted and talented children and youth. It is important to remember that this is a theoretical concept that can provide insights for facilitating the growth of the gifted and talented, not a diagnostic classification model (see Table 1).

Putting the Research to Use

It is essential that educators and parents understand the cognitive, emotional, and social needs of the gifted and talented. "Profiles of the gifted and talented" provides a framework for a better understanding of these students by looking closely at their feelings, behavior, and needs. Additional information is provided concerning adult and peer perceptions, identification, and home and school interactions. Parents and educators use the profiles to gain a deeper awareness of the gifted and talented. They are also able to use the information for inservice and courses concerning the nature and needs of the gifted and talented. Furthermore, educators can present the information directly to students in order to help them develop more insight into their own needs and behavior. "Profiles of the gifted and talented" is a starting point for those who want to develop a greater awareness and insight into these students. The application of the approach will provide deeper and greater understanding of our gifted and talented.

Additionally, children and youth should not be defined by any one of the following categories. The behavior, feelings, and needs of gifted and talented children change frequently when they are young, but as years pass there will be fewer abrupt changes and they may settle into one or two profile areas. This approach provides a new understanding of the gifted and talented and new opportunities for developing techniques and strategies for facilitating the cognitive, emotional and social growth of these children.

TYPE I: THE SUCCESSFUL

Perhaps as many as 90% of identified gifted students in school programs are Type I's. Children who demonstrate the behavior, feelings, and needs classified as Type I's have learned the system. They have listened closely to their parents and teachers. After discovering what "sells" at home and at school, they begin to display appropriate behavior. They learn well and are able to score high on achievement tests and tests of intelligence. As a result, they are usually identified for placement in programs for the gifted. Rarely do they exhibit behavior problems because they are eager for approval from teachers, parents and other adults,

These are the children many believe will "make it on their own." However, Type I's often become bored with school and learn to use the system in order to get by with as little effort as possible. Rather than pursue their own interests and goals in school, they tend to go through the motions of schooling, seeking structure and direction from instructors. They are dependent upon parents and teachers. They fail to learn needed skills and attitudes for autonomy, but they do achieve. Overall, these children may appear to have positive self-concepts because they have been affirmed for their achievements. They are liked by peers and are included in social groups. They are dependent on the system but are not aware that they have deficiencies because of the reinforcement they receive from adults who are pleased with them and their achievement. However, Goertzel and Goertzel (1962) concluded that the brightest children in the classroom may become competent but unimaginative adults who do not fully develop their gifts and talents. It seems that these children have lost both their creativity and autonomy.

Gifted young adults who may underachieve in college and later adulthood come from this group. They do not possess the necessary skills, concepts, and attitudes necessary for life-long learning. They are well adjusted to society but are not well prepared for the ever-changing challenges of life.

TYPE II

Type II's are the divergently gifted. Many school systems fail to identify Type II gifted children for programs unless the programs have been in place at least five years and substantial in-servicing has been done with teachers. Type II's typically possess a high degree of creativity and may appear to be obstinate, tactless, or sarcastic. They often question authority and may challenge the teacher in front of the class. They do not conform to the system, and they have not learned to use it to their advantage. They receive little recognition and few rewards or honors. Their interactions at school and at home often involve conflict.

These children feel frustrated because the school system has not affirmed their talents and abilities. They are struggling with their self-esteem. They may or may not feel included in the social group. Some Type II's also challenge their peers, and therefore are often not included or welcomed in activities or group projects; on the other hand, some Type II's have a sense of humor and creativity that is very appealing to peers. Nevertheless their spontaneity may be disruptive in the classroom. In spite of their creativity, Type II's often possess negative self-concepts.

Type II's may be "at risk" as eventual dropouts for drug addiction or delinquent behavior if appropriate interventions are not made by junior high. Parents of gifted high school students who drop out of school (Type IV) frequently note that their children exhibited Type II behaviors in upper elementary school or junior high. Although this relationship has not been validated empirically, it carries significant implications that merit serious consideration.

TYPE III: THE UNDERGROUND

The Type III gifted child is known as "the underground gifted." Generally, these are middle school females although males may also want to hide their giftedness. If a gifted boy goes underground, it tends to happen later, in high school, and typically in response to the pressure to participate in athletics.

In general, Type III's are gifted girls whose belonging needs rise dramatically in middle school (Kerr, 1985). They begin to deny their talent in order to feel more included with a non-gifted peer group. Students who are highly motivated and intensely interested in academic or creative pursuits may undergo an apparently sudden radical transformation, losing all interest in previous passions. Type III's frequently feel insecure and anxious. Their changing needs are often in conflict with the expectations of teachers and parents. All too often, adults react to them in ways that only increase their resistance and denial. There is a tendency to push these children, to insist that they continue with their educational program no matter how they feel. Type III's often seem to benefit from being accepted as they are at the time.

Although Type III's should not be permitted to abandon all projects or advanced classes, alternatives should be explored for meeting their academic needs while they are undergoing this transition. Challenging resistant adolescents may alienate them from those who can help meet their needs and long-term goals.

TYPE IV: THE DROPOUTS

Type IV gifted students are angry. They are angry with adults and with themselves because the system has not met their needs for many years and they feel rejected. They may express this anger by acting depressed and withdrawn or by acting out and responding defensively. Frequently, Type IV's have interests that lie outside the realm of the regular school curriculum and they fail to receive support and affirmation for their talent and interest in these unusual areas. School seems irrelevant and perhaps hostile to them. For the most part, Type IV's are high school students, although occasionally there may be an elementary student who attends school sporadically or only on certain days and has in essence "dropped out" emotionally and mentally if not physically.

Type IV students are frequently gifted children who were identified very late, perhaps not until high school. They are bitter and resentful as a result of feeling rejected and neglected. Their self-esteem is very low, and they require a close working relationship with an adult they can trust. Traditional programming is no longer appropriate for Type IV's. Family counseling is strongly recommended, and the Type IV youth should also be given individual counseling. Diagnostic testing is also necessary to identify possible areas for remediation.

TYPE V: THE DOUBLE-LABELED

Type V refers to gifted children who are physically or emotionally handicapped in some way, or who have learning disabilities. The vast majority of gifted programs do not identify these children, nor do they offer differentiated programming that addresses and integrates their special needs. Fortunately, research on the effective identification of these children has been promising, and suggestions

Table 1 Profiles of the Gifted and Talented

	Feelings and Attitudes	*Behaviors*	*Needs*	*Adults & Peers Perceptions of Type*	*Identification*	*Home Support*	*School Suport*
TYPE I: Successful	• Boredom • Dependent • Positive self-concept • Anxious • Guilty about failure • Extrinsic motivation • Responsible for others • Diminish feelings of self and rights to their emotion • Self-critical	• Perfectionist • High Achiever • Seeks teacher approval and structure • Non-risk taking • Does well academically • Accepts & conforms • Dependent	• To see deficiencies • To be challenged • To take risks • Assertiveness skills • Autonomy • Help with boredom • Appropriate curriculum	• Loved by teachers • Admired by peers • Loved & accepted by parents	• Grade point average • Achievement Test • IQ Tests • Teacher nominations	• Independence • Ownership • Freedom to make choices • Time for personal interests • Risk taking experiences	• Accelerated and enriched curriculum • Time for personal interests • Compacted learning experiences (pre-testing) • Opportunities to be with intellectual peers • Development of independent learning skills • In-depth studies • Mentorships • College & career counseling
TYPE II: Challenging	• Boredom • Frustration • Low self-esteem • Impatient • Defensive • Heightened sensitivity • Uncertain about social roles	• Corrects teacher • Questions rules, policies • Is honest, direct • Has mood swings • Demonstrates inconsistent work habits • Has poor self-control • Is creative • Prefers highly active & questioning approach • Stands up for convictions • Is competitive	• To be connected with others • To learn tact, flexibility, self-awareness, self-control, acceptance • Support for creativity • Contractual systems	• Find them irritating • Rebellious • Engaged in power struggle • See them as creative • Discipline problem • Peers see them as entertaining • Want to change them • Don't view as gifted	• Peer Recommendations • Parent nomination • Interviews • Performance • Recommendation from a significant, non-related adult • Creativity Testing • Teacher advocate	• Acceptance and understanding • Allow them to pursue interest • Advocate for them at school • Modeling appropriate behavior • Family projects	• Tolerance • Placement with appropriate teacher • Cognitive & social skill development • Direct and clear communication with child • Give permission for feelings • Studies in-depth • Mentorships • Build self-esteem • Behavioral contracting

(Continued)

Table 1 (Continued)

	Feelings and Attitudes	*Behaviors*	*Needs*	*Adults & Peers Perceptions of Type*	*Identification*	*Home Support*	*School Suport*
TYPE III: Underground	• Unsure • Pressure • Confused • Guilty • Insecure • Diminished feelings of self and rights to their emotions	• Denies talent • Drops out of G/T and advanced classes • Resists challenges • Wants to belong socially • Changes friends	• Freedom to make choices • To be aware of conflicts • Awareness of feelings • Support for abilities • Involvement with gifted peers • Career/college info. • Self-acceptance	• Viewed as leaders or unrecognized • Seen as average and successful • Perceived to be compliant • Seen as quiet/shy • Adults see them as unwilling to risk • Viewed as resistive	• Gifted peer nomination • Home nomination • Community nomination • Achievement testing • IQ Tests • Performance • Teacher advocate	• Acceptance of underground • Provide college & career planning experiences • Time to be with same age peers • Provide gifted role models • Model life-long learning • Give freedom to make choice	• Recognize & properly place • Give permission to take time out from G/T classes • Provide some sex role models • Continue to give college & career information
TYPE IV: Dropouts	• Resentment • Angry • Depressed • Explosive • Poor self-concept • Defensive • Burn-out	• Has intermittent attendance • Doesn't complete tasks • Pursues outside interests • "Spaced out" in class • Is self-abusive • Isolates self • Is creative • Criticizes self & others • Does inconsistent work • Is disruptive, acts out • Seems average or below • Is defensive	• An individualized program • Intense Support • Alternatives (separate, new opportunities) • Counseling (individual, group, and family) • Remedial help with skills	• Adults are angry with them • Peers are judgmental • Seen as loners, dropouts, dopers, or air heads • Reject them and ridicule • Seen as dangerous and rebellious	• Review cumulative folder • Interview earlier teachers • Descrepancy between IQ and demonstrated achievement • Incongruities and inconsistencies in performance • Creativity testing • Gifted peer recommendation • Demonstrated performance in non-school areas	• Seek counseling for family	• Diagnostic testing • Group counseling for young students • Nontraditional study skills • In-depth studies • Mentorships • Alternative out of classroom learning experiences • G.E.D.

(Continued)

Table I (Continued)

	Feelings and Attitudes	*Behaviours*	*Needs*	*Adults & Peers Perceptions of Type*	*Identification*	*Home Support*	*School Suport*
TYPE V: Double Labeled	• Powerless • Frustrated • Low self-esteem • Unaware • Angry	• Demonstrates inconsistent work • Seems average or below • May be disruptive or acts out	• Emphasis on strengths • Coping skills • G/T support group • Counseling • Skill development	• Seen as "dumb" • Viewed as helpless • Avoided by peers • Seen as average or below in ability • Perceived to require a great deal of imposed structure • Seen only for the disability	• Scatter of 11 points or more on WISC or WAIS • Recommendation of significant other • Recommendation from informed special ed. teacher • Interview • Performance • Teacher Advocate	• Recognize gifted abilities • Challenge them • Provide risk-taking opportunities • Advocate for child at school • Do family projects • Seek counseling for family	• Provide needed resources • Provide alternative learning experiences • Begin investigations and explorations • Give time to be with peers • Give individual counseling
TYPE VI: Autonomous	• Self-confident • Self-accepting • Enthusiastic • Accepted by others • Supported • Desire to know & learn • Accepts failure • Intrinsic motivation • Personal power • Accepts others	• Has appropriate social skills • Works independently • Develops own goals • Follows through • Works without approval • Follows strong areas of passion • Is creative • Stands up for convictions • Takes risks	• Advocacy • Feedback • Facilitation • Support for risks • Appropriate opportunities	• Accepted by peers and adults • Admired for abilities • Seen as capable and responsible by parents • Positive influences • Successful • Psychologically healthy	• Grade point average • Demonstrated performance • Products • Achievement Testing • Interviews • Teacher/Peer/Parent self-nominations • IQ tests • Creativity Testing	• Advocate for child at school and in community • Provide opportunities related to passions • Allow friends of all ages • Remove time and space restrictions • Do family projects • Include child in parent's passion	• Allow development of long-term, integrated plan of study • Accelerated and enriched curriculum • Remove time and space restrictions • Compacted learning experiences with pretesting • In-depth studies • Mentorships • College & career counseling and opportunities • Dual enrollment or early admission • Waive traditional school policies regulations

do exist for ways to provide programming alternatives (Daniels, 1983; Fox, Brody, & Tobin, 1983; Gunderson, Maesch, & Rees, 1988; Maker, 1977; and Whitmore & Maker, 1985).

Type V students often do not exhibit behaviors that schools look for in the gifted. They may have sloppy handwriting or disruptive behaviors that make it difficult for them to complete work, and they often seem confused about their inability to perform school tasks. They show symptoms of stress; they may feel discouraged, frustrated, rejected, helpless, or isolated.

These children may deny that they are having difficulty by claiming that activities or assignments are "boring" or "stupid." They may use their humor to demean others in order to bolster their own lagging self-esteem. They urgently want to avoid failures and are unhappy about not living up to their own expectations. They may be very skilled at intellectualization as a means of coping with their feelings of inadequacy. They are often impatient and critical and react stubbornly to criticism.

Traditionally, these students are either ignored because they are perceived as average or referred for remedial assistance. School systems tend to focus on their weaknesses and fail to nurture their strengths or talents.

TYPE VI: THE AUTONOMOUS LEARNER

The Type VI gifted child is the autonomous learner. Few gifted children demonstrate this style at a very early age although parents may see evidence of the style at home. Like the Type I's, these students have learned to work effectively in the school system. However, unlike the Type I's who strive to do as little as possible, Type VI's have learned to use the system to create new opportunities for themselves. They do not work for the system; they make the system work for them. Type VI's have strong, positive self-concepts because their needs are being met; they are successful, and they receive positive attention and support for their accomplishments as well as for who they are. They are well-respected by adults and peers and frequently serve in some leadership capacity within their school or community.

Type VI students are independent and self-directed. They feel secure designing their own educational and personal goals. They accept themselves and are able to take risks. An important aspect of the Type VI is their strong sense of personal power. They realize they can create change in their own lives, and they do not wait for others to facilitate change for them. They are able to express their feelings, goals, and needs freely and appropriately.

CONCLUSIONS

This matrix will be useful in a number of ways. One use is as a tool for inservicing educators about gifted and talented children and youth in general and about the differentiated social and emotional needs of the specified types in particular. The model can also be used as a teaching tool in order to expand students' awareness and understanding of the meaning of giftedness and the impact it has on their learning and relationships.

The model may also serve as a theoretical base for empirical research in the areas of definition, identification, educational planning, counseling, and child development. By looking closely at the behavior and feelings of gifted and talented youth, better educational programming may be developed to meet their diversified needs.

REFERENCES

Colangelo, N. and Parker, M. (1981). Value differences among gifted adolescents. *Counseling and Values, 26,* 35–41.

Daniels, P. R. (1983). *Teaching the gifted/learning disabled child.* Rockville, MD: Aspen Systems Corporation.

Delisle, J. R. (1982). Striking out: Suicide and the gifted adolescent. *Gifted/Creative/ Talented, 13,* 16–19.

Fox, L. H., Brody, L., and Tobin, D. (1983). *Learning-disabled/gifted children.* Baltimore: University Park Press.

Goertzel, V. and Goertzel, M. (1962). *Cradles of eminence.* Boston: Little, Brown and Company.

Gregory, E. H. and Stevens-Long, J. (1986). Coping skills among highly gifted adolescents. *Journal for the Education of the Gifted, 9,* 147–155.

Gunderson, C.W., Maesch, C., and Rees, J. W. (1988). The gifted/learning disabled student. *Gifted Child Quarterly, 31,* 158–160.

Kaiser, C. F., Berndt, D. J. and Stanley, G. (1987). Moral judgment and depression in gifted adolescents. Paper presented at the 7th World Conference on Gifted and Talented Children, Salt Lake City, Utah.

Kerr, B. (1985). *Smart girls, gifted women.* Columbus: Ohio Psychology.

Maker, J. (1977). *Providing programs for the gifted handicapped.* Reston, VA: Council for Exceptional Children.

Roeper, A. (1982). How the gifted cope with their emotions. *Roeper Review, 5,* 21–24.

Schlowinski, E. and Reynolds, C.R. (1985). Dimensions of anxiety among high IQ children. *Gifted Child Quarterly, 29,* 125–130.

Strang, R. (1965). The psychology of the gifted child. In W.B. Barbe, (Ed.). *Psychology and education of the gifted: Selected readings* (pp. 113–117). New York: Appleton-Century-Crofts.

Whitmore, J. R. and Maker, J. (1985). *Intellectual giftedness in disabled persons.* Rockville, MD: Aspen Systems Corporation.

9

Childhood Traits and Environmental Conditions of Highly Eminent Adults

Herbert J. Walberg, Shiow-Ling Tsai, Thomas Weinstein, Cynthia L. Gabriel, Sue Pinzur Rasher, Teresa Rosecrans, Evangelina Rovai, Judith Ide, Miguel Trujillo, and Peter Vukosavich

The extensive research of our team that has involved 76 scholars around the world reveals common psychological traits, as well as family, educational, and cultural conditions of more than 200 men (historically recognized as highly eminent) born between the 14th and 20th centuries, such as Mozart, Newton, and Lincoln. Ratings of their childhood characteristics and environments made on the basis of respected biographies show their distinctive intellectual competence and motivation, social and communication skills, general psychological wholesomeness, and both versatility as well as concentrated perseverance

Editor's Note: From Walberg, H. J., Tsai, S., Weinstein, T., Gabriel, C. L., Rasher, S. P., Rosecrans, T., Rovai, E., Ide, J., Trujillo, M., & Vukosavich, P. (1981). Childhood traits and environmental conditions of highly eminent adults. *Gifted Child Quarterly, 25*(3), 103–107.

during childhood. Most were stimulated by the availability of cultural stimuli and materials related to their field of eminence and by teachers, parents, and other adults. Although most had clear parental expectations for their conduct, they also had the opportunity for exploration on their own.

Our research combines psychology and "Cliometrics," the quantitative study of history, after Clio, the muse of history. The criterion of eminence employed (the number of words written about each man in biographical dictionaries and encyclopedias) proved technically reliable; but the ratings of traits and conditions are no doubt distorted to some extent by the accidents of what history and biography have recorded as well as the subjectivity involved in making the ratings. Our research proves little by itself; but since it corroborates recent studies on eminent living Americans (Arieti, 1976; Goertzel, Goertzel, & Goertzel, 1978; Passow, 1979; Stein & Heinze, 1964; Taylor & Barron, 1963; Taylor & Getzels, 1975) and accomplished, prize-winning adolescents in science and the arts (Walberg, 1969, 1971), it helps to maintain some balance both in research and policy between the need for minimal educational competencies and the desire to produce in our generations great men and women comparable to those of past centuries, through child-rearing and education practices and the provision of social and cultural opportunities.

Most research on educational effectiveness focuses on short-term gains made on standardized achievement tests in the usual school subjects such as reading, mathematics, and science. Although the importance of such learning cannot be denied, it is by no means the only intended outcome of schooling and child-rearing as school district goals and parental aspirations for their children attest. It is also well known that grades and achievement test scores for groups of students with the same amounts of education are at best only weakly predictive of adult happiness and accomplishments in the world outside school (Walberg, 1981). Thus it seems important to survey the psychological traits of eminent people and the educational and other environmental circumstances that may produce their development.

The sample of persons for our research traces back to the turn-of-the-century work of James McKean Cattell, founder of the biographical volumes *American Men of Science* (now called *American Men and Women of Science*). In 1903, Cattell listed in rank order of imputed eminence the 1,000 most eminent people according to the number of words that had been written about each in American, English, French, and German biographical dictionaries. The list included political and religious leaders, revolutionaries and militarists, scientists and philosophers, writers and artists, and aristocracy and nobility (Cattell, 1903).

Soon after Cattell's publication, Catherine Cox and the developer of the Stanford-Binet Intelligence Test, Frederick Terman, began a fascinating psychological study of part of Cattell's sample (Cox, 1926). They eliminated the least eminent half of the sample, persons who had apparently been included only because of aristocratic or noble birth, and those born before 1450. Cox and several associates combed more than 3,000 sources including encyclopedias, biographies, and collections of letters in the Stanford and Harvard University libraries for information on the mental development of each of the remaining 282 persons (including three women). From this information, Cox and two associates each independently estimated the IQ of each person. Cox's analysis and our own re-analysis of Cox's data show that the reliability of these careful estimates compares reasonably with that of group IQ tests now given to children in school classes (see Table 1).

INTELLIGENCE AND EMINENCE

The mean estimated IQ for the total group, 158.9, is far higher than the mean of about 100 which is found in unselected samples. The group ranges from Goethe, Leibnitz, and Grotius with estimated IQs between 195 and 200 to Massena, Grant, and Drake, between 120 and 125. Our analyses show philosophers to be significantly higher and militarists to be significantly lower in estimated IQ than the other groups: political and religious leaders, revolutionaries, scientists, writers, and artists.

For additional estimates of eminence, we counted the number of words in the primary biographical articles on each of the 282 persons in the 1935 New International Encyclopedia and the 1974 Encyclopedia Britannica. The indexes of eminence are in substantial agreement from one period to the next, but there are some interesting changes. For example, philosophers lost and musicians and artists gained in estimated eminence from 1903 to 1974. Individuals also shifted in estimated eminence: for example, starting with the most eminent, the top ten on the 1903 estimates are Napoleon, Voltaire, Bacon, Goethe, Luther, Burke, Newton, Milton, Pitt, and Washington; on the 1974 word counts, the top ten in order are Samuel Johnson, Luther, Rembrandt, Da Vinci, Napoleon, Washington, Lincoln, Goethe, Beethoven, and Dickens; on the 1974 citations, the top ten are Descartes, Napoleon, Newton, Leibnitz, Luther, Hegel, Kant, Darwin, Galileo, and Da Vinci.

Confirming Cox's analysis, we found that persons with the highest average of the four indexes of eminence had slightly higher estimated IQs (the correlation is + 0.33). There is no doubt that IQ and eminence are linked, but the linkage is by no means tight. Table 1 shows a sampling within each field of those near the top of the eminence and IQ distributions. It can be noted that the brightest are not necessarily the best. Research on recent samples of writers, scientists, and adolescents who have won awards and prizes suggests that outstanding performance in various fields requires minimal levels of intelligence. Intelligence higher than these levels, however, is less important than the presence of other psychological traits and conditions (Walberg, 1969, 1971).

CHILDHOOD TRAITS AND CONDITIONS

Our prior research concerns the traits of more than 2,000 American adolescents who won competitive awards and prizes in graphic and performing arts, music, writing, science, and social leadership. A number of traits were identified that characterize outstanding adolescents or that distinguish those who are outstanding in different fields. This research and that of other investigators on traits of recent samples of prize-winning adult artists, writers, scientists, and other groups helped the first author to formulate a list of 82 traits and conditions that appeared promising for the psychological study of Cox's sample.

But how can the incidence of the traits be estimated for a sample that lived between the years 1450 and 1850? Because Encyclopedia Britannica employs highly-screened historians and other scholars from throughout the world to write its biographical and other major articles, they constitute a group that may be as knowledgeable as can be found. For this reason, we asked biographers from the 1974 edition of Britannica to rate the presence or absence of the traits in the childhood through age 13 of the person from Cox's sample that he or she had written about. They were also asked to indicate the degree of confidence in their ratings.

A total of 76 rating forms with a reasonable degree of confidence were returned, and this sample was increased to 96 in two ways: In 1976, three graduate students, Eugenia Siepka, Jennifer Rautmen, and Barbara Fricke, made ratings of several eminent persons on Cox's list on the basis of the best available book-length biographies cited in the *Britannica* and ratings were obtained from Britannica biographers of persons in the upper part of Cattell's second set of 500, for example, Kierkegaard, Nietzche, and Turgenev. History not only continues to feature the adult accomplishments of persons in the sample but also has accumulated sufficient information to permit reasonably confident ratings of their childhood traits.

From 1978 through 1980, our team added to the sample by reading additional biographies cited in Britannica and also added 36 subjects whose lives spanned beyond 1850 such as Tschaikovsky, Whistler, and Marx so that there would be reasonable sample sizes for each of the ten spheres of eminence (see Table 1). In all, our researchers and the biographies made 297 ratings of 221 eminent men (ratings made more than once for some men were averaged).

In an effort to avoid bias, our team members, although trained through the master's level in educational and psychological research, were asked before joining the project, to avoid reading research literature on eminence and creativity and to carry out the ratings as independently of one another as possible. The first author who designed the research and rating form made no ratings.

CHARACTERISTIC TRAITS

Table 2 shows the percentages of the 221 eminent persons who possessed the cognitive, affective, and physical traits listed and who were exposed to the specific familial, educational, and cultural conditions. With the exception of cultural conditions, nearly all the results are statistically significant and corroborate research on accomplished adolescents and eminent adults in recent decades.

A principal components analysis showed that 14 sets of intercorrelated traits could be summed. The factors, their composition, and internal consistency reliabilities are: **eminence percentile:** normalized 1903 rank, 1936 word count, 1974 word count and number of citations to other articles (.81); **fluid:** complex, expressive, fantasizing, imaginative, and introspective (.80); **concentrated:** concentrated and discipline (.69); **persevering:** desired to excel, hard working, strong need to achieve, strove for distant goals, persistent, and serious (.82); **empirical:** attentive to detail, curious, and observant (.72); **versatile:** versatile and well-rounded (.52); **solid:** showed common sense, forthright, constructively reactive to crises, realistic, reliable, self-sufficient, and stable (.77); **challenging:** argumentative, *conforming, humble,* rebellious, critical, and *tolerant* (.75); **introverted:** brooding, inhibited, introverted, shy, and solitary (.80); **neurotic:** felt inferior, frustrated, and persecuted (.73); **opportunistic:** manipulative of others and opportunistic (.66); **firm:** dominant, firm, and strong will (.72); **popular:** loving, playful, and popular (.67); and **vitality:** athletic, healthy, and masculine (.74). The italicized traits are reversed in scoring.

The most distinctive of all the childhood traits is intelligence; 97% were rated intelligent, which confirms the Cox-Terman IQ estimates. Other more wide-ranging cognitive traits, however, are also highly characteristic of the sample. The group as a whole exhibited convergent and divergent ability ranging from concentration and perseverance to versatility and fluidity. The group, as children, also had superior communication skills. The one trait in Table 2 that is uncharacteristic of the sample is "economic;" only 38% were given this rating, which also corroborates research on eminent twentieth-century adults (although, in retrospect, the term seems a poor choice because it might mean penurious, pecuniary, or realistic economizing of scarce resources, including one's own energies to attain selected goals; and it is the last that probably promotes great accomplishments).

The majority of the sample also showed a large number of distinctive affective traits that collectively suggest psychological wholesomeness: ethical, sensitive, solid, magnetic, optimistic, and popular (Table 2). About a quarter to a third of the sample, however, showed introversion, neuroses, and physical sickliness. Only 38% were rated tall but the majority were handsome and possessed vitality.

Table 2 also shows the percentages of the sample exposed to family, educational, and cultural conditions during childhood. Only slightly more than half were encouraged by parents but a solid majority were encouraged by teachers and other adults and were exposed to many adults at an early age. Significantly more than half, 60%, were exposed to eminent persons during childhood.

About 80% were successful in school, the majority liked it, and less than a quarter had school problems. Seventy percent had clear parental expectations for their conduct; but nearly 9 out of 10 were permitted to explore their

Table 1 Samples of Eminent and/or Intelligent Persons and Groups Characteristics

Group and Sample Names	*IQ*	*Eminence Percentile*	*Group higher on:*	*Group lower on:*
32 Statesmen				
Franklin, Benjamin	160	88	Persuasive, economic, firm, magnetic, optimistic, popular, handsome, tall, liked by siblings, successful in school, cultural media in field of eminence restricted to privileged classes	Made analogies, concentrated, introverted, neurotic, single-minded, absence of father, only child, school problems, cultural emphasis on immediate gratification, strong external incentives and support of work in field of eminence
Grotius, Hugo	197	62		
Jefferson, Thomas	160	89		
Lincoln, Abraham	147	91		
17 Generals				
Bolivar, Simon	145	54	Questioning, tall, vitality, strong, external incentives and support in field of eminence	Made analogies, skill in writing, scholarly, handsome, encouragement of others, encouragement of teacher, exposed to many adults at an early age, presence of significant persons working in concert in field of eminence
Jackson, Thomas Jonathan	132	80		
Bonaparte, Napoleon	142	99		
Washington, George	135	93		
21 Religious Leaders				
Bossuet, Jacques B.	177	60	Concentrated, joy in work, scholarly, precocious, ethical, philosophical, religious, sensitive, encouragement of mother, encouragement of others, exposed to many adults at an early age, early exposure to eminent persons, strong external incentives and support for work in field of eminence	Versatile, impatient, permitted to explore, openness and receptivity to varied cultures and ideas
Calvin, John	165	92		
Luther, Martin	157	97		
Melanchthon, Philipp	180	68		
23 Essayists, Historians, Critics and Sociologists				
John, Samuel	165	87	Fluid, made analogies, persevering, intelligent, precocious, religious, sensitive, solid, challenging, absence of father, encouragement of mother, clear parental expectations of conduct, cultural stimuli or materials related to field of eminence available, cultural emphasis on immediate gratification, strict social class structure with little mobility, openness and receptivity to varied cultures and ideas	Economic, empirical and opportunistic
Macaulay, Thomas	180	57		
Rousseau, J. J.	150	91		
Sarpi, Paolo	187	10		
43 Poets, Novelists and Dramatists				
Goethe, J.W.	200	96	Concentrated, challenging, neurotic, absence of father, only child, liked school	Persuasive, questioning, persevering, scholarly, competent, empirical, intelligent, philosophical, religious, magnetic,
Leopardi, Giacomo	185	13		
Milton, John	167	88		
Voltaire, Arouet, de	185	92		

(Continued)

Table 1 (Continued)

Group and Sample Names	*IQ*	*Eminence Percentile*	*Group higher on:*	*Group lower on:*
				optimistic, popular, handsome, tall, encouragement of mother, liked by siblings, permitted to explore, clear parental expectations of conduct, cultural stimuli or materials related to field of eminence available, revolutionary period in field of eminence, openness and receptivity to varied cultures and ideas
21 Musicians				
Bach, J. Sebastian	152	77	Competent, opportunistic, single-minded, popular, encouragement of father, encouragement of teacher, cultural emphasis on immediate gratification	Questioning, skill in speaking, empirical, intelligent, precocious, ethical, solid optimistic, absence of father, absence of mother
Beethoven, Ludwig Van	157	92		
Mendelssohn, Felix	162	56		
Mozart, W. A.	162	88		
18 Artists				
Dürer, Albrecht	150	86	Fluid, competent, empirical, ethical, wholesome, challenging, optimistic, popular, handsome, vitality, liked by siblings, revolutionary period in field of eminence, openness and receptivity to varied cultures and ideas, presence of significant persons working in concert in field of eminence, strong external incentives and support of work in field of eminence	Sensitive, single-minded, successful in school, cultural media in field of eminence restricted to privileged classes
Buonarroti, Michelangelo	170	94		
Rubens, Peter Paul	155	87		
Vinci, Leonardo da	167	94		
19 Philosophers				
Bacon, Francis	172	94	Questioning, empirical, intelligent, versatile, philosophical, challenging, clear parental expectations of conduct, permitted to explore	Concentrated, economic, religious, sensitive, opportunistic, popular, handsome, sickly, tall, vitality, encouragement of father, encouragement of mother, encouragement of teacher, only child, liked school, successful in school, cultural emphasis on immediate gratification, strong external incentives and support of work in field of eminence
Descartes, René	175	93		
Leibnitz, Gottfried Wilhelm, von	200	92		
Spinoza, Baruch	172	84		
22 Scientists				
Darwin, Charles R.	160	89	Opportunistic, single-minded, absence of mother	Fluid, sensitive, clear parental expectation of conduct
Haller, Albrecht	185	33		
Newton, Isaac	170	92		
Pascal, Blaise	192	81		

environments on their own, obviously a delicate, important balance in child rearing and teaching.

SOCIAL AND CULTURAL CONDITIONS

The social and cultural ratings (Table 2) require special caution in interpretation. The list of environmental conditions that were rated for each man's childhood was taken from Silvano Arieti's (1976) book, which contains arguments and anecdotes suggesting that the conditions are associated with creativity. Unlike the traits and other conditions, much opinion but little systematic evidence for corroboration is published. Our ratings, nonetheless, support Arieti's hypotheses in the sense that from 30 to 77% of the sample were raised under the conditions he specified. To take the extreme cases, for example, less than a third were exposed to a cultural emphasis on immediate gratification but more than three-quarters had cultural stimuli and materials available in their field of evidence. More research on these conditions may or may not confirm these findings.

DIFFERENTIATING TRAITS AND ENVIRONMENTS

Note that in Table 1, the last two columns show the traits and conditions that appear significantly (probability less than .05) more (and less) prominently in each field as compared to the other fields. The distinguishing characteristics of men in each field generally support previous research and match what might be considered personality traits and conditions required to some extent for excellence. Statesmen, for example, had superior personal attractiveness and social skills, and less intense cognitive traits and psychic disorders than those in other groups. Scientists were more single-minded and less sensitive. Essayists made more analogies and were more challenging, precocious, and persevering.

CONCLUSION

"The childhood shows the man, as morning shows the day," wrote John Milton in 1667. Our research on childhood traits of highly eminent people confirms the poet's wisdom. Outstanding traits and conditions of childhood can be identified that foreshadow the degree and the kind of eminence that history records. But, as rainy afternoons sometime follow sunny mornings contrary to expectations, the childhood traits and conditions are possible clues or indications of adult eminence rather than certain predictors.

Table 2 Traits and Environmental Conditions of 221 Eminent Men

Traits		Environments	
Cognitive		**Family and Educational Conditions**	
Fluid	91*	Absence of father	29*
Made analogies	74*	Absence of mother	22*
Persuasive	75*	Encouragement of father	60
Questioning	91*	Encouragement of mother	55
Skill in speaking	79*	Encouragement of others	78*
Skill in writing	82*	Encouragement of teacher	70*
Concentrated	77*	Exposed to many adults at an early stage	80*
Joy in work	87*	Early exposure to eminent persons	60
Persevering	91*	First born	36*
Scholarly	77*	Only child	13*
Competent	79*	Liked by siblings	77*
Economic	38*	Clear parental expectations of conduct	70*
Empirical	93*	Permitted to explore	82*
Intelligent	97*	Liked school	67*
Precocious	79*	School problems	23*
Versatile	86*	Successful in school	79*
Affective and Physical			
Ethical	85*	**Social and Cultural Conditions**	
Philosophical	73*	Cultural stimuli or materials related to field of eminence available	77*
Religious	67*	Cultural emphasis on immediate gratification	30*
Sensitive	68*	Revolutionary period in field of eminence	51
Solid	84*	Strict social class structure with little mobility	62*
Wholesome	70*	Cultural media in field of eminence restricted to privileged classes	46
Challenging	54	Openness and receptivity to varied cultures and ideas	46
Impatient	44	Presence of significant persons working in concert in field of eminence	57
Introverted	36*	Strong external incentives and support of work in field of eminence	57
Neurotic	26*		
Opportunistic	56		
Single-minded	60		
Firm	81*		
Magnetic	64*		
Optimistic	77*		
Popular	73*		
Handsome	62*		
Sickly	29*		
Tall	38*		
Vitality	61*		

* Significantly different from a 50–50 even split at the .05 level

REFERENCES

Arieti, S. *Creativity: The magic synthesis.* NYC: Basic Books, 1976.

Cattell, J. M. A statistical study of eminent men. *Popular Science Monthly,* February 1903, 359–377.

Cox, C. M. *The early mental traits of three hundred geniuses.* Stanford, CA: Stanford University Press, 1926.

Goertzel, M.G., Goertzel, V., & Goertzel, T. G. *300 eminent personalities.* San Francisco: Jossey-Bass, 1978.

Passow, A. H. *The gifted and the talented.* Chicago: National Society for the Study of Education, 1979.

Stein, M. E., & Heinze, S. J. *Creativity and the individual.* Chicago: Free Press of Glencoe, 1964.

Taylor, C. W., & Barron, F. *Scientific creativity: Its recognition and development.* NYC: Wiley & Sons, 1963.

Walberg, H. J. A portrait of the artist and scientist as young men. *Exceptional Children,* September 1969, 5–11.

Walberg, H. J. Varieties of adolescent creativity and the high school environment. *Exceptional Children,* October, 1971, 111–116.

Walberg, H. J. A psychological theory of educational productivity. In N. Gordon & F. H. Farley (Eds.), *Psychology and education: The state of the union.* Berkeley, CA: McCutchan, 1981.

10

Developmental Potential of the Gifted

Michael M. Piechowski

Nicholas Colangelo

Many authors have addressed the question of the nature of giftedness and talent only to discover that many factors, components, traits, facets, and potentialities are not captured by the tests in use (Bloom, 1963; Gallagher, 1975; Hoyt, 1966; Nicholls, 1972; Passow, 1981; Wing & Wallach, 1971). That a gifted child is not reliably the parent to a gifted adult—not all gifted children fulfill their promise and adult late bloomers are not counted earlier among the gifted—has been established over and over again; it has been said that the psychometric approach has failed in its predictive promise (Feldman, 1977; Gruber, 1982; Renzulli, 1978). But the problem of what makes for mature giftedness and talent remains; what are all those contributing skills, endowments, or personal powers by which true giftedness is recognized?

Inevitably our approaches are a function of our definitions, be they explicit or implicit. Terman's definition of intellectual giftedness as the top one percent

---

Editor's Note: From Piechowski, M.M., & Colangelo, N. (1984). Developmental potential of the gifted. *Gifted Child Quarterly, 28*(2), 80-88. © 1984 National Association for Gifted Children. Reprinted with permission.

of the population on a standardized measure established a method of deciding who was gifted and who was not. Now Renzulli's (1978) proposal to use three clusters of ingredients of giftedness—above average ability, task commitment, and creativity—provides a new, explicit definition and a new strategy. Implicit in this definition is the criterion of social usefulness: the three clusters are found together in people who are productive and who make creative contributions in their fields of endeavor. Newland (1976) went so far as to suggest periodic adjustment of the definition of who is gifted, based on social demand.

The criteria of productivity and social usefulness deal only with the optimal combination of many capabilities and fail to look at them individually, independently of their social application. Albert (1975), for example, defined genius in terms of early start and sustained productivity but left out of the picture the structure of a mind that works in unprecedented ways. A person with a 160 IQ who is not creative or productive still possesses a set of unusual mental gifts. A chess champion's extraordinary capacity for solving chess problems does not make him or her creative, nor does it make him or her productive—winning prizes produces little except a perpetuation of chess competitions. Yet, a chess master has unusual and fascinating mental capabilities whose workings can be studied to produce knowledge and *understanding of human intelligence.*

From the point of view of research and theory, studying a phenomenon in its pure form is the more fruitful approach. A criterion of social usefulness would limit us to a social definition of a phenomenon which is not of social origin. Giftedness begins with some form of native endowment, the organism's original equipment. Feldman (1979), Gardner (1982), and Sternberg (1980) take the more basic approach: they strive to identify specific units of mental equipment, or, as Gardner is fond of calling them, "specific computational devices." Investigating the workings of such units or devices, one can uncover the way they are designed (that is, the way they evolved to carry out specific functions) and then see how their different versions combine in each individual. The purest examples of such units operating without connection with other critical units of the mental apparatus are found in *idiots savants,* autistic children, child prodigies, and patients with localized brain damage (Gardner, 1975). Gardner (1982, p. 51) says:

> I propose that human cognitive competence be thought of as consisting of a number of autonomous, or semi-autonomous, domains of intellect. Each of these intellectual competences has its own genetic origins and limitations as well as its own neuroanatomical substrate or substrates . . . These intellectual competences or "intelligences" have evolved over millions of years in order to carry out specific hominoid problem-solving and production activities, including finding one's way around the environment, making tools, and communicating and interacting successfully with other individuals . . . All normal individuals possess some potential for developing each of the intellectual competences, but individuals differ from one another in the extent to which they can and will realize each competence.

The advantage of this approach is that it provides the logical basis for individual psychology, that is, for the study of structure and design of mental processes and the manner in which their elements vary across individuals, as opposed to the study of individual differences in terms of group norms and deviations from such norms. This structural or "faculties" approach is eminently suited for the study of the gifted individual.

THE MODEL OF DEVELOPMENTAL POTENTIAL

The model to be presented here follows similar principles. It defines five parallel dimensions or modes of mental functioning assumed to be genetically independent of one another. In this model, the strength of these five dimensions is taken to be a measure of the person's developmental potential (DP), hence, also of the person's giftedness (Piechowski, 1979). Everything we have discovered so far—intellective factors, motivational factors, special aptitudes, Gardner's "intelligences"—all are part of a picture which is always incomplete. The model of developmental potential *fills in certain broad and important areas.*

The five modes encompassed by the model are represented by five forms of so-called psychic overexcitability. This term was first introduced by Dabrowski (1938) to describe an expanded and intensified manner of experiencing in the psychomotor, sensual, intellectual, imaginational, and emotional areas. The prefix *over* in overexcitability is meant to convey that this is a special kind of responding, experiencing, and acting, one that is enhanced and distinguished by characteristic forms of expression.

As personal traits, overexcitabilities are often not valued socially, being viewed instead as nervousness, hyperactivity, neurotic temperament, excessive emotionality, and emotional intensity that most people find uncomfortable at close range. Dabrowski, perceiving their developmental significance, deliberately gave these manifestations a new name. He was not the first to see the positive side of such a temperament which, in a still earlier epoch, was called "psychopathic." William James (1902, p. 26) saw in the intensity and overemphasis of highly emotional people a necessary condition of being genuinely rather than superficially moral:

> Few of us are not in some way infirm, or even diseased; and our very infirmities help us unexpectedly. In the psychopathic temperament we have the emotionality which is the *sine qua non* of moral perception; we have the intensity and tendency to emphasis which are the essence of moral vigor; and we have the love of metaphysics and mysticism which carry one's interests beyond the surface of the sensible world . . . If there were such a thing as inspiration from a higher realm, it might well be that the neurotic temperament would furnish the chief condition of the requisite receptivity.

And further (p. 24–25).

> But the psychopathic temperament . . . often brings with it ardor and excitability of character. The cranky person has extraordinary emotional susceptibility. He is liable to fixed ideas and obsessions. His conceptions tend to pass immediately into belief and action; and when he gets a new idea, he has no rest till he proclaims it, or in some way "works it off." "What shall I think of it?" a common person says to himself about a vexed question; but in a "cranky" mind "What must I do about it?" is the form the question tends to take . . . Thus, when a superior intellect and a psychopathic temperament coalesce—as in the endless permutations and combinations of human faculty, they are bound to coalesce often enough—in the same individual, we have the best possible condition for the effective genius that gets into the biographical dictionaries. Such men do not remain mere critics and understanders with their intellect. Their ideas possess them, they inflict them, for better or worse, upon their companions or their age.

Here James connects superior intellect and heightened emotional excitability. His "effective genius that gets into the biographical dictionaries" is the operational genius of Albert and Renzulli. He describes characteristics which endow certain individuals with capabilities absent in others, capabilities that open doors to other realms, that make these individuals see certain truths with unusual vividness, and that compel them to seek answers to questions which to others are only matters of opinion. Gallagher (1975, p. 64), more recently, echoes an aspect of James' insight in his view that hyperactivity might, under some conditions, be an asset to intellectual development. Both James and Gallagher describe what are, in Dabrowski's appellation, forms of psychic overexcitability. Let us review these five forms briefly. All of the illustrative examples given below are direct quotes from gifted adolescents (see Note 1). A more detailed description exists (Piechowski, 1979).

Psychomotor overexcitability (P) may be viewed as an organic excess of energy, or heightened excitability of the neuromuscular system. It may manifest itself as a love of movement for its own sake—rapid speech, pursuit of intense physical activity, impulsiveness, restlessness, pressure for action, or drivenness; the capacity for being active and energetic.

> When I am around my friends, I usually come up with so much energy I don't know where it came from. Also when I am bored, I get sudden urges and lots of energy that can be dealt with by doing a physical sport or activity such as bike riding, jogging, walking, or playing basketball. Sometimes during class (it happens quite often) I get bored because I understand what is being taught, and get a lot of energy. This energy is used to goof off, even though I know I shouldn't. The energy seems to just swell up inside of me, then just flows over. Honestly, some classes are boring and I wish those who understand could go ahead and work, then maybe I wouldn't use my energy so harmfully. (Female, age 13)

[I have the greatest urge to do something] mainly when I haven't been doing anything. Like when I've been doing a long homework assignment or sitting typing more of my book I suddenly get the urge to shoot some baskets or bike ride or something. Usually I just get up and walk around for a while if I'm really in need of finishing my homework. If not I usually go outside and let my dog chase me around for a while. (Male, age 15)

Sensual overexcitability (S) is expressed in the heightened experience of sensual pleasure and in seeking sensual outlets for inner tension. Beyond desires for comfort, luxury, stereotyped or refined beauty, and the pleasure in being admired and taking the limelight, sensual overexcitability may be expressed in the simple pleasure of taste and smell, for instance, the smell of car exhaust. In short, it is the capacity for sensual enjoyment.

I love to have something that tastes good in my mouth. I just really enjoy good tasting things. If I taste something I like I can't stop eating it. (Male, age 14)

[What kind of physical activity (or inactivity) gives you the most satisfaction?] If I said sex would you die laughing or just be shocked? (Female, age 16)

[Is tasting something very special to you?] Yes, it is. Maybe that's why I'm so "picky." Taste depends on flavor, texture, consistency, smell, color and appearance. Beans are so gross! They are just *there,* they don't *do* anything for you. Whipped potatoes in butter—*they* are fun! You can do anything with them! Not that food has to be fun—simply being good in flavor is all right, too! (I don't mean to sound like a Jell-O commercial. Watch it shimmer!). (Female, age 16)

Intellectual overexcitability (T) is associated with an intensified activity of the mind. Its strongest expressions—persistence in asking probing questions, avidity for knowledge and analysis, preoccupation with logic, and theoretical problems—have more to do with striving for understanding and truth than with academic learning and achievement. Other expressions are: a sharp sense of observation, independence of thought (often expressed in criticism), symbolic thinking, development of new concepts, striving for synthesis of knowledge; a capacity to search for knowledge and truth.

I can't resist math puzzles, or brain teasers of any kind, and I go to ridiculous lengths to figure them out. When I'm being sensible I know they're a waste of time, but I can't see one without working it out. I guess I'm conceited—I don't like to think that there is anything I can't figure out. My favorite puzzles are the logic puzzles in which they give a set of facts that must be combined in order to find the answer. (Female, age 16)

> Yes. [I think about my own thinking,] sometimes I get a long line of thinking and I go back and trace from where I started, and usually it is from the most insignificant thing, or, I am appalled at how I have compared something. (Male, age 14)
>
> I don't very often [catch myself seeing or imagining things that aren't really there.] Instead, I analyze things that are there in different ways. I read stories deeper, read into questions, find catchy puns or mistakes of words in people's writings, etc. If something has no meaning I try to give it some. If it means something I wonder why. I usually find when given a topic to write about, for example, I usually have a completely different approach to the same topic than does the rest of the class. (Male, age 16)

Imaginational overexcitability (M) is recognized through rich association of images and impressions, inventiveness, vivid and often animated visualization, use of image and metaphor in speaking and writing. Dreams are vivid and can be retold in detail. Living in the world of fantasy, predilection for fairy and magic tales, poetic creations, imaginary companions, or dramatizing to escape boredom are also observed.

> I like to think about things not too many people do. Like what will fire hydrants look like in the future.
>
> Sometimes I used to pretend I had a little brother or sister, or I would imagine myself in a rabbit hole watching thousands of wild horses galloping over me. (Female, age 13)
>
> I also have one [fantasy] in which I can get inside people's heads to see what "makes them go" or can make everything and everyone freeze in their tracks (everyone except me) so I can go around and see what they are doing. (Male, age 15)
>
> In a real event, if it does not particularly interest me, I only see a few highlights. If it is a real event that terrifically interests me I only see the main highlights and supporting details. If it is imaginary I can visualize it down to the last detail. I do this a lot. I also take real events and change them around in my imagination to make them appeal more to me. (Male, age 15)

Emotional overexcitability (E) is recognized in the way emotional relationships are experienced, in strong attachments to persons, living things or places, and in the great intensity of feeling and awareness of its full range. Characteristic expressions are: inhibition (timidity and shyness) and excitation (enthusiasm); strong affective recall of past experiences, concern with death, fears, anxieties, depressions; there may be an intense loneliness, and an intense desire to offer love, a concern for others. There is a high degree of differentiation of interpersonal feeling. Emotional overexcitability is the basis of one's relation to self through self-evaluation and self-judgment, coupled with a sense of responsibility, compassion, and responsiveness to others.

> When I kill a fly or an ant or any other insect, I suddenly get a feeling like, "Should I have done that? That's really just like going and killing a human being. I bet the animals have their own life, feelings, they must because they are really very intelligent." The next time a fly gets in the way, I usually just let it go, because I feel guilty. (Female, age 13)
>
> I spend my time writing poetry once in a while. Every time I write a poem, it comes out as a poem about someone I love, something I love, something that won't always be around or something special to me. Sometimes I write of sad things to take the hurt out of me. I can never write poetry unless it is something *very special* to me. (Male, age 13)
>
> [If you ask yourself, "Who am I" what is the answer?] Usually the answer is: An insignificant human speck in the vast universe trying to make something out of itself but will probably not succeed. A biological imperfect being destined for certain death in the end and being forgotten even though it attempted to make something of itself. But sometimes I get an irrational response: You are a perfect intelligence. You are destined to become a powerful person. This response sometimes scares me. (Male, age 15)

The above examples are taken from responses given by gifted youngsters to the Overexcitability Questionnaire (OEQ). The method and the different studies to be compared here are described below.

This study is an attempt to assess components of giftedness defined by the model of developmental potential, that is, the strength of the five modes of mental functioning. The model combines both the intellective—represented by T—and the nonintellective components—represented by E, M, S, and P—of giftedness.

By choosing to compare overexcitability profiles of gifted adolescents with those of gifted and nongifted adults we sought to obtain a cross-sectional view of the development of these variables.

METHOD

Subjects

Subject samples come from several studies. Iowa gifted adolescents ($N = 49$), 26 girls and 23 boys, age 12–17, mean age 14.8, were drawn from gifted programs in seven schools scattered throughout the state, part of a study by Colangelo, Piechowski, and Kelly (Note 1). Their entry into these gifted programs was based on a combination of test scores, grades, and teacher nominations. Volunteer participants formed this sample and all the other samples in the study. The intellectually gifted adults, $N = 28$, 21 women and 7 men, age 22–55, mean age 36.4, are from a study by Silverman and Ellsworth (1981). They were either Mensa members (98th percentile or better on a standard test of intelligence) or persons qualified for similar status on the basis of high GRE, SAT, IQ scores, former placement in gifted classes, or known and recognized scholarly achievement. The artists, $N = 19$, 12 women and 7 men, age 18–59, mean age 33.9, are from a study by Piechowski, Silverman, Falk, and Cunningham (Note 2). They include writers, poets, singers (rock and classical), film producers, dancers-choreographers, a graphic designer, and a weaver. The graduate students, $N = 42$, 30 women and 12 men, age 22–50, mean age 29, are taken from a study by Lysy and Piechowski (1983). They include students in counseling, history, linguistics, natural science, education, library science, political science, and religious studies. We assume most of them are not gifted, based partly on the content of their responses and partly on the fact that their mean overexcitability scores are nearly identical to those of a sample of community women ($N = 51$) whose mean number of years of schooling (15.12) and general level of achievement are lower than those of graduate students (Beach, 1980).

Instrument

The Overexcitability Questionnaire (OEQ) is a 21-item, free-response instrument with half a page blank per item. It is derived from an earlier longer questionnaire (Piechowski, 1979; Lysy & Piechowski, 1983). Subjects write their responses at their leisure. On each of the 21 items, one point is scored for each OE that can be identified in the response. For example, in the following excerpt in answer to the question, "What kinds of things get your mind going," we can identify an element of intellectual overexcitability in the girl's interest in math problems and in her urge to pursue problems to completion, imaginational overexcitability in her eidetic-like experience while reading, and emotional overexcitability in her feeling for the characters in the story:

> Right now, the problems we are doing in Senior Math get my mind going. I really don't like to leave things unanswered but sometimes they are pretty frustrating. I can also get pretty involved in some of the books I read. Sometimes I feel as though I am right there where it is happening and I can feel emotion for the characters. (Female, age 17)

This response is scored one point for each of the three forms of OE: T, M, and E. The total score is thus a simple frequency count of the number of responses in which a given OE was observed. The highest possible score is 21 for each of the five OEs. The questions, as also illustrated in the foregoing example, do not predetermine the OE mode of the response because for many people, not only intellectual stimuli but emotions, images, sensual pleasures, or sports can get their mind going as well.

The scoring procedure is conservative: responses minimally adequate to be regarded as expression of an OE are given the same weight of 1 as responses

Figure 1 Intellectual overexcitability scores in four different samples

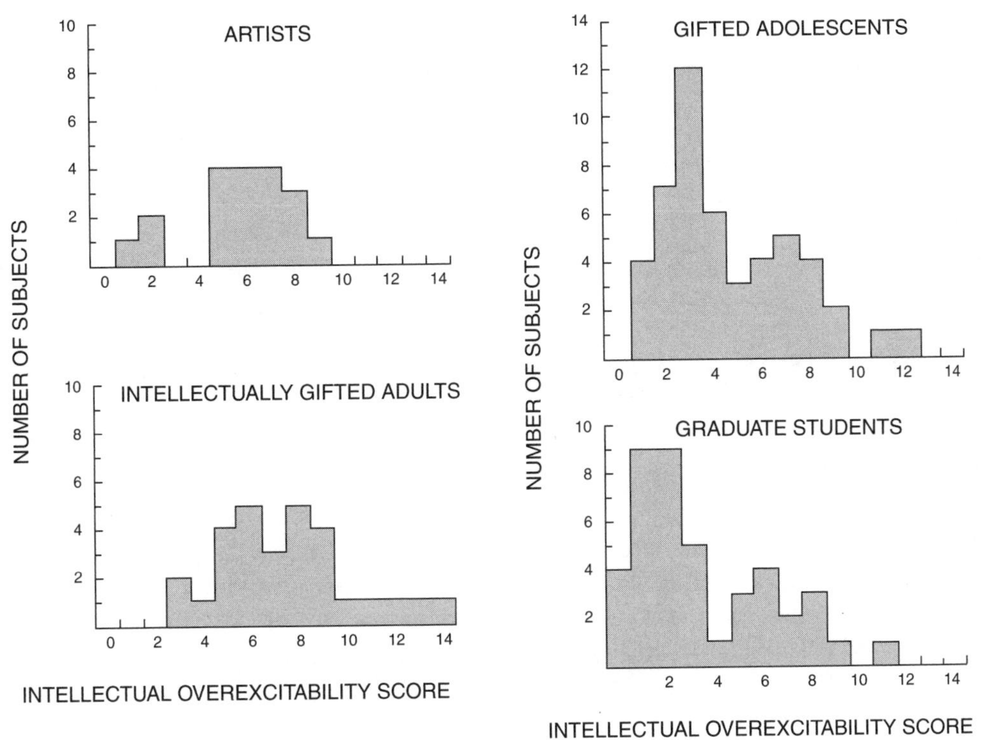

containing richly elaborated and multiple expressions of an OE. What compensates for this to some degree is that subjects with abundant OEs tend to generate OE material more often,—more items of their OEQ protocols receive OE scores.[1]

The OEQ protocols are rated independently by two raters. Disagreements on item scores are resolved by arriving at a consensus. The interrater correlation coefficients (Pearson's *r*'s), obtained with different pairs of raters prior to consensus, range from .60 to .95, most commonly from .70 to .80. The correlation between the individual rater's score and the final consensus scores is on the average .82 (Piechowski, Silverman, Falk, & Cunningham, Note 2).

Data Analysis

Figure 1 shows that the scores in our samples are not normally distributed. For this reason, the nonparametric Mann-Whitney two-sample rank test was used in all comparisons. Also, this procedure allows a comparison between samples of unequal size. The Mann-Whitney test gives a p value for the probability of the two samples having an identical distribution of scores. The smaller the p, the farther apart are the sample distributions. Hence, the more different they are from each other in regard to the variable measured.

Table 1 Mean Overexcitability Scores of Intellectually Gifted Adults, Gifted Adolescents, and Graduate Students

Overexcitability (OE)	*A Gifted Adults N=28*	P_{AB}	*B Gifted Adolescents N=49*	P_{BC}	*C Graduate Students N=42*	P_{AC}
Psychomotor: P	3.61	.071	7.31	.55	3.00	.18
Sensual: S	4.43	.0000	4.96	.0014	3.36	.11
Intellectual: T	7.46	.0001	4.59	.015	3.40	.0000
Imaginational: M	5.18	.86	1.76	.033	3.69	.11
Emotional: E	7.39	.40	2.90	.0002	4.79	.01

Note: The value of p, obtained by the Mann-Whitney test, represents the probability of the two samples having an identical distribution of scores.

RESULTS

Table 1 shows the mean overexcitability scores of three groups: intellectually gifted adults (A), gifted adolescents (B), and graduate students (C). Three comparisons are made: gifted versus nongifted adults (A versus C), young versus adult gifted (A versus B), and gifted adolescents versus nongifted adults (B versus C). The first comparison shows that gifted adults are characterized by significantly higher scores on T, and E OEs than nongifted adults. The second comparison shows that the younger gifted group is characterized by lower scores on S and T OEs but similar to the adult gifted on M and E OEs. The third comparison combines the gifted versus nongifted and young versus adult tests of difference. The gifted adolescents are again lower than the adult graduate students on S, leading to the conclusion that sensuality has more to do with age (maturity) than with giftedness. The gifted adolescents, like the adults in the first comparison, are higher than the graduates on T and E OEs, supporting the conclusion that these two OEs are characteristic of giftedness. The gifted adolescents are also significantly higher on M OE lending support to the significance of a similar difference on M between the gifted adults and graduate students.

Psychomotor OE provided no significant differences between these three groups. The level of sensual OE appears to be a function of age. We are left with T, E, and M OEs as the significant variables distinguishing a gifted from a nongifted sample. The graduate students' significantly lower scores on these three principal OEs are consistent with the assumption of the graduates' largely nongifted status.

If the gifted adolescents' lower S scores are a function of age, is their lower T score also a function of age? It could be that the lower mean score of the younger group is not a function of age but of a heterogeneity in the score distribution. Figure 1 shows that this is so. The distribution of T scores for gifted adolescents is bimodal. The same is true of the graduate group. The lower graduate group has T scores from 0 to 3, the higher from 5 on up. The lower adolescent group has T scores from 1 to 4, the higher from 5 on up. Ninety percent of the gifted adults (25 out of 28) have T scores of 5 or more. Eighty-four percent

Figure 2 Bimodality in the distribution of intellectual overexcitability scores when the samples depicted in Figure 1 are combined (*N* = 138). Dotted line represents the scores of gifted children, ages 9, 11, and 13, from the University for Youth in Denver (*N* = 41)

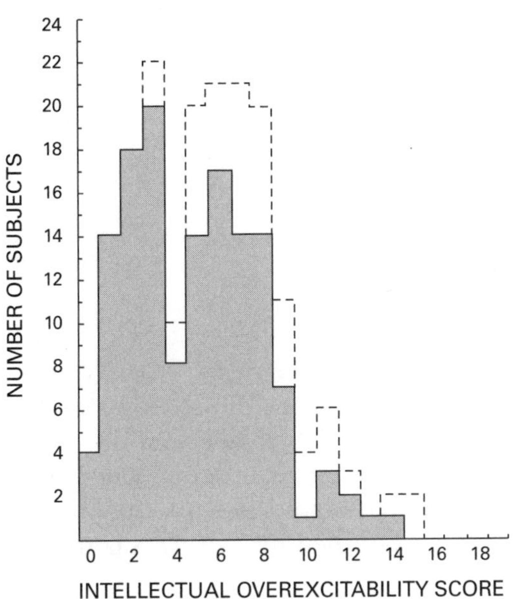

of the artists (16 out of 19) also have a score of 5 or more (this is why this group is included here). We are simply noting that a numerical cliff between the scores of T = 4 and T = 5 occurs in four independent samples. When all the samples are added together (N = 138) the deep cleft at T = 4 is clearly visible (Figure 2).

The bimodality of the T score distribution suggests that it might be interesting to divide the adolescents and the graduates into two groups, one with T ≤ 4 and one with T ≥ 5, and examine their OE profiles. We want to know how these subgroups compare on the remaining OEs particularly M and E. Table 2 shows that in regard to the distribution of M and E OE scores, the subgroups of gifted adolescents and graduates selected on the basis of T ≥ 5 are indistinguishable from each other and from the gifted adults. Although we have no other supporting data, it is plausible that the 14 graduate students so selected are gifted.

When gifted adolescents with T ≤ 4 are compared with their graduate counterparts (Table 3), they show significantly higher mean scores on T, M, and E. When the two subgroups of gifted adolescents (B′ and B?) and the two subgroups of graduates (C′ and C?) are compared with each other. (Table 4), it is evident that the adolescents' mean scores on M and E are unchanged: they retain their gifted profile on these two dimensions. The lower scoring graduates, however, are also significantly lower on E ($p < .01$). Whether the lower T score of the B? group is the result of a developmental lag or a different selection procedure awaits resolution.

Table 2 Mean OE Scores of Intellectually Gifted Adults, Gifted Adolescents, and Graduate Students Whose T OE Score Is 5 or More

Overexcitability (OE)	*A′ Gifted Adults N = 28*	$P_{A'B'}$	*B′ Gifted Adolescents N = 20*	$P_{B'C'}$	*C′ Graduate Students N = 14*	$P_{A'C'}$
Psychomotor: P	3.56	.033	3.15	.41	3.57	.85
Sensual: S	4.32	.0001	1.50	.004	4.14	.79
Intellectual: T	7.96	.51	7.35	.52	6.93	.24
Imaginational: M	5.28	.72	5.35	.64	4.93	.79
Emotional: E	7.88	.76	7.35	.50	7.00	.39

Note: See note to Table 1.

The consistent pairing of T, M, and E scores in the higher scoring groups could be the result of a high correlation between these variables which would argue against the assumption of their independence. Table 5 shows that the three variables do not correlate highly, nor are they uniform in the pattern of correlations across groups examined here. This is consistent with the assumption of their independence.

DISCUSSION

Our results show that both gifted adolescents and gifted adults, as a group, are characterized by two nonintellective factors, imaginational (M) and emotional (E) overexcitabilities, and by intellectual (T) overexcitability. Intellectual overexcitability occupies a special position. On the one hand it is related to intellective capabilities; on the other, as intellectual fervor and a drive to pursue existential and moral questions, it goes beyond the purely intellective. The level of these variables shows no age trends; the younger group's mean scores on E and M OEs are equal to those of the adults. In regard to T OE, a subsample in the younger group is equal to the adults; the subsample with lower T OE scores is, nevertheless, significantly above a corresponding sample of graduate students.

The bimodality in the distribution of T scores becomes plainly visible when the data from all the samples are pooled together as shown in Figure 2. This is further supported by data on another group of gifted children, age 9–13, recruited from among the participants at the University for Youth, a program for gifted and talented children at the University of Denver (Piechowski, Note 3). The admission requirements of this program are the students' attaining achievement test scores of 2.0 or more grade levels higher than their current placement. Ninety percent of these children (37 out of 41) have T scores of 5 or more. Added to the four previous samples (dotted line in Figure 2) they further accentuate the deep cleft at T = 4. This group, like the gifted adults, is unimodal in regard to T OE, and in its profile of OE scores it is also like them and the B? group of the gifted Iowa adolescents as well.

In contrast to T, the distributions of E and M scores are not bimodal, although there is a sharp drop in M scores between 5 and 6.

One of the unexpected findings of this study is the constancy of the group OE scores across different ages. The youngest gifted groups (age 9 and 11 in the Denver sample) have each the same OE profile of T, M, and E as the gifted adults. This constancy supports the idea of developmental potential as original equipment (Piechowski, 1975). Studies of younger children will be critical for testing the validity of this idea; the need for a longitudinal study starting at a very young age is evident.

In individuals, the three variables are not consistently linked, although the correlation between M and E is always positive (Table 5). The correlations between T and M, and between T and E have no consistent pattern and can even be negative. The *individual* scores of the gifted can be as low as 1 and as high as 16, and perhaps even more; the lower scores overlap with the non-gifted range. A gifted child may be high or low on any of the three over-excitabilities, T, M, or E, but will not be low on all of them at once and is very likely to have elevated scores on any two. This allows for a great deal of individual variation.

The OEs are not like the specific domains that Feldman and Gardner identified as areas of competence, excellence, and prodigious achievement. Rather, they represent the kind of endowment that feeds, nourishes, enriches, empowers and amplifies talent. Without the overexcitabilities a talent would be no more than a bare computational device.

Overexcitabilities are modes of enhanced mental functioning; they can be thought of as channels of information flow. They can be widely open, narrow, or operating at a bare minimum. They certainly are wide open in artists. Artists are the creative *par excellence.* As a group they score higher than anybody else on M and E (Piechowski, Silverman, Falk, & Cunningham, Note 2). This suggests forcibly that to be truly creative, and creatively productive, one must have a higher endowment on these two dimensions. The model presented here suggests also a possible distinction between intellectual and creative giftedness. The intellectually gifted and the artists share a higher than average endowment on the three principal OEs. But while both groups display similar levels of intellectual overexcitability (though probably different in content); the artists have, in addition, much more of imaginational and emotional overexcitability.

In conclusion, although the level of each OE varies considerably across gifted individuals, the OEs are consistently and reliably present in a gifted group of any age (i.e., as low as age 9). The OEs appear to be a promising ground in which to find those endowments and potentialities that make for "the effective genius that gets into the biographical dictionaries."

Table 3 Mean OE Scores of Gifted Adolescents and Graduate Students Whose T OE Score Is 4 or Less

Overexcitability (OE)	*B″ Gifted Adolescents N = 29*	$P_{B''C''}$	*C″ Graduate Students N = 28*
Psychomotor: P	2.72	.96	2.71
Sensual: S	1.87	.027	2.96
Intellectual: T	2.69	.0008	1.64
Imaginational: M	4.69	.004	3.07
Emotional: E	7.27	.0001	3.68

Note: See note to Table 1.

Table 4 Probabilities of the High and Low T OE Groups Having an Identical Distribution of OE Scores

Overexcitability (OE)	*PB′B″*	*PB′C″*
Psychomotor	.72	.072
Sensual	.33	.19
Intellectual	.0000	.0000
Imaginational	.39	.10
Emotional	.79	.0009

Note: PB′B″ compares the distribution of OE scores in gifted adolescents with a T OE score of 5 or more (B′) with that of gifted adolescents with a T OE score of 4 or less (B″). Analogously, PC′C″ compares the distribution of OE scores in the two groups of graduate students (C′ and C″). The mean OE scores for the four groups are shown in Table 1.

Table 5 Correlations Between Intellectual (T), Imaginational (M), and Emotional (E) Overexcitabilities

	T with M	*T with E*	*M with E*
Gifted adolescents (B′)	−.061	−.153	.537
Graduate students (C′)	−.528	−.127	.389
Gifted adults	.436	.051	.083
Gifted adolescents (B″)	.420	.346	.166
Graduate students (C″)	−.182	.231	.230
Total gifted adolescents (B′ + B″)	.166	.054	.294
Total Grads (C′ + C′)	.148	.407	.426

Note: B′ and C′ designate groups with a score of T of 5′ or more, B″ and C″ designate groups with a score of T of 4 or less.

SUMMARY

Two nonintellective variables, representing the imaginational (M) and the emotional (E) dimensions of mental life, and one broadly intellective variable (T) have been identified as characteristic of giftedness. A cross-sectional comparison showed no age trend when groups of gifted children (as young as age 9) and adolescents are compared with gifted adults. The broadly intellective variable T showed bimodal distribution creating two subsamples, one with T scores lower than 5, and one with T scores of 5 or more. This did not affect the M and E mean scores of the two subsamples of gifted adolescents. The three variables, E, M, and T are viewed here as critical contributors to the creative power and productivity of gifted people.

REFERENCE NOTES

1. Colangelo, N., Piechowski, M. M., & Kelly, K. R. Differentiating two types of gifted learners: Accelerated and enriched. Presentation given at the National Elementary/Middle School Guidance Conference, Purdue University, July, 1982.
2. Piechowski, M. M., Silverman, L. K., Cunningham, K., & Falk, R. F. A comparison of intellectually gifted and artists on five dimensions of mental functioning. Paper presented at the annual meeting of the American Education Research Association, New York City, March, 1982.
3. Piechowski, M. M. Assessing overexcitabilities by questionnaire and interview. Unpublished manuscript, Northwestern University, 1983.

FOOTNOTE

1. More recently, weights of 1, 2, and 3 are given to each single OE score in order to take into account the degree of richness and intensity of the response. Comparison with other samples which were not scored this way is, of necessity, limited to the conservative procedure outlined here.

REFERENCES

Albert, R. S. Toward a behavioral definition of genius. *American Psychologist*, 1975, *30*, 140–151.

Beach, B. J. *Lesbian and nonlesbian women: Profiles of development and self-actualization.* Ph.D. thesis, University of Iowa, Iowa City, 1980.

Bloom, B. S. Report on creativity research by the examiner's office of the University of Chicago. In C. W. Taylor & F. Barron (Eds.), *Scientific creativity: Its recognition and development.* NYC: Wiley, 1963.

Dabrowski, K. Typy wzmozonej pobudliwosci psychicznej (Types of increased psychic excitability). *Biul. Inst. Hig. Psychicnzej*, 1938, *1* (3–4), 3–26.

Feldman, D. H. *Review of the intellectually gifted: An overview,* W. Dennis & M. Dennis (Eds.), *Harvard Educational Review*, 1977, *47*, 576–581.

Feldman, D. H. The mysterious case of extreme giftedness. In A. H. Passow (Ed.), *The gifted and the talented: Their education and development.* NSSE, 78th yearbook. Chicago: University of Chicago Press, 1979.

Gallagher, J. J. *Teaching the gifted child* (2nd ed.). Boston: Allyn & Bacon, 1975.

Gardner, H. *The shattered mind.* NYC: Knopf, 1975.

Gardner, H. Giftedness: Speculations from a biological perspective. In D. H. Feldman (Ed.), *Developmental approaches to giftedness and creativity.* San Francisco: Jossey-Bass, 1982.

Gruber, H. E. On the hypothesized relation between giftedness and creativity. In D. H. Feldman (Ed.), *Developmental approaches to giftedness and creativity.* San Francisco: Jossey-Bass, 1982.

Hoyt, D. P. College grades and adult accomplishment: A review of research. *The Educational Record,* 1966 (Winter), 70–75.

James, W. *The varieties of religious experience. A study of human nature.* NYC: Modern Library, 1902.

Lysy, K., & Piechowski, M. M. Personal growth: An empirical study using Jungian and Dabrowskian measures. *Genetic Psychology Monographs,* 1983, *108,* 267–320.

Newland, T. E. *The gifted in socioeducational perspective.* Englewood Cliffs, NJ: Prentice-Hall, 1976.

Nicholls, J. G. Creativity in the person who will never produce anything creative or useful: The concept of creativity as a normally distributed trait. *American Psychologist,* 1972, *27,* 717–727.

Passow, A. H. The nature of giftedness and talent. *Gifted Child Quarterly,* 1981, *25,* 5–10.

Piechowski, M. M. A theoretical and empirical approach to the study of development. *Genetic Psychology Monographs,* 1975, *92,* 231–297.

Piechowski, M. M. Developmental potential. In N. Colangelo & R. T. Zaffrann (Eds.), *New voices in counseling the gifted.* Dubuque, IA: Kendall/Hunt, 1979.

Renzulli, J. S. What makes giftedness? Reexamining a definition. *Phi Delta Kappan,* 1978, *60,* 180–184.

Silverman, L K., & Ellsworth, B. The theory of positive disintegration and its implications for giftedness. In N. Duda (Ed.), *Theory of positive disintegration: Proceedings of the third international conference.* Miami, FL: University of Miami School of Medicine, 1981.

Sternberg, R. J. Sketch of a componential subtheory of human intelligence. *Behavioral and Brain Sciences,* 1980, *3,* 573–584.

Wing, C. W., Jr., & Wallach, M. A. *College admissions and the psychology of talent.* NYC: Holt, Rinehart, 1971.

11

Child Prodigies: A Distinctive Form of Giftedness

David Henry Feldman

Tufts University

The basic premise of this article is that the child prodigy is a distinct form of giftedness which must be understood on its own terms. In contrast with the child of great general ability, the prodigy tends to have a more focused, specialized, and domain-specific form of giftedness. Studies of prodigies have contributed to changing theories about the nature of giftedness (e.g., from single to multiple) and will likely continue to do so. Along with the related phenomenon of savant syndrome, the prodigy points to a set of complex relationships between psychometric intelligence in the traditional sense and expression of talent within specific domains like music or mathematics. Based in part on findings from studies of prodigies, it is likely that there are important roles for both general and specific abilities in most forms of giftedness and that they represent two distinct evolutionary trends to maximize the likelihood of human survival.

Editor's Note: From Feldman, D. H. (1993). Child prodigies: A distinctive form of giftedness. *Gifted Child Quarterly, 37*(4), 188–193.

The prodigy has been known for millennia, known but hardly understood. In fact, part of the early meaning of the word *prodigy* was intended to capture the mysteriousness of a wide variety of events and processes. In its earliest use, prodigy referred to any event that seemed to be "out of the usual course of nature" or "inexplicable" or "monstrous" (Gove, 1961). It did not refer necessarily even to human behavior and was not originally associated with exceptional mental ability. Over the centuries, there has been a narrowing and focusing of the notion of the prodigy; a recent definition all but lost the distinctiveness of the word by defining a *prodigy* as a "highly gifted or academically talented child" (Gove, 1961, p. 1810).

Were this definition of a prodigy as a high-IQ child to be accepted, it would mean that a prodigy and an academically talented child were indistinguishable. In fact, the relationship between the prodigy and psychometric intelligence is not at all straightforward, all examination of this relationship is a major purpose of the present discussion.

A more recent definition of the child prodigy offered by the author and his colleagues is intended to distinguish prodigies from other forms of extreme intellectual capability, as well as to recapture some of the ancient meaning of the term. The definition that we offered for the prodigy was a child (typically younger than 10 years old) who is performing at the level of a highly trained adult in a very demanding field of endeavor. This definition has a number of features: it emphasizes *performance* as a criterion for calling someone a prodigy as opposed to psychometric intelligence, which tries to measure potential; it labels the prodigy as a distinctly *human* phenomenon that can only occur with the support and assistance of other human beings; it emphasizes the *specific* realms within which prodigious behavior appears as opposed to psychometric intelligence, which aims at assessing general intellectual ability; and it has a *comparative* feature which allows for reasonable measurement of the degree of prodigiousness in relation to the standards of performance within a given field.

Although there is growing consensus that a definition of the prodigy such as the one just proposed is a reasonable one, it would be going too far to say that such a consensus exists without controversy. There may, for example, be some wisdom in the view of Radford (1990), who has argued that there are so many problems with specifying at what age, and against what standard, a child would have to perform to be called a prodigy, that it is folly to try to be precise in a definition. It is true enough that each field has its own standards, that these standards change, and that what might be an extremely early age for achievement in one field might be fairly routine in another, making it inherently difficult to classify behavior as prodigious out of the context of a specific field. Still, it seems better to try to specify what is uniquely characteristic of the child prodigy even if ambiguities in doing so are inevitable.

Putting the Research to Use

As we move into the next milennium, the diversity of the population, including the population we think of as "gifted," is likely to increase markedly. Although there is growing consensus that our notions of giftedness have to respond to the changes in our population, it is not always clear how to go about transforming ideas and practices so that they are more responsive to the changing needs of our children. Although prodigies represent extreme examples of diversity, and although it is rare that a prodigy appears, the study of prodigies helps us begin to lay out the dimensions of a notion of giftedness that can guide future practice. In particular, prodigies represent one of the profiles of giftedness that has been more or less excluded from most current definitions: the highly specialized and focused talent for a particular domain or field. Prodigies also help us begin to sort out the relationship between broad, general academic talent and more domain-specific talents. It appears that any of several combinations can occur: general academic talent can exist in combination with domain-specific talents, or each can occur in the relative absence of the other. Prodigies seem to be individuals with average or above average general academic talent and profoundly powerful domain-specific talents. By showing how, in extreme cases, giftedness takes on a distinct form not found elsewhere, the prodigy helps show what identification of giftedness might look like in the next century.

Definitions notwithstanding, what has happened during the past decade or so is that there is renewed interest in the prodigy as one of the more striking manifestations of human potential, and recognition that the prodigy, along with other examples of extreme talent such as savants and very high-IQ cases, is increasingly seen as worthy of careful study (Morelock & Feldman, 1991). The study of prodigies therefore offers an opportunity both better to understand the nature and limitations of the concept of psychometric intelligence and to offer a unique avenue into some of the least understood aspects of intellectual development.

It must be emphasized, however, that there have been an amazingly small number of scientific studies of prodigies. In the entire psychological research literature, only three books have reported major studies, and two of these appeared in German more than 50 years ago (Baumgarten, 1930; Revesz, 1925/1970). In spite of the many centuries of anecdotes and stories and legends about prodigies, from the young David of the Old Testament to Joan of Arc in medieval times and Yehudi Menuhin in this century, the scientific knowledge base is extremely modest. Fewer than 20 cases have been studied in depth (Feldman, 1991a).

We know that prodigies have appeared in many but far from all fields of human endeavor. There is no accurate estimate of the number of prodigies in general, nor are there accurate counts within various fields, but there are some domains in which prodigies are relatively more frequent, others in which they are less frequent, and still others in which prodigies have not yet been identified.

Music is probably the field in which prodigies appear with greatest frequency, and chess has also had many prodigies. Mozart is often cited as the most extraordinary child prodigy that the field of classical music composition has produced, and the American chess player Bobby Fischer was acclaimed as the most exceptional prodigy of the 1960s. Although mathematics is generally believed to be the specialty of prodigies, most known cases have actually been calculators, more akin to savants than prodigies (Smith, 1983). When original mathematical reasoning is included as a criterion for calling a child a mathematical prodigy, there are actually a relatively small number of documented cases (Feldman, 1991a; Radford, 1990).

There have been no more than a few writing prodigies: the best known is probably the English girl Daisy Ashford, who wrote a popular novel *The Young Visiters* before the turn of the last century. Even fewer prodigies have been found in the visual arts. Until recently, the only clear case of an artistic prodigy was that of Nadia, a disturbed English girl whose artistic ability diminished as her autism responded to treatment (Selfe, 1977). More recently, a mainland Chinese girl, Wang Yani, has achieved considerable fame for her exceptionally deft watercolors of monkeys and other subjects that she began producing at age 3 (Ho, 1989). If sports fields are included within the definition of prodigy, then the number of cases increases considerably, particularly in fields like gymnastics and swimming where an early start seems necessary to achieve the highest levels of performance.

There have been few if any prodigies who have been identified in the natural sciences, philosophy, dance, or the plastic arts. Fields like law and business and medicine also seem to require a greater number of years of preparation before the heights are scaled, although there have been a few instances of individuals who have achieved entry-level status while still in their teens; a Florida boy named Steven Baccus took the oath to practice law before his 18th birthday (Hicks, 1986). Computer programming appears to be a field in which prodigies may appear, although none younger than 10 has come to widespread public attention thus far.

Another feature of the prodigy phenomenon has been that vastly more boys than girls have been identified (Goldsmith, 1987). This seems to be true for at least two reasons: the fields in which prodigies are found have tended to be populated more by males than females (e.g., chess) and there has been a long history of prejudice against girls participating in and/or receiving recognition for their work in fields like music or mathematics. If allowed to participate in a field, girls have often been relegated to amateur status or been required to pursue their interests in a field outside of the professional community. In the only published article specifically on girl prodigies, this example is given:

Sophie Germain began an informal study of mathematics when she was 13, and in six years had mastered the field to such a degree that her work came to the attention of mathematician Joseph Lagrange. Working almost exclusively outside of the established (male) community, Germain nonetheless made a substantial contribution to the field of number theory. . . . (Goldsmith, 1987, p. 77)

As social and cultural restrictions on women have broken down, the number of girl prodigies has begun to increase. The most striking change has been in the field of music performance, where girls are now found in numbers more or less equal to boys. Girls have also moved toward greater parity in the field of chess; a Hungarian girl named Judit Polgar has achieved the rank of grandmaster at age 15 years, 5 months, a month earlier than the great prodigy and eventual World Champion Bobby Fischer (McFadden, 1992). It is reasonable to hypothesize that the number of girl prodigies will increase, and increase rapidly, during the next few decades as opportunities for participation increase, barriers are lowered, and rewards for high-level achievement are equalized.

RECENT RESEARCH

In the mid 1970s, the first modern study of child prodigies was begun at Tufts University under the direction of the author (Feldman, 1991a). This study followed six boy prodigies over a nearly 10-year period. The boys were between 3 and 10 years old when first observed and were involved in fields ranging from writing to chess to mathematics to music. Two of the children were difficult to classify as pure prodigies, one because his abilities seemed so diverse, the other because he was originally identified in mathematics but became more interested in science over time.

In contrast to earlier studies, which tended to concentrate on the mental abilities of the child subjects as revealed in tests of various kinds, more recent studies have focused on broader processes of development, including aspects of the prodigies' family and educational experiences, personal and emotional qualities, and interactions with the various domains in which they are involved (Bamberger, 1982; Feldman, 1991a). The questions of interest to current research have more to do with the processes through which a prodigy achieves such high levels of mastery than with the amounts of intelligence or more specific abilities that give rise to high levels of performance. Earlier studies focused more on the kinds of logical, spatial, musical, and linguistic abilities the children possessed: they also established the distinctive mixture of child and adult qualities that so often marks the prodigy's profile both intellectually and emotionally (Baumgarten, 1930; Revesz, 1925/1970).

DEVELOPMENT IN PRODIGIES

Contrary to what seems to be a common view of the prodigy as an adult mind that happens to be constrained by a child's body, the evidence suggests that a more accurate description would be that a prodigy is a child who happens to have a powerful and highly focused talent along with a powerful drive to develop it. Based on observations of the six prodigies in *Nature's Gambit,* the impression is consistent with earlier accounts that prodigies are indeed remarkably advanced within their specific areas of expertise but not particularly advanced emotionally or in their social development.

Indeed, to some degree the kinds of lives that prodigies have been encouraged to lead stand in the way of their normal development in other areas. The focus of resources, both those of the child and of those around her or him, can be so intense that there is little emphasis on making sure that the child learns to do things independently. The weight of the responsibility for making sure the child's talent is fully developed can lead to a tendency to relieve the child of other responsibilities (Feldman, 1991a). The turn-of- the-century piano prodigy Erwin Nyiregyhazi could not tie his own shoes at 21 (Revesz, 1925/1970).

On the other hand, prodigies are sometimes given responsibilities far beyond their years, responsibilities to earn money to support their families. Particularly in fields such as music and sports and show business, the pressure on children to perform often and in settings inappropriate for them can lead to precocious adultlike attitudes about professionalism and about money. The Jackson Five, a popular singing group of the seventies, included the children from a single family, one of whom was then 5-year-old Michael. This group was earning millions of dollars before its oldest member had reached the age of maturity; the youngest has become one of the world's most famous entertainers.

Exploitation of prodigies by parents and other adults has been an unfortunate aspect of the history of the phenomenon. Stories of arithmetical calculating prodigies being put on display as freaks were not uncommon during the Middle Ages (Smith, 1983). Even the great Mozart at age 8, as well as his older sister, were advertised in the newspaper as "Prodigies of Nature" well into the so-called Age of Enlightenment (MacLeish, 1984).

The experience of being a prodigy and the experience of raising a prodigy are unusual. It should not be surprising that there are unusual qualities characteristic of both prodigies and their parents. Prodigies tend to be unusually focused, determined, and highly motivated to reach the highest levels of their fields. They are often marked as well by great confidence in their abilities, along with a naive sense of these abilities in relation to those of others. It is often a surprise to prodigies that other people do not have the same talents, or the same preoccupations, that they do. In this respect there can be both the appearance of overconfidence in the prodigy and at the same time a strong sense that doing what she or he does is both natural and comfortable, indeed that doing anything else would be detrimental to the child's well-being.

Parents of prodigies are often involved in the same or related fields as their offspring (Bloom, 1985). Picasso's father was an artist, Mozart's father a musician, Nijinsky's parents were dancers. Often older when they have their children, parents of prodigies are generally willing to devote major portions of their own time and energy to the development of their children's talents. One or both parents may reduce or give up entirely their own careers, may move long distances to be where their children can receive the best instruction, may sacrifice their own comfort and security so that the very best equipment, technology, competition, and promotion can be provided.

Parents of prodigies are also sometimes driven to extreme behavior because of unresponsiveness or even outright hostility to the needs of their offspring. Prodigies in the United States are faced with substantial difficulties in public (and some private) schools. Schools are often rather inflexible in accommodating the special needs of prodigies, such as allowing time for travel to tournaments or competitions or providing special instructional resources. Parents also find themselves at odds with school authorities over the extra resources needed to respond to the exceptional talents of their children. A number of parents of prodigies have found that their children are better served by home instruction. Alternatively, parents find that they must continuously search for appropriate settings for their children, with school changes as frequent as twice a year not unusual (Feldman, 1991a).

PRODIGIES AND PSYCHOMETRIC INTELLIGENCE

Recent research on prodigies has established (or reestablished) that the prodigy is a distinctive form of human intelligence not reducible to any other form (Feldman, 1991a). This means that prodigies must be understood on their own terms, but it does not mean that the processes that govern expression of potential in the prodigy are fundamentally different from those same processes in other human beings. Prodigies, like others, are endowed with certain talents and interests, have access to greater or fewer resources, live in families with varying commitments to helping their children achieve their potential, must deal with difficult transitions, confront developmental changes in their bodies and minds and emotions (Bamberger, 1982), and live in cultures where various fields are more or less valued and more or less available; in short, proceed as best they can with the demanding process of developing their talents.

The question of just what role psychometric intelligence might play in the prodigy's development and expression of potential has not been answered systematically. Possible answers have ranged from the prodigy being nothing more than a very high-IQ child (cf. Cox, 1926; Hollingworth, 1942/1975), to prodigies being nothing more than individuals with a peculiar gift unrelated to more general intellectual functioning, in short, a savant (Marshall, 1985). Based on what is now known about prodigies, a more reasonable answer would acknowledge that psychometric intelligence plays a role in the process of prodigy development, but a supporting rather than a central one.

In the six cases studied in *Nature's Gambit,* for example, IQs were known in two of the cases, SAT college entrance examination scores in two others (highly correlated with IQ), and school achievement scores (also highly correlated with IQ) in the other two (Feldman, 1991a). In all six cases, their IQs were above average by at least one standard deviation. That is, these six boys were all well above average in their general ability to succeed in traditional academic pursuits. One of the boys had a measured IQ of above 200 while a preschooler. Their IQ scores could be reasonably estimated to fall in the range of about 120 (low) to well above 200 (high).

Although IQ scores are of course not available for most of the famous prodigies of history, it seems reasonable to guess that most of them were also generally able, if not exceptionally gifted (Feldman & Goldsmith, 1989). Mozart, for example, wrote quite well, picked up languages with relative ease, and had a keen ability to judge both musical and nonmusical qualities in other people (Feldman, 1991b; Marshall, 1985). This is not to say that Mozart's gifts in verbal areas were equal to his exquisite musical gifts but rather to suggest that his musical gift was supported and enhanced by his somewhat more modest gifts in verbal (and also interpersonal) intelligence (Feldman, 1991b; Gardner, 1983).

There are cases of individuals whose striking gifts in highly specific areas are *not* supported by more general intellectual abilities. These cases have been studied more extensively than have prodigies and are now labeled *savant syndrome* (Howe, 1989; Treffert, 1989).

A savant may be someone who is able to carry out highly complex arithmetic calculations quickly and seemingly effortlessly or who can play back any piece of music perfectly, holding that piece of music permanently in memory. Savants have been found in many of the same areas as prodigies: mathematics, music, art, and occasionally chess. There are also savants who are able to memorize great volumes of verbal material (e.g., the Manhattan telephone book) or who can provide the correct day of the week for any date in history (Treffert, 1989). Although it would be overly simplified to say that prodigies and savants differ only with respect to the amount of psychometric intelligence available to them, it is clearly one way that they do differ, and a vitally important one.

EXPLAINING THE PRODIGY PHENOMENON

It should be clear from what has been presented above that the prodigy is a distinctive form of giftedness, marked by unusually strong talent in a single area such as music or mathematics, reasonably high but not necessarily exceptionally high IQ, focused energy and sustained effort to achieve the highest levels of the target field, and unusual self-confidence. Although the prodigy shares some qualities with other forms of giftedness, it nonetheless would be a distortion of the phenomenon to try to reduce it to one or another of the other forms such as general academic talent or savant-like isolated talent. It would also impede progress in deepening our understanding of all forms of giftedness to fail to attend to the distinctive qualities of the prodigy.

Although there is no theory which can adequately explain the various forms that giftedness has been known to take, some features of such a theory can be identified. Whatever else turns out to be true, it is clear that the traditional notion of intelligence as IQ will not serve as an adequate theoretical basis from which to analyze the now differentiated forms of giftedness. This does not mean that IQ is an irrelevant construct necessarily, but it is likely to be a component of the theoretical landscape rather than its foundation in future work.

The main reason that IQ is inadequate to organize research on giftedness is that it altogether misses the prodigy as well as the savant (Morelock & Feldman, 1991, 1992, 1993). In fact, the prevalence of IQ interpretations of intelligence is likely to have impeded research on various distinctive extreme forms of giftedness by suggesting that they all represent high IQ, which in fact they do not (Feldman, 1979, 1991a). A theory like Howard Gardner's multiple intelligences (Gardner, 1983) is a better fit to the prodigy phenomenon. In fact, the existence of prodigies in particular fields was one of the eight criteria that Gardner used to support the claim for a particular form of intelligence. This theory, which claims that there are at least seven distinct forms of intelligence, each existing more or less independently of the others in any person, certainly comes closer to capturing the prodigy (and the savant, another criterion for calling a candidate ability an intelligence) than IQ.

Yet it must be acknowledged that the presence or absence of more general adaptive qualities differentiates the prodigy from the savant. Therefore, to leave out general academic talent would seem to be problematic if an adequate overall account of the prodigy is ever to be achieved. General academic talent seems to play an enabling role for the prodigy, allowing the prodigy to develop her or his more focused talent in ways that afford a successful career and full participation in social and cultural life (in contrast with the savant).

A model that might begin to integrate the two kinds of capabilities that seem central to the prodigy's development—general academic talent and specific field talent—is one that proposes an evolutionary explanation for the existence of the two forms of giftedness (Feldman, 1991a). In this model, it is assumed that over the course of evolution *two* quite distinctive forms of intelligence have evolved. One of these, what we now usually call general intelligence or IQ, has the purpose of permitting the maximum degree of adaptability under the widest variety of environmental circumstances. It is what has made it possible for human beings to gain dominion over the planet, to control or destroy other inhabitants of the same space, to exploit natural resources of staggering variety for their own purposes, and to form adaptive yet stable societies and cultures. To function well in any society requires at least a reasonable dose of this kind of intelligence. The other form of intelligence that has evolved is a highly specific talent for a relatively constrained dimension of experience, often associated with one or another of the sensory channels. If someone has highly sensitive visual capabilities, for example, it makes it more likely that she or he will be visually oriented, will gravitate toward visual experience, and may develop visual skills to a high degree through the mastery of a domain like architecture or art.

The kind of theory that is necessary to capture the prodigy would encompass both the more general and the more specific forms of intellectual functioning and would assume that human beings were born with potential of both sorts to varying degrees. In other words, one person might be blessed with great general intellectual talent and more modest specific capabilities, while another might have a very powerful specific talent but more modest general intellectual ability. Someone else might have more than one specific talent or have great general intellectual capability as well as a very powerful specific talent.

All the combinations of general and specific intelligences are possible and likely to be found in the human population. One is in fact a hedge for the other; the specific talents are there to make maximum use of heightened potential for experience within fairly narrowly constrained domains: the more general talents tend to be used for sustaining and extending culture. The title of my book on prodigies, *Nature's Gambit,* is intended to capture this evolutionary tendency to play one type of intelligence off against the other as a way to ensure the long-term survival of the human species.

The specific talents tend to require environments very well-suited to their development and will thrive only under a limited range of variations of environmental conditions. General adaptive talent is useful in almost any environment and makes it possible to use the widest variety of environmental resources to ensure survival and well-being. The specific talents are more likely to be called upon when major changes in bodies of knowledge come about; more general talents tend to be used to sustain steady growth and stable progress in most fields.

"Nature's gambit," then, is the remarkable evolutionary tendency to produce a small number of extremely specialized talents that depend upon finely tuned environmental circumstances for their expression (as in prodigies) and therefore only rarely develop fully, balanced by a much larger number of general talents that make survival possible even when environmental circumstances are not favorable for specific talent development. Often both kinds of talents exist in the same individual, but not necessarily; thus the savant, the prodigy, and the high-IQ individual represent extreme variations in the evolutionary process of general and specific talent distribution.

CONCLUSION

Comparative studies of various forms of extreme intellectual giftedness would go a long way toward helping answer some of the many questions remaining about prodigies and would also add to our understanding of giftedness in its many forms. Although we know more than we did even a few years ago about prodigies, the study of extreme giftedness is still rarely done despite pioneering efforts by some of our predecessors (Hollingworth, 1942/1975; Silverman, 1990). Some of the questions that need answers are: What are the essential similarities and differences between prodigies and savants? Between high IQ and extreme talent? Is it possible to use general academic ability to achieve high levels of performance in specific fields and would there be differences between this way of accomplishing high-level performance and accomplishing it through the use of specific talent? Why are there both prodigies and savants in certain fields (such as music or drawing) but not in others? Are there fields in which there are prodigies, but not savants? And vice versa?

These and many other questions can be more productively pursued now that the prodigy has begun to establish a distinctive place among the recognized manifestations of human giftedness. We are also aided in our efforts by changing theories of giftedness itself. As it becomes clearer and clearer that giftedness must be conceived as multiple in nature, as domain specific, and as developmental (cf. Feldman, 1992; Gardner, 1983), better conceptualizations and better research questions will emerge. During the coming decades, we may hope that some of the many questions raised by the prodigy, this most fascinating form of human intelligence, will be answered. It is likely that these answers will deepen our understanding of all forms of giftedness.

REFERENCES

Bamberger, J. (1982). Growing up prodigies: The midlife crisis. In D. H. Feldman (Ed.), *Developmental approaches to giftedness and creativity* (pp. 61–77). San Francisco: Jossey-Bass.

Baumgarten, F. (1930). *Wunderkinder: Psychologische Untersuchungen* [Child prodigies: Psychological examinations]. Leipzig: Johann Ambrosious Barth.

Bloom, B. (Ed.). (1985). *Developing talent in young people.* New York: Ballantine Books.

Cox, C. (1926). *Genetic studies of genius: Vol 2. The early mental traits of three hundred geniuses.* Stanford, CA: Stanford University Press.

Feldman, D. H. (1979). The mysterious case of extreme giftedness. In H. Passow (Ed.), *The gifted and the talented: 78th yearbook of the NSSE* (pp. 335–351). Chicago, IL: University of Chicago Press.

Feldman, D. H., with Goldsmith, L. T. (1991a). *Nature's gambit: Child prodigies and the development of human potential.* (Paperback Edition) New York: Teachers College Press.

Feldman, D. H. (1991b, December). *Mozart and the transformational imperative.* Paper presented at the symposium Mozart and the Perils of Creativity, Smithsonian Institution, Washington, DC.

Feldman, D. H. (1992). Has there been a paradigm shift in gifted education? In N. Colangelo, S. Assouline, & D. Ambroson (Eds.), *Talent development: Proceedings for the 1991 Henry B. and Jocelyn Wallace National Research Symposium on talent development* (pp. 89–94). Unionville, NY: Trillium.

Feldman, D. H., & Goldsmith, L. T. (1989). Child prodigies: Straddling two worlds. In the *Encyclopedia Britannica Medical and Health Annual* (pp. 32–51). Chicago, IL: Encyclopedia Britannica, Ltd.

Gardner, H. (1983). *Frames of mind: The theory of multiple intelligences.* New York: Basic Books.

Goldsmith, L. T. (1987). Girl prodigies: Some evidence and some speculations. *Roeper Review, 10,* 74–82.

Gove, P. B. (Ed.). (1961). *Webster's third new international dictionary of the English language unabridged.* Springfield, MA: G.& C. Merriam Co.

Hicks. D. F. (1986, November 15). At 17, prodigy will take his oath as a new lawyer. *Miami Herald,* p. 1.

Ho, W. C. (Ed.). (1989) *Wang Yani: The brush of innocence.* New York: Hudson Hills.

Hollingworth, L. (1975). *Children above 180 IQ.* New York: Arno. (Original work published 1942)

Howe, M. J. A. (Ed.). (1989). *Fragments of genius.* London: Routledge.

Marshall, R. L. (1985). Mozart/Amadeus: Amadeus/Mozart. *Brandeis Review, 5,* 9–16.

McFadden, R. D. (1992, February 4). Youngest grandmaster ever is 15, ferocious (and female). *The New York Times,* pp. A1, C15.

MacLeish, R. (1984). The mystery of what makes a prodigy. *Smithsonian Magazine, 14,* 12, 70–79.

Morelock, M. J., & Feldman, D. H. (1991). Extreme precocity. In N. Colangelo & G. Davis (Eds.), *Handbook of gifted education* (pp. 347–364). Boston: Allyn and Bacon.

Morelock, M. J., & Feldman, D. H. (1992). The assessment of giftedness in preschool children. In E. B. Nuttall, I. Romero, & J. Kalesnik (Eds.), *Assessing and screening preschoolers: Psychological and educational dimensions* (pp. 301–309). Boston: Allyn and Bacon.

Morelock, M. J., & Feldman, D. H. (1993). Prodigies and savants: What they tell us about giftedness and talent. In K. A. Heller, F. J. Monks, & A. H. Passow (Eds.), *International handbook for research on giftedness and talent* (pp. 161–181). Oxford, UK: Pergamon.

Radford, J. (1990). *Child prodigies and exceptional early achievers.* New York: The Free Press.

Revesz, G. (1970). *The psychology of a musical prodigy.* Freeport, NY: Books for Libraries Press. (Original work published 1925)

Selfe, L. (1977). *Nadia: A case of extraordinary drawing ability in an autistic child.* London: Academic Press.

Silverman, L. K. (Ed.). (1990). A tribute to Leta Stetter Hollingwolth [Special issue]. *Roeper Review, 12* (3).

Smith, S. B. (1983). *The great mental calculators: The psychology, methods, and lives of calculating prodigies.* New York: Columbia University Press.

Treffert, D. (1989). *Extraordinary people: Understanding "idiot savants."* New York: Harper & Row.

12

A Developmental View of Giftedness

Frances Degen Horowitz

The University of Kansas

Our most precious resources for the future of our society are human resources. We made an important commitment of scientific talent and financial support about 25 years ago to enhancing the developmental potential of the retarded among us. The progress in this area has been gratifying. A concomitant commitment has not been made to understanding the developmental potential of the gifted among us. The time is past due for that commitment. It is important to draw out the developmental issues related to the gifted and the talented in such a way as to frame productive scientific questions. The model presented in this essay has been used to frame such a set of questions.

How early might we identify a child with special gifts? How best might those gifts be nurtured? What developmental course can be expected for a

Editor's Note: From Horowitz, F. D. (1987). A developmental view of giftedness. *Gifted Child Quarterly, 31*(4), 165–168. © 1987 National Association for Gifted Children. Reprinted with permission.

gifted child and how is that course different from that of the non-gifted child? When a child is gifted in one domain, what effect does this have on development in other domains?

Considering the importance of nurturing and conserving the human resources represented in the gifted among us, it would be reasonable to expect that we would have the answers to these questions or that we could cite large scale on-going research programs devoted to these topics. It is for this reason that the American Psychological Association in cooperation with the American Psychological Foundation decided to commission a volume entitled: *The Gifted and the Talented: Developmental Perspectives* edited by myself and my colleague, Marion O'Brien (Horowitz and O'Brien, 1985). As author after author in that volume notes, our knowledge about the development and nurturance of giftedness and talent, in most domains, is much smaller than our knowledge base about normal development in those domains.

Our knowledge base about development and individual differences in various domains is quite uneven. For example, we have a relatively good map of normal motor development and a growing understanding of the developmental course of cognitive and intellectual development and of language development. Systematic attempts to understand social and emotional development have only recently been renewed (Campos et al., 1983). Our developmental knowledge with respect to musical and artistic domains is meager indeed. The mapping of development requires reliable measurement techniques; in the area of intelligence our measurement strategies are the most sophisticated and reliable, if controversial. As recent efforts of both Gardner (1983) and Sternberg (1985) attest, alternative conceptualizations of intelligence will likely produce different measurement strategies and perhaps new definitions of giftedness.

The most extensive interest in individual differences is in the area of intellectual development; however, attention has been concentrated much more on the lower end of the continuum of intelligence than on the upper end. Considering that, with a reasonably symmetric distribution, 1% to 3% of the population is identified as retarded and that 3 to 5% of the population is designated as gifted (Marland, 1972), the disparity of research efforts is remarkable. Some aspects of this disparity are understandable. We know what developmental path a retarded child is supposed to traverse if retardation did not exist. Though there is a debate over whether retardation is basically a case of delayed or arrested development as opposed to a different quality of functioning (Zigler and Balla, 1982), the path not taken (i.e., normal development) is available for comparative purposes. With the gifted individual we are often looking not only at precocious development but unique developmental characteristics so that the normal developmental path is less effective as a prospective guide. Nevertheless, the overall dearth of developmental research on giftedness is regrettable. In the light of this situation this essay will concentrate on a general model of development that might serve to stimulate a developmentally oriented research agenda aimed at understanding the development of gifted and talented individuals.

Figure 1 A model of organism-environment interaction. (Adapted from Gowen, 1952)

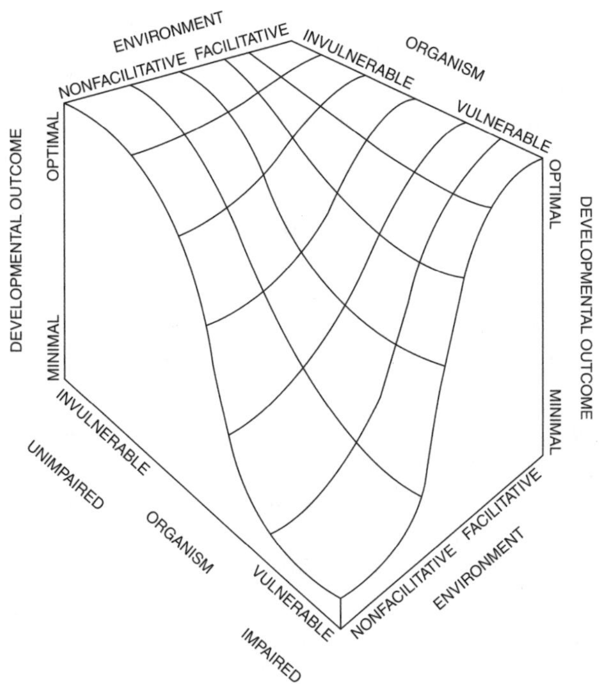

A MODEL OF DEVELOPMENT

Rather than dwelling upon apportioning genetic and environmental contributions to development as some previous models have done, we might consider a model such as that shown in Figure 1. This model of development is not, in a real sense, uniquely different from other models, nor is it a model to be tested, per se. It is, however, a *structural* model designed to diagram the sources of influence on development and to stimulate the asking of developmental questions in the form of equations in which variables are specified, weighted, and given a set of functional relationships for the prediction of developmental status or outcome (Horowitz, 1987).

The surface of the figure represents the level of adequacy of development at a given point in time in a given domain. Highly adequate or optimal development is represented at the far upper surface; poorer or minimal development toward the nearer low quadrant of the surface. A child's developmental adequacy is represented by the placement on the surface of the diagram. In this diagram these two determinants of developmental adequacy are shown as the two main dimensions of the model: environmental and organismic.

The environmental dimensions can be described as ranging on a continuum from facilitative of development to nonfacilitative of development. A challenge facing us today is documenting those elements of the environment which make the child's experience facilitative of development. In this model it is assumed that an environment that is facilitative of development in one period of development may not be facilitative in another period. Similarly, an environment that is facilitative of development in one domain of development may not necessarily be facilitative of development in another domain. For example, an environment that provides strong contingencies for verbal behavior will be facilitative of language development but not necessarily of spatial development unless it also provides strong contingencies in this area. Alternatively, because spatial information feedback is more inherently available to the child as the child interacts with the physical world, specially arranged environmental contingencies may be less critical for good spatial development. Therefore, environments that provide differential levels of contingent reinforcement for different domains of development may be equally facilitative at very different levels of mediated contingencies.

The organismic dimension is described along two, non-correlated, continua. One relates to the presence and degree of physical impairment while the other relates to the individual's vulnerability or resiliency. These organismic characteristics interact with the nature of the environment to produce the level of development that describes the child. Several concrete examples will be useful here. In the area of motor development a child may be severely impaired by a handicap such as cerebral palsy. At the present time there is no known environment that will be facilitative of normal motor development for a severely impaired cerebral palsied child. Thus, as regards motor development, that child's developmental level will be placed in the near, lower quadrant of the surface of Figure 1. On the other hand, some environments and surgical treatments can aid the cerebral palsied child's motor development. The result would move the adequacy of motor development up on the surface, away from the near low quadrant to some degree.

This same child may be quite unimpaired with respect to cognitive development. However, children have different degrees of dependence upon the environment for its facilitative effects. There are some children who show excellent cognitive development even in relatively non-facilitative environments. These children might be described as "invulnerable" or "resilient." These children will show cognitive development that might be nearly optimal, with resulting placement in the upper far quadrant of the developmental outcome surface in this domain. These same children may be more dependent upon the nature of the facilitative environment for comparable development, let us say, in the social domain. They would be described as being more vulnerable or less independently resilient in the social development area in the cognitive development area.

The reader can spin out other combinations and permutations using the model's dimensions. One principle involved is that the structural combination that accounts for development in one domain may be different from that which accounts for development in another domain. A second principle is also involved:

The structural combination that exists in one period of development may not be the same as in another period of development. For example, in the first two years of life a child's cognitive development may be excellent, relatively independent of the specific facilitative nature of the environment. We would say the child is highly invulnerable or very resilient in the cognitive area. However, after two years of age the child's relative vulnerability in this domain may change. For the same level of development to continue, the child's environment may need to be very facilitative. It should be obvious that the model can accommodate the effects of intervention programs since changes in environments may increase their facilitative effects. The model being proposed can also account for instances of continuity and discontinuity in development without having to resort to an entirely hereditarian or an entirely environmental point of view.

A perspective on the results of the early intervention programs some of which were disappointing, is that we probably do not fully understand the nature of the elements that constitute highly facilitative environments and therefore our "interventions" or alterations of environmental input were not as individually matched, precise, or effective as they ultimately could be. Indeed, when initial gains were made only to be lost later, we reacted as though the intervention had been analogous to an innoculation program. No one claims that adequate doses of vitamin C at age four will prevent vitamin C deficiency at age ten. If cognitive and intellectual development is a dynamic continuing process, and if our model is a valid one, then the functional equation that describes the relationships between conditions and intellectual development may well change for different periods of development.

Some children, according to our model, will show optimal development independent of environmental input. Or, for some presently unknown reasons, these children make very efficient and effective use of whatever environment they find themselves in. They are "invulnerable" or "resilient." Sometimes they are referred to as "gifted."

APPLYING THE MODEL OF GIFTEDNESS AND TALENT

Giftedness is defined in many different ways—as precocity, as a different quality of functioning, as unique development. The gifted child according to this model is one who shows superior development in a given domain. That superior development could be the result of a highly facilitative environment and/or characteristics in the child that enable the child to make extremely good use of any and all environmental input. Giftedness may be confined to one domain or be a characteristic in several domains of development. Even though giftedness is thought of as an enduring individual difference characteristic, there are many instances in which early giftedness does not continue; in other instances early development in a particular domain is quite normal with gifted performance in evidence only at later periods of development in that domain.

The model is most useful in helping us think about the conditions that result in gifted performance, the development of giftedness, and the maintenance of giftedness. According to this model there is no one set of conditions that accounts for all instances of giftedness. Rather, a multiple set of conditions (or developmental equations) can result in giftedness or the expression of a high level of talent. In one instance giftedness may be an individual difference characteristic that exists relatively independent of the nature of environmental input. Thus, for some children raised in seemingly quite adverse circumstances with respect to cognitive or language stimulation, extraordinary early cognitive or language development may be in evidence. These children are able to use to the maximum whatever minimal environmental input exists. Other children may show similar levels of extraordinary development but only under conditions when the environment is maximally facilitative of such development. Two similarly gifted children may thus be the result of quite different combinations of circumstances.

In some domains of development environmental input may be essential if an initial level of giftedness or talent is to progress. For example, a very musically gifted child with potential for extraordinary performance capabilities on a violin or piano will not develop these gifts in the absence of having a violin or piano accessible. Further, the ultimate level of the realization of the gifted potential is unlikely in the absence of systematic instruction. Some domains are more environmentally dependent for their development than others.

The combinatorial approach applies, equally, to different periods of development. Initially precocious or gifted development may not continue if during a subsequent period of development the proper combination of circumstances is not present. For example, there may be shifts in organismic reliance on environmental input. At an early stage of development a child may be more independent of the nature of environmental input and show precocity or special gifts. However, subsequently, if those gifts are to be maintained and developed, a particularly facilitative environment may be necessary. This need for a particularly facilitative environment may be individually determined or may be characteristic of the given behavioral domain. Early mathematical gifts may, inherently, require environmental input in the form of instruction if they are to be realized in their mature form.

In her study of musical prodigies Bamberger (1982) has noted that there is a transitional period which requires the earlier intuitive musical competence to be integrated with a higher level of formal representations. Those prodigies who accomplish that integration continue to perform in the gifted ranks; those who do not perform at less gifted levels. This failure to integrate to a higher level and thus to maintain highly gifted performance may represent a change in the combinatorial set that accounted for the earlier level of performance. If we better understood the individual character of the required combinatorial set to maintain gifted performance across developmental periods, then it might be possible to manipulate the environmental input for maximal developmental effect.

Children who give no early hint of giftedness in a particular domain but later show extremely gifted performance may represent a variety of combinatorial circumstances. Early on the environmental input to facilitate highly gifted performance may be absent but be present at a later stage. This would require that a level of requisite skill be achieved in the early period upon which later gifted performance could be built. Alternatively, there may be an organismically controlled shift which makes the individual less dependent upon environmental input for performance at gifted levels. For example, the physical changes during adolescence may make highly gifted motor performance possible when such gifted performance was not previously in evidence.

As noted at the outset of this essay, there is little truly developmentally oriented research related to giftedness and talent. We tend to think of giftedness in a developmental sense as being equated to precociousness. But this is too simple and ultimately not useful. The basic issue involves the conditions of the result in highly competent performance in one or more behavioral domains. Are there developmentally critical periods for different domains where environmental input matched to the individual's characteristics is especially important? How do we identify the combinations of conditions for individual children which will most foster gifted performance and maintain giftedness throughout the developmental course? Is early identification essential? More essential in some areas than others?

Our developmental perspective for the identification of the gifted is sometimes like a wedge; the probability of identifying giftedness narrows as development proceeds. But this may not, in fact, be inherent in giftedness. Because the early frames of development, or of learning for that matter, are not extraordinary does not mean that a combination of circumstances will not result in giftedness at later epochs. Sometimes we treat later discoveries of giftedness as delayed discoveries, assuming the individual's gifts have just been overlooked or not fostered in earlier years. However, if development is a continuous process of possibility, it is not unreasonable to suppose that a set of combinatorial circumstances that results in gifted levels of performance can come into existence at various points along the developmental time line. Thus the "grandmother" artist may have come to artistic gifts late in life not in terms of discovering a latent talent but of developing a talent at that point in time.

Equally compelling from the developmental point of view is the notion that early identification of giftedness and proper nurturance of talent can insure continued optimal development that would not otherwise continue in the absence of nurturance. The nature of that nurturance may have to change developmentally as the requisite combinatorial circumstances change. This does not mean that the combinatorial aspects must change, only that they may change. Learning how to track those changing needs effectively is an extremely challenging task.

It is relatively clear that giftedness in a given area is not developmentally detrimental to performance in other areas. Indeed, the evidence from a number of directions is that children highly gifted in a given domain tend to show relatively strong development in other domains as well (Horowitz and O'Brien, 1985). We might expect this under conditions where giftedness is being fostered by environmental input on the theory that the general nature of that environmental input will have relevance to a wide number of behavioral domains and not be specific to a single domain.

CONCLUDING COMMENTS

A systematic, developmentally oriented program designed to increase our understanding of giftedness requires a useful model or theory to guide the research. We also need good measures of individual differences in a variety of domains and good measures of the nature of functional environments. In some domains such as intelligence and cognition, strides are being made in the development of new individual difference measures (e.g., Sternberg, 1985). In the more social, more artistic, and more personal domains our measures are weaker. Our measures of functional environments are crude at best, relying as they do on gross observational techniques or microanalytic strategies that are shot-gun in their approach and little guided by theory. The work to be done in more effectively identifying critical elements of the environment is extensive.

Our most precious resources for the future of our society are our human resources. We made an important commitment of scientific talent and financial support about 25 years ago to enhancing the developmental potential of the retarded among us. The progress in this area has been gratifying. A concomitant commitment has not been made to understanding the developmental potential of the gifted among us. The time is past due for that commitment.

It is important to draw out the developmental issues related to the gifted and the talented in such a way as to frame productive scientific questions. The model presented in this essay has been used to frame such a set of questions. It is not the only model that might be employed, but it has a level of complexity that permits the formation of a set of questions with a strong developmental perspective. It goes beyond the descriptive approach to a functional analysis of the conditions that could produce and maintain gifted development. Other models that might be developed need to approximate, at least, the complexity inherent in the model described here. If we are to conserve the benefit from the power of the resources represented by the gifted we must have a better understanding of the development of giftedness and, ultimately, of how we may nurture the gifted potential in our society. Our world, for all its advances and sophistication, is fragile and vulnerable to the most destructive of forces. Maximizing the possibility of contributions by gifted individuals to the problems we face is imperative. Hopefully, more and more developmentalists will carry out the basic research that might enable us to achieve this goal.

REFERENCES

Bamberger, J. (1982). Growing up prodigies: The midlife crisis. In D. H. Feldman (Ed.), *Developmental approaches to giftedness and creativity.* San Francisco: Jossey-Bass, Inc., 61–78.

Campos, J. J., Barrett, K., Lamb, M. E., Goldsmith, H. H., and Stenberg, C. (1983). Socioemotional development. In P. H. Mussen (Ed.) *Handbook of child psychology.* 4th Edition, Vol. 2: M. M. Halth and J. J. Campos (Eds.), *Infancy and developmental psychobiology.* New York: Wiley, 783–915.

Gardner, H. (1983). *Frames of mind: The theory of multiple intelligence.* New York: Basic Books.

Gowen, J. W. (1952). Humoral and cellular elements in natural and acquired resistance to typhoid. *American Journal of Human Genetics.* Vol. 4, No. 4, 285–302.

Horowitz, F. D. (1987). *Exploring developmental theories: Toward a Structural/behavioral model of development.* Hillsdale, N.J.: Lawrence Erlbaum.

Horowitz, F. D. and O'Brien, M. (1985). *The gifted and the talented: Developmental perspectives.* Washington, DC: The American Psychological Association.

Marland, S. P. (1972). *Education of the gifted and talented: Report to the Congress of the United States by the U.S. Commissioner of Education.* Washington, DC: U.S. Government Printing Office.

Sternberg (1985). *Beyond I.Q.* Cambridge: Cambridge University Press.

Zigler, E. and Balla, D. (Eds.) (1982). *Mental retardation: The developmental difference controversy.* Hillsdale, NJ: Lawrence Erlbaum.

13

Wherefore Art Thou, Multiple Intelligences? Alternative Assessments for Identifying Talent in Ethnically Diverse and Low Income Students

Jonathan A. Plucker
University of Maine
Carolyn M. Callahan
The University of Virginia
Ellen M. Tomchin
The University of Virginia

The recent popularity of Multiple Intelligences (MI) theory corresponds with current efforts to move away from the use of standardized measures of achievement and ability to more authentic assessment techniques, including portfolio and performance-based assessment. Gardner and his

Editor's Note: From Plucker, J.A., Callahan, C.M., & Tomchin, E.M. (1996). Wherefore art thou, multiple intelligences? Alternative assessments for identifying talent in ethnically diverse and low income students. *Gifted Child Quarterly, 40*(2), 80–92.

colleagues have strongly encouraged the application of MI theory to performance-based assessment. This study investigates the reliability and validity of a battery of instruments based on MI theory, including teacher checklists and performance-based assessment activities. The purpose in developing the instruments was the identification of talent in culturally diverse and/or low income kindergarten and first grade students. Results suggest acceptable evidence of reliability but raise questions about the validity of the assessments. This study has implications for both future research efforts and the application of MI-based, performance measures to the assessment and identification of talent.

Discussions of the considerable difficulty encountered in identifying talented minority and disadvantaged children and the differential effects of special programs based upon student ethnicity pervade the literature (Ascher; 1988; Baldwin, 1987; High & Udall, 1983; Maker & Schiever, 1989; Ogbu, 1988). Theorists suggest that assessment procedures relying on broader definitions of *talent* and *intelligence* and the use of alternative assessment strategies will assist school personnel in more accurate identification of exceptional student abilities than do traditional measures (Gardner, 1988; Sternberg, 1988) and will increase representation of children from ethnically diverse populations in programs for the gifted (Patton, 1992). As part of a larger study designed to increase the participation and performance of ethnically diverse and/or economically disadvantaged students in programs for the highly able in a large, urban school district, we have investigated one approach to applying Multiple Intelligences (MI) theory (Gardner, 1983) to the process of identifying potential talents. Similar programs are nearly non-existent in the United States (Patton, Prillaman, & VanTassel-Baska, 1990). The larger study contains five components: talent identification (which is addressed in this study), student instruction, parent outreach, mentoring, and evaluation of project outcomes. The talent identification component is comprised of alternative assessments, including checklists and performance assessments based on MI theory.

Putting Research to Use

The results of this preliminary study suggest that Gardner's multiple intelligences theory can be translated into reliable assessment instruments, but that creating valid assessments is quite difficult. The adults who administer and score alternative assessments apparently tend to exhibit a bias toward linguistic and logical-mathematical intelligence, which results in measures with little construct validity outside of the assessment of verbal and mathematical skills.

Intensive staff training is necessary with any large-scale, high-stakes alternative assessment effort, especially considering this bias toward areas which are traditionally assessed with standardized tests. The research also suggests that development of measures to assess the "personal" intelligences should focus on avoiding the use of indicators that rely on assessment of verbal interactions of the child, which appear to confound the construct validity of the assessments.

Assessment terminology can be confusing and often contradictory (e.g., compare classifications used by Meyer, 1992, and Puckett and Black, 1994). For the purposes of this study, *alternative assessment* is used as the encompassing term for measures of student achievement and ability that do not employ the traditional fixed-response format, such as teacher ratings, peer nominations, and performance-based assessments. Recent use of the term "authentic assessment" implies that fixed-response tests do not provide valid estimates of student ability and achievement.

The interest in alternative assessments as a more accurate measure of student achievement and ability is relatively constant across educational disciplines, including science education (Collins, 1993; Doran, Boorman, Chan, & Hejaily, 1993; Finson & Beaver; 1994; Lawrenz, 1992; Reichel, 1994; Shavelson, Baxter, & Pine, 1991), the education of young children (Hills, 1992; Puckett & Black, 1994), mathematics education (Lane, 1993), reading (Peers, 1993), teacher education (Collins, 1993; Delandshere & Petrosky, 1994; Smith, Millet, & Joy, 1988), special education (Greenwood, 1994; Rivera, 1993), creativity (Baer, 1994), education of the gifted and talented (Baldwin, 1994; Clasen, Middleton, & Connell, 1994), and educational measurement (Reckase, 1993; Stiggins & Plake, 1991). The use of performance assessments has been quite widespread in both the United States and abroad (Maeroff, 1991; Nuttall, 1992; Semple, 1992). A 1990 study by the Center for Research on Evaluation, Standards, and Student Testing (CRESST) found that 23 states were using, developing, or considering the use of performance assessment at a statewide level (Aschbacher; 1991).

The increase in emphasis upon alternative assessment techniques has coincided with the popularity of Multiple Intelligences theory (Gardner, 1983, 1993b). Current understandings of intellectual development and extensive observation of brain-damaged individuals and other special populations (e.g., autistic children, children with learning disabilities) caused Gardner to become dissatisfied with unitary models and measures of intelligence and to develop a new theory of intellectual abilities (Gardner, 1993a). The resulting theory posits seven *intelligences,* although they may also be referred to as *talents* or *abilities*

(Walters & Gardner, 1986): linguistic; logical-mathematical, or the mathematical, scientific, and logical abilities; spatial, which involves knowledge and manipulation of physical things; musical; bodily-kinesthetic, the use of the body to solve problems and accomplish tasks; interpersonal, the ability to understand and interact with other people; and intrapersonal, or the ability to understand one's self and use that knowledge in one's life (see Waters & Gardner, 1985, for an overview of MI theory). Although the linguistic and logical-mathematical intelligences have been historically accented in western societies and, therefore, systems of education, Gardner (1993a) believes all seven intelligences to be of equal importance and relative worth.

However, performance assessment techniques and MI theory are not without controversy. Several intelligence and measurement specialists have cautioned educators that MI theory still has relatively little research support (Matthews, 1988; Sternberg, 1984; Weinberg, 1989). Logistical issues such as increased cost, the need for intensive teacher/observer training, more involved scoring, balance of breadth and depth of coverage, and collection of assessment materials are frequently mentioned in discussions of potential problems with performance-based assessment (Aschbacher, 1991; Darling-Hammond, 1994; Frechtling, 1991; Guskey, 1994; Marzano, 1994; Miller & Legg, 1993; O'Neil, 1992; Stiggins, 1991; Wolf, LeMahieu, & Eresh, 1992).

Psychometric issues are also raised during consideration of the quality of alternative assessments, specifically performance assessments (Burger & Burger, 1994; Dunbar; Koretz, & Hoover; 1991; Haertel, 1994; Herman & Winters, 1994; Linn, 1994; Linn & Burton, 1994; MacGinitie, 1993; Messick, 1994; Miller & Legg, 1993). As Worthen (1993) stated:

> [S]ome evidence that the technical quality of the assessment is good enough to yield a truthful picture of student abilities is essential. To succeed, alternative assessment must show that its tasks and measures are authentic (not merely authentic-looking) assessment. Otherwise, the promise it holds for improving teaching and learning will go unfulfilled. (p. 448)

Several authors question whether traditional standards of reliability and validity should be applied to alternative assessments, and if so, what types of reliability and validity should be considered (Baker, O'Neil, & Linn, 1993; Linn, Baker, & Dunbar, 1991; Swezey, 1981; Wolf, Bixby, Glenn, & Gardner, 1991). Wiggins (1993) expresses concern over the use of content, concurrent, and construct validity to demonstrate validity of performance assessments and suggests that the authenticity and face validity of the tasks are most worthy of educators' concern. Linn, Baker, and Dunbar (1991) stress the importance of transfer and generalizability of assessment results, while noting (along with Dunbar, Koretz, and Hoover, 1991) the difficulties encountered when generalizing across performance tasks. Other recommendations for establishing evidence of validity include reliance upon criterion validity and normative data

(Burger and Burger, 1994) and content, concurrent, and predictive validity (Swezey, 1981). Baker, O'Neil, and Linn (1993) note that certain generalizability and reliability issues are less important when assessments are used at the group level, and similarly, Haertel (1994) recommends that, until adequate reliability and validity are assured for performance assessments, results *not* be interpreted at the individual level.

Few how-to and/or pro-performance assessment publications mention psychometric concerns (see Herman, Aschbacher, & Winters, 1992 and Moon, 1993 for exceptions). To what extent are these technical issues the concern of practitioners? Robinson (1994) believes that psychometric concerns regarding alternative assessments "are to be battled over by measurement experts" (p. 22). This attitude is misleading since "internal self-criticism is rather scarce among proponents of alternative assessment . . . The more broadly accepted [alternative assessment] becomes, the less frequently it will be challenged" (Worthen, 1993, p. 447). This lack of attention will eventually slow the development of quality alternative assessments and lessen their long-term impact upon education. Additional research into the psychometric qualities and proper use of performance assessment techniques is needed in order to guide their proper use (Baker, Aschbacher, Niemi, & Sato, 1992; Hambleton & Murphy, 1992; Miller & Legg, 1993; Stiggins, 1991; Worthen, 1993).

MI Theory and Performance-Based Assessment

Gardner (1991) and his colleagues at Project Spectrum (Adams & Feldman, 1993; Hatch & Gardner, 1990; Kornhaber & Gardner, 1993; Krechevsky, 1991; Walters, 1992) strongly support the use of alternative assessment techniques, especially those involving performance-based assessment, to identify and evaluate student abilities with respect to MI theory. Maker (1992, 1993) and her colleagues at Project Discover (Maker, Nielson, & Rogers, 1994) are developing a series of MI-based, performance assessments, and similar projects are under way across the country (see Gardner, 1993b; Maker, Nielson, & Rogers, 1994). However, published research involving these efforts is not plentiful and has involved small sample sizes (Gardner & Hatch, 1989).

The study of the psychometric properties of alternative assessments based on MI theory is the purpose of this paper. The following objectives were addressed:

1. to confirm whether a particular set of activities and checklists based on MI theory assess different abilities or intelligences or assess only linguistic and logical-mathematical abilities;
2. to determine the reliability and validity of each subscale logically derived from the set of activities;
3. to assess the gender, ethnic, or school differences on the assessments.

METHOD

Sample

The sample for this study consisted of 1,813 children enrolled in kindergarten and first grade in 16 schools in a large school district during the 1992–1993 school year. The school district is situated in one of the 30 largest cities in the country, and recent desegregation efforts result in a student population drawn from urban, suburban, and rural areas. The target population for testing the instruments was ethnically diverse and/or low socioeconomic kindergarten and first grade students. Female students comprised 48.2% (*n*=873) of the sample, and ethnic composition of the students was as follows: Caucasian, 18.8%; African American, 71.3%; Asian American, 1.8%; Hispanic American, 2.5%; and other ethnic groups, 3.5%. Socioeconomic status (SES) was determined by participation in the federal government's free/reduced lunch program. The lunch status could not be determined for 59.8% of the sample. Of the remaining 729 students, 48.4% (*n*=353) received free or reduced lunch.

Validity sample. Data on additional measures of attitude, self-concept, and achievement (see below) were obtained for the 371 children who entered the talent development program. In the following sections that report evidence of concurrent validity, only results from students in the validity sample were used. Since these students generally received higher scores on the assessment activities, the results of the analyses which employed the restricted sample should not be generalized to the entire sample. In the validity sample, 49.6% (*n*=184) of the students were female, and the ethnic composition of the students was as follows: Caucasian, 23.5%; African American, 63.6%; Asian American, 6.5%; Hispanic American, 2.7%; and other ethnic groups, 3.8%. Nearly half of the students (48.2%, *n*=179) received free or reduced lunch.

Instrumentation

In the spring of 1993, the subjects were assessed using the Multiple Intelligences Assessment Technique (Udall & Passe, 1993), which is based upon the work of Project Spectrum at Harvard and that of C. June Maker at the University of Arizona (Maker, 1992; Maker, Nielson, & Rogers, 1994; Maker, Rogers, & Nielson, 1992) with local modifications. The technique consists of 13 performance-based activities, teacher ratings, and observational checklists corresponding to four of the multiple intelligences: logical-mathematical, linguistic, spatial, and interpersonal. The 13 checklists, ratings, and activities are summarized by subscale in Table 1. For purposes of illustrating, a complete set of instructions for activity 2 (Pablo Blocks and Connectors) is included in the Appendix. It includes a materials list, teacher/observer scripts, a sample student evaluation sheet, and a suggested scoring rubric. Scoring rubrics were developed by project staff after initial field tests of the assessments, and

Table 1 Activities Used in Alternative Assessment Categorized by Intelligence

Activity Title	*Type of Assessment*
Spatial intelligence	
1 spatial checklist	teacher rating
2 Pablo	students construct 3-D animal from puzzle pieces
3 mechanical pump	students take pump apart, put it back together
4 tangrams	students manipulate puzzle pieces
5 artwork	students draw or paint a picture
Logical-mathematical intelligence	
6 math-logical checklist	teacher rating
7 bus activity	board game
8 math activity	students solve mathematical problems
Linguistic intelligence	
9 linguistic checklist	teacher rating
10 story-telling activity	students tell a story using various objects
11 pictorial writing prompt	students write or draw a story
Interpersonal intelligence	
12 interpersonal checklist	teacher rating
13 interpersonal skills	observation checklist

teachers and observers were encouraged to add to the rubric sheets as they gained experience with administering the assessments and evaluating student performance.

For each activity, student performance was rated on a scale as "not evident or not observed" in a given setting (0), "evident" (1), or "extremely evident" (2). Teachers and external observers were given training on administration of the assessments, and guidelines were provided with respect to typical behaviors that should be rated 0, 1, or 2 for each assessment activity (Udall & Passe, 1993). In order to obtain estimates of concurrent validity, the Iowa Test of Basic Skills (ITBS; language arts, mathematics, reading comprehension, and vocabulary sub-tests) were administered.

Data Analysis

Reliability. Because of logistical problems associated with large-scale assessments, test-retest and inter-rater reliability could not be obtained for the performance assessments, although obtaining this evidence is a priority of future administrations of the assessments. Cronbach's alpha was calculated as a measure of internal consistency for each of the four subscales.

Validity. Correlations among the assessment subscales and ITBS subscale scores were computed to obtain evidence of construct validity. Factor analysis was used to determine whether the activities assess the corresponding four intelligences.

Gender, ethnic, and school differences. Fixed effect analyses of variance (ANOVAS) were computed using the subscale scores as dependent variables to determine the presence of any differences based on gender, ethnicity, or school. Eta squared (η^2), the percent of variance accounted for by significant effects, was calculated as a measure of effect size (Tabachnik & Fidell, 1989), and recommended guidelines for interpreting effect sizes (Rosenthal & Rubin, 1979; Rosnow & Rosenthal, 1988) were followed.

RESULTS

Reliability

For each of the subscales included in Table 1, Cronbach's alpha was calculated. Resulting values for alpha (α) are acceptably large (Thorndike & Hagen, 1955): spatial, $\alpha = .74$; logical-mathematical, $\alpha = .73$; linguistic, $\alpha = .72$; interpersonal, $\alpha = .87$.

Validity

Factor analysis. Factor analysis was used to confirm the presence of four intelligences in the battery of activities. Principal factors extraction with varimax rotation was performed using SPSSx on the 13 activities, using principal components extraction to define the four factors (Table 2). Variables were generally well-defined by the four resulting factors, with communality values (h^2 or variance shared by all four factors together) ranging from .57 to .78. Overall, the four factors accounted for 67.5% of the variance of student scores on the 13 activities before rotation.

With a minimum loading of .40 for inclusion of a variable in the interpretation of a factor; only activity 6 loads on more than one factor. The activities designed to assess linguistic and interpersonal intelligence (activities 9 through 13) all load onto the first factor; logical-mathematical activities (6, 7, and 8) load onto the second factor; and the five spatial activities load on the third (activities 1, 3, and 5) and fourth factors (2 and 4).

Construct validity. Inter-item correlations appear in Table 3. High correlations among the teacher rating scales and the observation checklists (with the exception of the spatial scale) were noted.

A multitrait-multimethod matrix (Campbell & Fiske, 1967) appears in Table 4. Values in the validity diagonal (italicized values) are moderate for the math subscales and low for the language/linguistic subscales. The different trait-different method correlations are sufficiently low to provide evidence of discriminant validity, with the exception of the relatively high correlation between the ITBS

Table 2 Factor Loadings and Communalities (h_2) for Principal Factors Extraction and Varimax Rotation for Performance-Based Assessment Activities

Activity	F_1[a]	F_2	F_3	F_4	h^2
12 – interpersonal checklist (I)[b]	.78	.38	.05	.18	.78
9 – linguistic checklist (V)	.76	.33	.17	.13	.74
13 – interpers. observation (I)	.72	.38	.03	.22	.71
10 – storytelling (V)	.71	-.10	.34	.04	.63
11 – pictorial activity (V)	.56	.31	.39	-.01	.57
7 – bus activity (M)	.15	.77	.10	.10	.64
8 – math worksheet (M)	.25	.70	.24	.11	.63
6 – math-logical checklist (M)	.40	.63	.35	.17	.71
3 – pump activity (S)	.08	.13	.80	.16	.70
5 – artwork activity (S)	.35	.31	.56	.24	.59
1 – spatial checklist (S)	.32	.35	.55	.33	.63
4 – tangrams activity (S)	.00	.22	.16	.82	.75
2 – Pablo activity (S)	.26	.02	.18	.78	.70

[a]Factor labels: F1 linguistic – verbal
F2 logical – mathematical
F3 spatial – general
F4 spatial – tangrams
[b]Theoretical subscales in parentheses: (V) linguistic; (M) math; (S) spatial; (I) interpersonal

language subscale and the math performance assessments. Unfortunately, this correlation exceeds the correlation between the ITBS language subscale and linguistic performance assessments. The ITBS language subscale also correlates more highly with the math teacher checklist than the linguistic teacher checklist.

Gender, Ethnic, SES, and School Differences

The full sample of 1,813 students was used to investigate whether gender, SES, and school differences exist on the battery of assessment tasks and rating scales. The Bonferroni procedure was used to adjust for the influence of multiple analyses upon the study-wide alpha level (α=.05/16=.003). A two-way, between subjects design with school (16 levels) and gender as independent variables revealed that a significant school effect is present for all four subscales, although the corresponding effect sizes are small (Table 5). Post hoc analysis utilizing the Tukey-b procedure at the .05 level indicate that school 4 has significantly lower scores on the math-logical and interpersonal subscales than over half of the other schools (although no pattern was apparent with respect to the other schools). For the linguistic subscale, schools 13, 12, and 16 scored significantly higher than a majority of the other schools. On the spatial subscale, schools 12 and 13 scored significantly higher than schools 14, 15, 4, 3, 2, and 7; school 15 scored significantly lower than 12 schools. No discernible,

Table 3 Inter-item Correlations Among Assessment Activities and Checklists

Act.	1(S)b	2(S)	3(S)	4(S)	5(S)	6(M)	7(M)	8(M)	9(V)	10(V)	11(V)	12(I)	13(I)
1	1.00a	.13	.11	.08	.17	.22	.14	.13	.19	.13	.13	.19	.17
2		1.00	.19	.30	.27	.28	.22	.23	.26	.23	.19	.23	.24
3			1.00	.41	.30	.27	.18	.20	.19	.13	.19	.20	.20
4				1.00	.45	.27	.20	.22	.19	.09	.20	.19	.23
5					1.00	.47	.33	.36	.42	.31	.54	.40	.44
6						1.00	.47	.53	.61	.33	.47	.58	.53
7							1.00	.38	.35	.22	.34	.38	.37
8								1.00	.41	.27	.42	.40	.40
9									1.00	.47	.54	.69	.63
10										1.00	.36	.37	.36
11											1.00	.50	.47
12												1.00	.78
13													1.00

[a]For all coefficients, $p < .01$

[b]Subscales in parentheses: (V) linguistic; (M) math; (S) spatial; (I) interpersonal

Table 4 Multi-Trait Multi-Method Matrix

		Pref. Assessments			Teacher Checklists			ITBS	
		Math	*Ling.*	*Spatial*	*Math*	*Ling.*	*Spatial*	*Math*	*Ling.*
	Math	1.00							
Performance	Ling.	.14*	1.00						
Assessments	Spatial	.11	.09	1.00					
	Math	.41**	.24**	.16*	1.00				
Teacher	Ling.	.16*	.46**	.12	.36*	1.00			
Checklists	Spatial	.09	.20*	.47**	.50**	.27**	1.00		
	Math	.29**	.11*	.15*	.22**	.06	.09	1.00	
ITBS	Lang.	.25**	.16**	.06	.17**	.08	.07	.70**	1.00

*$p < .05$ **$p < .01$ (2-tailed)

overarching pattern emerges from the analysis, suggesting inconsistency rather than systematic bias: Schools whose students scored high on one subscale scored lower on others and vice-versa. With respect to the two significant gender effects, female students scored higher than male students on both the linguistic and interpersonal subscales, although the effect sizes are rather small.

Because the number of African American and Caucasian students greatly exceeded the number of Hispanic American and Asian American students in the sample, students were randomly selected from the larger ethnic groups to equalize group size in the corresponding one-way ANOVA. Resulting ANOVAS with the Tukey-b post hoc procedure indicate that Asian students scored or were rated significantly higher than all other ethnic groups on all four subscales: math-logical, $F(4, 149)=12.57$, $p<.0001$, $\eta^2=.252$; linguistic, $F(4, 142)=4.49$, $p<.002$, $\eta^2=.112$; spatial, $F(4, 79)=13.42$, $p<.0001$, $\eta^2=.405$; and interpersonal, $F(4, 157)=5.01$, $p<.001$, $\eta^2=.113$. The only other difference between specific ethnic groups occurred on the spatial subscale—students classified ethnically as "other" by the school district (e.g., students of Asian Indian or mixed ethnicity) had significantly higher scores than Hispanic American students.

DISCUSSION

Reliability evidence suggests that the subscales are internally consistent. The factor analysis confirmed the presence of the linguistic and logical-mathematical subscales, but the presence of the two remaining subscales could not be confirmed. The combination of linguistic and interpersonal intelligence activities on the first factor is not surprising, since interpersonal communication contains a major verbal component. Analysis of the Interpersonal Checklist (Udall & Passe, 1993, p. 62) reveals that many of the items on the checklist can be interpreted with an emphasis on verbal-linguistic talent (e.g., "Acts as peacemaker," "shows humor in interactions," "Is listened to and sought out by other children"). The split of spatial activities between the third and fourth factors is more puzzling. Activities 2 (Pablo) and 4 (Tangrams) are very similar, so their loadings on the fourth factor were expected, but their separation from the other spatial activities is not easily explained. Since the fourth factor accounts for little explained variance (when a three-factor model is used, the third and fourth factors collapse), the split of spatial activities may have little practical significance.

No meaningful gender differences were found on the assessments, but the relatively high ratings of Asian American students are cause for concern. Teacher subjectivity may be influencing the assessments, or the use of performance assessments to avoid ethnic bias on standardized tests may simply be misguided. Significant differences in ratings among schools exist (although they are associated with small effect sizes), which supports previous research on the inconsistency associated with performance-based assessments (e.g., Aschbacher, 1991; Haertel, 1994).

Analysis of the multitrait-multimethod matrix yields limited evidence of both convergent and discriminant validity. A possible explanation for the relatively large correlations among the mathematical-logical subscale and the other subscales and ITBS sub-tests may be that the activities and checklist associated with the math-logical subscale are the most objectively scored of those in the MI-based alternative assessment batter.

Establishing evidence of concurrent validity of new assessment tools based on alternative assessments of intelligence presents a difficult challenge to test developers and educators who wish to use the assessments. The construct validity issue becomes immediately apparent as we examine our data. On the one hand, the definitions of logical-mathematical intelligence and linguistic intelligence would lead us to expect that ability in these areas would correlate

Table 5 ANOVA Results for Assessment Subscales

	School Effects			*Gender Effects*			*School X Gender*		
Subscale	*F*	*p*[a]	$\eta 2$	*F*	*p*	$\eta 2$	*F*	*p*	$\eta 2$
Math-logical	3.04	.001	.026	.01	.945	n/a	1.32	.182	n/a
Linguistic	6.16	.001	.051	12.22	.001	.007	1.43	.123	n/a
Spatial	7.28	.001	.060	4.12	.043	n/a	1.38	.150	n/a
Interpersonal	4.13	.001	.035	21.21	.001	.012	1.40	.140	n/a

[a]$\alpha = (.05/16) = .003$
η^2 = effect size

Suggested Scoring Rubric

Pablo Rubric

Extremely Evident (2)	*Evident (1)*	*Not Evident (2)*
Original Ideas	Copies And Adds Own Details	Copies with No Additions
3-D	Simple Design	1 Shape (Animal Body) With 4 Connectors for Legs
Something That Stands Up	Common Objects—People, Turtle, Etc.	2-D
Symmetry With More Than 4 Pieces		
Moveable Parts		
Complex Design Many Pieces/Connectors		
Object Is Recognizable Representational Art		
Absorbed, Excited, or Enthusiastic		Bored, Frustrated
Makes Many Creations		Makes 1 Simple Creation

* A set of scoring guidelines for giving scores to student work. Please add to these lists as you work with your students.

with high scores on achievement tests which assess outcomes relating to high ability in those areas. On the other hand, the writings of Gardner (1984) are clearly critical of traditional assessment tools as being too narrowly conceived to capture the richness of aptitude and performance. If this is true, then how can the validity of MI-based assessments be established? Is MI theory essentially unable to be proven? Gardner and Hatch (1990) address this issue directly:

> Some critics have suggested that MI theory cannot be disconfirmed . . . If future assessments do not reveal strengths and weaknesses within a population, if performances on different activities prove to be systematically correlated, and if constructs (and instruments) like the IQ explain the preponderance of the variance on activities configured to tap specific intelligences, then MI Theory will have to be revamped. (p. 8)

We strongly believe that, for legal, educational, and ethical reasons, performance assessments used for high-stakes purposes such as identifying potentially talented students need to be reliable, valid, appropriately normed, and equally fair to students regardless of gender and ethnicity. This belief is voiced by others who are concerned with the proper use of alternative assessment techniques (O'Neil, 1992). Miller and Legg (1993) believe that "when the stakes for assessment scores are high, the traditional notion of valid and reliable interpretation of scores remains critical" (p. 10), and Messick has argued that

> [S]uch basic assessment issues as validity, reliability, comparability, and fairness need to be uniformly addressed for all assessments because they are not just measurement principles, they are social values that have meaning and force outside of measurement wherever evaluative judgment and decisions are made. (Messick, 1994, p. 13)

Future Directions

This study will be replicated with successive cohorts, with determination of evidence of stability and inter-rater agreement as a high priority. Teacher attitudes and experiences relative to the assessments, which are generally mentioned in the literature but not explored (see King, 1991; Peers, 1993 for exceptions), will also be examined, as well as the predictive validity of the assessments.

MI theory and alternative assessments may hold substantial implications for education of gifted and talented students, and it is not surprising that many educators are enthusiastically applying these innovations to the classroom. But educators using MI theory, alternative assessments, and combinations of the two should subject the programs to rigorous evaluation. Only then can the potential contributions of Multiple Intelligences theory and alternative assessment to education be known.

REFERENCES

Adams, M. L., & Feldman, D. H. (1993). Project Spectrum: A theory-based approach to early education. In R. Pasnak & M. L. Howe (Eds.), *Emerging themes in cognitive development. Volume II: Competencies.* New York: Springer-Verlag.

Aschbacher, R. R. (1991). Performance assessment: State activity interest, and concerns. *Applied Measurement in Education, 4,* 275–288.

Ascher, C. (1988). Improving the school-home connection for poor and minority urban students. *The Urban Review, 20,* 109–123.

Baer, J. (1994). Performance assessments of creativity: Do they have long-term stability? *Roeper Review, 17,* 7–11.

Baker, E. L., Aschbacher, P. R., Niemi, D., & Sato, E. (1992). *CRESST performance assessment models: Assessing content area explanations.* Los Angeles: National Center for Research on Evaluation, Standards, and Student Testing.

Baker, E. L., O'Neil, H. F., Jr., & Linn, R. L. (1993). Policy and validity prospects for performance-based assessment. *American Psychologist, 48,* 1210–1218.

Baldwin, A. Y. (1987). I'm Black but look at me. I am also gifted. *Gifted Child Quarterly, 31,* 180–185.

Baldwin, A. Y. (1994). The seven plus story: Developing hidden talent among students in socioeconomically disadvantaged environments. *Gifted Child Quarterly, 38,* 80–84.

Burger, S. E., & Burger, D. L. (1994). Determining the validity of performance-based assessment. *Educational Measurement: Issues and Practices, 13*(1), 9–15.

Campbell, D. T., & Fiske, D. W. (1967). Convergent and discriminant validation by the multitrait-multimethod matrix. In D. N. Jackson & S. Messick (Eds.), *Problems in human assessment* (pp. 124–132). New York: McGraw Hill.

Clasen, D. R., Middleton, J. A., & Connell, T. J. (1994). Assessing artistic and problem solving performance in minority and non-minority students using a nontraditional multidimensional approach. *Gifted Child Quarterly, 38,* 27–32.

Collins, A. (1993). Performance-based assessment of biology teachers: Promises and pitfalls. *Journal of Research in Science Teaching, 30,* 1103–1120.

Darling-Hammond, L. (1994). Performance-based assessment and educational equity. *Harvard Educational Review, 64,* 5–30.

Delandshere, G., & Petrosky, A. R. (1994). Capturing teachers' knowledge: Performance assessment. *Educational Researcher, 23*(5), 11–18.

Doran, R. L., Boorman, J., Chan, F., & Hejaily, N. (1993). Alternative assessment of high school laboratory skills. *Journal of Research in Science Teaching, 30,* 1121–1131.

Dunbar, S. B., Koretz, D. M., & Hoover, H. D. (1991). Quality control in the development and use of performance assessments. *Applied Measurement in Education, 4,* 289–303.

Finson, K. D., & Beaver, J. B. (1994). Performance assessment: Getting started. *Science Scope, 18*(1), 44–49.

Frechtling, J. A. (1991). Performance assessment: Moonstruck or the real thing? *Educational Measurement: Issues and Practice, 10*(4), 23–25.

Gardner, H. (1983). *Frames of mind.* New York: Basic Books.

Gardner, H. (1984). Assessing intelligences: A comment on "Testing intelligence without I.Q. tests.' *Phi Delta Kappan, 65,* 699–700.

Gardner, H. (1988). Beyond the IQ: Education and human development. *National Forum, 68*(2), 4–7.

Gardner, H. (1991). Assessment in context: The alternative to standardized testing. In B. R. Gifford & M. C. O'Connor (Eds.), *Changing assessments: Alternative views of aptitude, achievement, and instruction* (pp. 77–120). Boston: Kluwer.

Gardner, H. (1993a). In a nutshell. In H. Gardner, *Multiple intelligences* (pp. 5–12). New York: Basic Books.

Gardner, H. (1993b). *Multiple intelligences.* New York: Basic Books.

Gardner, H., & Hatch, T. (1989). Multiple intelligences go to school: Educational implications of the theory of multiple intelligences. *Educational Researcher, 18*(8), 4–9.

Gardner, H., & Hatch, T. (1990). *Multiple intelligence go to school: Educational implications of the theory of multiple intelligences* (Technical Report No. 4). New York: Center for Technology in Education. (ERIC Document Reproduction Service No. 324–366)

Greenwood, C. R. (Guest Ed.). (1994). Technology-based assessment within special education [Special Issue]. *Exceptional Children, 61*(2).

Guskey, T. R. (1994). What you assess may not be what you get. *Educational Leadership, 51*(6), 51–54.

Haertel, E. H. (1994). Theoretical and practical considerations. In T. R. Guskey (Ed.), *High stakes performance assessment: Perspectives on Kentucky's educational reform* (pp. 65–75). Thousand Oaks, CA: Corwin Press.

Hambleton, R. K. (1992). A psychometric perspective on authentic measurement. *Applied Measurement in Education, 5,* 1–16.

Hatch, T., & Gardner, H. (1990). If Binet had looked beyond the classroom: The assessment of multiple intelligences. *International Journal of Educational Research, 14,* 415–429.

Herman, J. L., Aschbacher, P. R., & Winters, L. (1992). *A practical guide to alternative assessment.* Alexandria, VA: Association for Supervision and Curriculum Development.

Herman, J. L., & Winters, L. (1994). Portfolio research: A slim collection. *Educational Leadership, 52*(2), 48–55.

High, M. H., & Udall, A. J. (1983). Teacher ratings of students in relation to ethnicity of students and school ethnic balance. *Journal for the Education of the Gifted, 6,* 154–165.

Hills, T. W. (1992). Reaching potentials through appropriate assessment. In S. Bredekamp & T. Rosegrant (Eds.), *Reaching potentials: Appropriate curriculum and assessment for young children. Vol. 1* pp. 43–63). Washington, DC: National Association for the Education of Young Children.

King, B. (1991). Teachers' views on performance-based assessments. *Teacher Education Quarterly, 18,* 109–119.

Kornhaber, M., & Gardner, H. (1993). *Varieties of excellence: Identifying and assessing children's talents.* New York: The National Center for Restructuring Education, Schools, and Teaching.

Krechevsky, M. (1991). Project Spectrum: An innovative assessment alternative. *Educational Leadership, 48,* 43–48.

Lane, S. (1993). The conceptual framework for the development of a mathematics performance assessment instrument. *Educational Measurement: Issues and Practices, 12*(2), 16–23.

Lawrenz, F. (1992). Authentic assessment. In F. Lawrenz, K. Cochran, J. Krajcik, & R. Simpson (Eds.), *Research matters . . . to the science teacher* (NARST Monograph No. 5) (pp. 65–70). Manhattan, KS: National Association of Research in Science Teaching.

Linn, R. L. (1994). Performance assessment: Policy promises and technical measurement standards. *Educational Researcher, 23*(9), 4–14.

Linn, R. L., Baker, E., & Dunbar, S. (1991). Complex, performance-based assessment: Expectations and validation criteria. *Educational Researcher, 20*(8), 15–21.

Linn, R. L., & Burton, E. (1994). Performance-based assessment: Implications of task specificity. *Educational Measurement: Issues and Practices, 13*(1), 5–8, 15.

MacGinitie, W. H. (1993). Some limits of assessment. *Journal of Reading, 36,* 556–560.

Maeroff, G. I. (1991). Assessing alternative assessment. *Phi Delta Kappan, 73,* 273–281.

Maker, C. J. (1992). Intelligence and creativity in multiple intelligences: Identification and development. *Educating Able Learners: Discovering & Nurturing Talent, 17,* 12–19.

Maker, C. J. (1993). Creativity, intelligence, and problem solving: A definition and design for cross-cultural research and measurement related to giftedness. *Gifted Education International, 9,* 68–77.

Maker, C. J., Nielson, A. B., & Rogers, J. A. (1994). Giftedness, diversity and problem-solving. *Teaching Exceptional Children, 27*(1), 4–18.

Maker, C. J., Rogers, J. A., & Nielson, A. B. (1992). *Assessment/observation of problem solving abilities.* Tucson, AZ: University of Arizona.

Maker, C. J., & Schiever, S. W. (Eds.). (1989). *Critical issues in gifted education: Defensible programs for cultural and ethnic minorities. Vol. II.* Austin, TX: Pro-ed.

Marzano, R. J. (1994). Lessons from the field about outcome-based performance assessments. *Educational Leadership, 51*(6), 44–50.

Matthews, D. (1988). Gardner's multiple intelligence theory: An evaluation of relevant research literature and a consideration of its application to gifted education. *Roeper Review, 11,* 100–104.

Messick, S. (1994). The interplay of evidence and consequences in the validation of performance assessments. *Educational Researcher, 23*(2), 13–23.

Miller, M. D., & Legg, S. M. (1993). Alternative assessment in a high-stakes environment. *Educational Measurement: Issues and Practices, 12*(2), 9–15.

Moon, T. R. (1993). *A teacher's guide to developing performance-based assessments.* Charlottesville, VA: Bureau of Educational Research, University of Virginia.

Nuttall, D. L. (1992). Performance assessment: The message from England. *Educational Leadership, 49*(8), 54–57.

Ogbu, J. U. (1988, spring). Human intelligence testing: A cultural-ecological perspective. *National Forum, 68*(2), 23–29.

O'Neil, J. (1992). Putting performance assessment to the test. *Educational Leadership, 49*(8), 14–19.

Patton, J. M. (1992). Assessment and identification of African-American learners with gifts and talents. *Exceptional Children, 59,* 150–159.

Patton, J. M., Prillaman, D., VanTassel-Baska, J. (1990). The nature and extent of programs for the disadvantaged/gifted in the United States and territories. *Gifted Child Quarterly, 34,* 94–96.

Peers, M. G. (1993). A teacher/researcher's experience with performance-based assessment as a diagnostic tool. *Journal of Reading, 36,* 544–548.

Puckett, M. B., & Black, J. K. (1994). *Authentic assessment of the young child.* New York: Merrill.

Reckase, M. (Ed.). (1993). Performance assessment [Special Issue]. *Journal of Educational Measurement, 30*(3).

Reichel, A. G. (1994). Performance assessment: Five practical approaches. *Science and Children, 32*(2), 21–25.

Rivera, D. (1993). Performance, authentic, and portfolio assessment: Emerging alternative assessment options in search of an empirical basis. *Diagnostique, 18,* 325–348.

Robinson, A. (1994). Assessment, identification, and evaluation. *Tempo, 14*(2), 1, 22–23.

Rosenthal, R., & Rubin, D. B. (1979). A note on percent variance explained as a measure of the importance of effects. *Journal of Applied Social Psychology, 9,* 395–396.

Rosnow, R. L., & Rosenthal, R. (1988). Focused tests of significance and effect size estimation in counseling psychology. *Journal of Counseling Psychology, 35,* 203–208.

Semple, B. McL. (1992). *Performance assessment: An international experiment* (ETS Report No. 22-CAEP-06). Princeton, NJ: IAEP/ETS.

Shavelson, R. J., Baxter, G. P., & Pine, J. (1991). Performance assessment in science. *Applied Measurement in Science, 4,* 347–362.

Smith, G. P., Miller, M. C., & Joy, J. (1988). A case study of the impact of performance based testing on the supply of minority teachers. *Journal of Teacher Education, 39,* 45–53.

Sternberg, R. J. (1984). Fighting butter battles. *Phi Delta Kappan, 65,* 700.

Sternberg, R. J. (1988, spring). Beyond IQ testing. *National Forum, 68*(2), 8–11.

Stiggins, R. J. (1991). Facing the challenges of a new era of educational assessment. *Applied Measurement in Education, 4,* 263–273.

Stiggins, R. J., & Plake, B. (Eds.). (1991). Performance assessment [Special issue]. *Applied Measurement in Education, 4*(4).

Swezey, R. W. (1981). *Individual performance assessment: An approach to criterion-referenced test development.* Reston, VA: Reston Publishing.

Tabachnik, B. G., & Fidell, L. S. (1989). *Multivariate statistics (2nd ed.).* New York: HarperCollins.

Thorndike, R. L., & Hagen, E. (1955). *Measurement and evaluation in psychology and education.* New York: Wiley & Sons.

Udall, A. J., & Passe, M. (1993). *Gardner-based/Performance-based Assessment Notebook.* Charlotte, NC: Charlotte-Mecklenburg Schools.

Walters, J. (1992). Application of multiple intelligences research in alternative assessment. In *Focus on Evaluation and Measurement.* Washington, DC: National Research Symposium on Limited English Proficient Student Issues. (ERIC Document Reproduction Service No. ED 349 812)

Walters, J. M., & Gardner, H. (1985). The development and education of intelligences. In F. Link (Ed.), *Essays on the intellect* (pp. 1–21). Washington, DC: Curriculum Development Associates.

Walters, J., & Gardner, H. (1986). The theory of multiple intelligences: Some issues and answers. In R. J. Sternberg & R. Wagner Eds.), *Practical intelligences* (pp. 163–181). New York: Cambridge University Press.

Weinberg, R. A. (1989). Intelligence and IQ: Landmark issues and great debates. *American Psychologist, 44,* 98–104.

Wiggins, G. (1993). Assessment: Authenticity, context, and validity. *Phi Delta Kappan, 75,* 200–214.

Wolf, D., Bixby, J., Glenn III, J., & Gardner, H. (1991). To use their minds well: Investigating new forms of student assessment. In G. Grant (Ed.), *Review of research in education: Volume 17* (pp. 31–74). Washington, DC: American Educational Research Association.

Wolf, D. P., LeMahieu, E. G., & Eresh, J. (1992). Good measure: Assessment as a tool for educational reform. *Educational Leadership, 49*(8), 8–13.

Worthen, B. R. (1993). Critical issues that will determine the future of alternative assessment. *Phi Delta Kappan, 74,* 444–454.

APPENDIX

Description of Pablo Task (Activity 2)

Taken from Udall and Passe (1993) with the permission of the authors. Readers are reminded that teachers and observers received extensive training in the administration of the assessments and that research evidence of the assessments' effectiveness is inconclusive at this time. The following material is provided for illustrative purposes only.

Materials Needed

- 1 classroom set of Pablo Blocks and Connectors, individual cups or bowls for connectors
- Color photos of building or mountains
- Script and directions
- Student folders/evaluation sheets

Instructions for Teachers

Please allow 30–35 minutes for this series of activities. Move as rapidly as possible through steps 1–4. Allow a major portion of the time for steps 5 and 6.

Children should be divided into four groups, with one observer in each group. Each group should be seated around a table. A Pablo set should be located in the center of the group.

Teacher Says: You may take just a few minutes to make something with the pieces in front of you. (approximately 5 minutes)

> I am holding a picture of some tall buildings. Find one or more pieces that look like tall buildings. Make your buildings on the table in front of you. (approximately 3 minutes)
>
> Please put all pieces in the middle. Which pieces could you use to make mountains? Make your mountains on the table in front of you. (approximately 3 minutes)
>
> Please put all pieces back in the middle.

Teacher Action: Give an equal number of Connectors to each child and demonstrate use of Connectors.

Teacher Says: Make an animal with as many pieces as you need. Make any animal you want to make. You can tell about it if you want.

Teacher Action: Allow time for observers to draw a picture of or describe in words each student's construction(s). (approximately 10 minutes)

Teacher Says: Please put all pieces back in the middle. Now you may make anything you would like to make using as many pieces as you want to use. (again, allow at least 10 minutes)

(At conclusion of activity) Put all of the Pablos and Connectors in their separate bags.

Instructions for Observers

Introduce yourself to the children at your table. Make certain you know how to pronounce each child's name. Record their names on the observation sheet.

Observer Action: During the "warm up" (free play, tall buildings, mountains) phase of this activity, encourage the children as they work and record any creative behaviors in the comments section. Use the codes to note behaviors.

Teachers will give directions about Connectors.

Observer Action: Give each child at the table an equal number of Connectors in a cup or bowl. Give as many as possible. Encourage children to make an animal. They can make any animal they want—real or imaginary (children can make more than one animal if they have time).

Ask them to tell you about their animal(s) and record as much as possible of what they say. Always make a sketch of the animal(s) on the observation sheet. If several children make the same animal, be sure to record which child made it first. Note which children make the same animal but make it in a different way. This is not considered copying. Show equal approval for all constructions and descriptions.

Please Note: Accept all constructions, whether or not they are animals. Show approval for anything children make and encourage everyone in the group.

Encourage the children to take apart their animals completely and place all pieces back in the middle when the teacher directs them to do so. Suggest that they use different pieces in their next activity.

For the open-ended construction activity, encourage children to make whatever they would like to make. Show appreciation for animals if they continue to make them but encourage them to make other things as well. Ask them to explain or tell you about what they make. Show equal approval and appreciation for all constructions and descriptions.

In each section of the observations form, be sure to record the number of Pablo pieces used and the number of connectors beside the drawing of a construction. Note whether the construction is complex (Cx), shows humor (Hu), is two-dimensional (2-D) or three-dimensional (3-D), is symmetrical (Sy) or asymmetrical (As). Record on observation sheet if child only uses the connectors. Encourage the use of Pablo pieces but accept whatever the child creates.

In the comments section write any other observations, such as children who helped others, conversations among children, storytelling about their products, interest and absorption in the task, and the problem-solving process each child seemed to use. *Be sure to record actual behaviors rather than your interpretations of these behaviors.*

In the final section, some important problem-solving behaviors are listed. Check *only* those behaviors you observed in each child. This can be done during the activity or immediately after it is over.

Note: Remember after each activity to place Pablo pieces in the middle of table so all children have equal access to pieces. Shuffle them around if necessary.

Sample Student Evaluation Sheet

CODE
AS = ASYMMETRICAL
S = SYMMETRICAL
CS = VERY COMPLEX
H = HELPED OTHERS
2D = 2 DIMENSIONAL
3D = 3 DIMENSIONAL

CODE
RH = RECEIVED HELP
C = COPIED IDEA OF OTHERS
M = MOVEMENT IN CONSTRUCTION
HU = HUMOR

PABLO

OBSERVER 10

SCHOOL Bryant

TEACHER Diaz

DATE 3/13

PCS = PIECES **CNT** – CONNECTORS

NAME	ANIMALS	PCS	CONSTRUCTION	PCS	COMMENTS	CHECK ONLY THOSE APPLY	overall
Juan	Turtle	2 / CNT 4	Building	6 / CNT 6	Helped others get structure to stand	√ CONTINUOUSLY WORKING √ SHOWS ENJOYMENT — ATTENTION TO DESIGN — CLEAR RESEMBLANCE — INTERPERSONAL — INVENTS NEW METHODS — PREFERS OPEN ENDED PROBLEMS √ FOCUSED ON OWN TASK — STRONG LINGUISTIC SKILLS	1
Sue	Man	4 / CNT 6	M Machine	5 / CNT 6	HLL Enjoyed talking & working with group	√ CONTINUOUSLY WORKING — SHOWS ENJOYMENT — ATTENTION TO DESIGN √ CLEAR RESEMBLANCE √ INTERPERSONAL — INVENTS NEW METHODS — PREFERS OPEN ENDED PROBLEMS — FOCUSED ON OWN TASK √ STRONG LINGUISTIC SKILLS	2
Carmen	Dog	1 / CNT 4	House	2 / CNT 1	Distracted, Frustrated	— CONTINUOUSLY WORKING — SHOWS ENJOYMENT — ATTENTION TO DESIGN — CLEAR RESEMBLANCE — INTERPERSIONAL — INVENTS NEW METHODS — PREFERS OPEN ENDED PROBLEMS — FOCUSED ON OWN TASK — STRONG LINGUISTIC SKILLS	0
Taj	Horse	6 / CNT 11	Invention	7 / CNT 12	HLL Told story about invention to group	√ CONTINUOUSLY WORKING √ SHOWS ENJOYMENT — ATTENTION TO DESIGN — CLEAR RESEMBLANCE √ INTERPERSONAL √ INVENTS NEW METHODS — PREFERS OPEN ENDED PROBLEMS √ FOCUSED ON OWN TASK √ STRONG LINGUISTIC SKILLS*	2
Lia	c Turtle	2 / CNT 4	TV	2 / CNT 2	Copied Others	— CONTINUOUSLY WORKING — SHOWS ENJOYMENT — ATTENTION TO DESIGN — CLEAR RESEMBLANCE — INTERPERSONAL — INVENTS NEW METHODS — PREFERS OPEN ENDED PROBLEMS — FOCUSED ON OWN TASK — STRONG LINGUISTIC SKILLS	0

2: Extremely Evident **1: Evident** **0: Not Evident**

Suggested Scoring Rubric

PABLO RUBRIC

EXTREMELY EVIDENT (2)	EVIDENT (1)	NOT EVIDENT (2)
Original Ideas	Copies And Adds Own Details	Copies With No Additions
3-D	Simple Design	1 Shape (Animal Body) With 4 Connectors For Legs
Something That Stands Up	Common Objects — People, Turtle, Etc.	2 - D
Symmetry With More Than 4 Pieces		
Moveable Parts		
Complex Design Many Pieces/Connectors		
Object Is Recognizable Representational Art		
Absorbed, Excited, or Enthusiastic		Bored, Frustrated
Makes Many Creations		Makes 1 Simple Creation

* A set of scoring guidelines for giving scores to student work. Please add to these lists as you work with your students.

Index

Note: References to tables or figures are indicated by *italic type* and the addition of "*t*" or "*f*" respectively.